Prentice Hall's

One-Day
MBA
in
MARKETING

*A complete education for the
busy professional*

Michael Muckian

**Prentice
Hall Press**

Library of Congress Cataloging-in-Publication Data

Muckian, Michael.
    Prentice Hall's one-day MBA in marketing / Michael Muckian.
        p. cm.
    ISBN 0-7352-0207-9 — ISBN 0-13-028156-5
    1. Marketing. I. Title: One-day MBA in marketing. II. Prentice Hall, Inc.
    III. Title.

HF5415.M74 2001
658.8-dc21   2001018543

This publication is designed to provide accurate and authoritative information in
regard to the subject matter covered. It is sold with the understanding that the
publisher is not engaged in rendering legal, accounting or other professional
service. If legal advice or other expert assistance is required, the services of a
competent professional person should be sought.

—From a Declaration of Principles jointly adopted by a Committee of the
American Bar Association and a Committee of Publishers and Associations.

Printed in the United States of America
10 9 8 7 6 5 4 3 2 1

ISBN 0-7352-0207-9

> **ATTENTION: CORPORATIONS AND SCHOOLS**
>
> Prentice Hall books are available at quantity discounts with bulk purchases for
> educational, business, or sales promotional use. For information, please write to:
> Prentice Hall Special Sales, 240 Frisch Court, Paramus, NJ 07652. Please supply:
> title of the book, ISBN number, quantity, how the book will be used, date needed.

Prentice Hall Press

Paramus, NJ 07652

Visit us at www.phdirect.com

To market, to market
to sell a fat pig.
Home again, home again,
Jiggedy Jig.

Oh, if it were only that simple . . .

Contents

Chapter 4   Making Plans   47

Chapter 5   Building Your Marketing Budget   65

Chapter 6   The Marketing Gestalt   83

Chapter 7   From Creative Thinking
to Strategic Planning   89

Chapter 10   Working with an Ad Agency   137

Chapter 11   Preparing Your Product Launch   155

Chapter 15   Serious Sales
Part 2~Mastering Educated Selling   215

Chapter 16   The Media Explosion   231

Chapter 17   The New Demographics   243

Chapter 18   Online Marketing Part 1~Background   257

If we could only learn to learn in time.

—*Enrique Solari*

Acknowledgments
and Appreciations

Nearly 20 years ago I met a group of marketers who told me that their discipline, above all others, was the engine of enterprise, the catalyst of commerce and the most important aspect of business since sliced budgets. "All is marketing," they said. "At least in enlightened firms."

At the time, I dismissed their claims to the arrogance of self interest. But I have come to see over time—as has much of the rest of the business world, it would seem—that customers and consumers do, indeed, drive the success or failure of business. We've come a long way from railroad tycoon J.P. Morgan's advice that, "The public be damned!," to an online world in which ragtag groups of e-mailers and Web crawlers can make or break an enterprise.

Marketing in its broadest sense—and that goes well beyond promotion to the intrinsic positioning and development of both products and firms—is not only the sails but the sextant that drives the ship of business and directs it to deep waters and smooth sailing. My thanks go to those members of the Financial Marketing Association and, subsequently, the CUNA Marketing Council who, both individually and as a body politic, made this point perfectly clear. Thanks, too, to Jeanne Klemm for getting this whole process underway.

I also thank Luis Gonzalez of Prentice Hall for his conception and support of this project, as well as his patience for the usual challenges. His stewardship is greatly appreciated.

My wife, Jeanie, also provided great insight and assistance, if only in the patience she exercised during an interminable number of nights spent at the word processor. She is my strength and is as much responsible for this book as I am.

Finally, an enormous amount of gratitude goes out to those marketing experts and gurus who have contributed to all our educations over the years. Those responsible for trading up the process from posters and tabloid ads to a sophisticated, scientific discipline are too numerous to name. But my personal heroes, individuals who helped increase my understanding and education, deserve to be mentioned. It's the very least I can do.

In no particular order, my thanks to David Ogilvy, Dr. Michael Porter, Dr. Theodore Levitt, Al Ries, Jack Trout, Don Peppers, Martha Rogers, Faith Popcorn, Ivy Lee, Edward L. Bernaise, Zig Ziglar, Peter Mayle, Michael Knapstein, Sergio Zyman and a host of others who have contributed to my overall understanding of marketing and its various related enterprises.

Thanks, too, to Arthur Miller. I reread *Death of a Salesman* while preparing the chapters on selling. Miller reminds us all of the danger of illusion and the tragedy of lost dreams, both so intrinsic to the discipline of marketing. We would all do well to embrace the hope while, at the same time, paying heed to the warning.

Introduction:
We Are All Marketers

What is marketing? I mean, what is it *really?*

Q: You're walking down the aisle at the grocery store and you see a large display of Pepsi-Cola products emblazoned with characters from the latest *Star Wars* film. There are price discounts corresponding with the opening of the film and Pepsi and Lucasfilms' co-branded merchandise available to purchasers. Is this marketing?

A: That's certainly a part of it. But so are the research and demographic studies that helped executives at both Pepsico and Lucasfilms understand and develop the advantages of the co-branded campaign. Not to mention the work done to create and establish both the soft drink and the film series concept in the first place.

Q: You open the *Wall Street Journal* and spot an ad for United Airlines in which the Chicago-based carrier announces it has removed several rows of seats from its economy cabin and spaced the remaining rows farther apart to give passengers more leg room. This can't be marketing, can it?

A: If the move was made in response to formal and informal customer feedback with ideas of a) satisfying regular customers and encouraging repeat business, b) attracting new flyers tired of the cramped spaces of United's competitors, and c) increasing market share for the airline, then the answer is a resounding yes. The smart money—and the competition—assumed this was the strategy and quickly followed suit.

Q: You know that for more than a decade, the McDonald's Corporation has helped thousands of families nationwide by offering the Ronald McDonald House as a cost-effective place to stay while their children are hospitalized. In fact, for many families, the Ronald McDonald House was the only alternative and the only way they could afford to be near their children during this important time of need. Surely, there can't be a marketing element to this, can there?

A: The Ronald McDonald Houses have provided a wonderful service for families nationwide, it's true. But the fact that a) the service is targeted to those customers (low- to moderate-income families with young children) who comprise the restaurant's major client base and b) that the name of the charity is identified both by the company's name (McDonald's) and its main advertising icon (Ronald McDonald) says a lot about the firm's marketing savvy. Add to that the fact that customers can participate in supporting the charitable effort through the donation of change from their purchases at the point of sale and you have a marketing master stroke that serves the needs of both McDonald's and the families the Ronald McDonald House serves.

These examples show how pervasive marketing can be in our lives, both at passive and at active levels. Marketing is all around us in the form of advertising messages stuck to billboards, posted on the sides of buses and inserted in our favorite television programs. It's also evident in the types of products we buy and, quite honestly, many of the needs we have, all the result of assiduous marketing research. Did we know we needed e-mail or, for that matter, a telephone before they were introduced? Now I doubt many of us would believe that we could get along without them.

Marketing thought also is evident in deciding whether those products are high quality, high-priced heirloom-type items, or quick, low-cost serviceable pieces that can get the job done with little fanfare. A well-to-do couple may spend several thousand dollars on a dining room set handcrafted by Amish carpenters for the style, beauty and residual value available to subsequent generations of family who will inherit the set. But this same couple will likely drop in at the local discount store to pick up a cheap plastic-handled broom to sweep the adjoining kitchen. Those types of buying decisions are made with the help of the marketers who have already researched the proposition, thought through the alternatives and answered the couple's question even before it was asked.

Marketing is everywhere and we're all part of it, both as buyers and as sellers. You can't escape it and, in fact, would be wise to embrace it. Mastery of the marketing equation is critical to helping you succeed individually, on behalf of your department or firm and in the world at large. Providing you with the knowledge and tools to enable this success is the focus of this volume.

Prentice Hall's One-Day MBA in Marketing is designed to give you a comprehensive view of the marketing landscape with an eye toward instruction on how marketing can affect the way you operate your business now and in the future. You won't have the depth and breadth of knowledge that a formal MBA program in marketing will provide. No single volume can accomplish that. But what this text will do is offer a level of knowledge from which you can build your personal and professional expertise to greater and higher levels.

If we all are marketers, as this introduction has been postulating to this point, exposure to basic marketing principles, as well as some advanced thinking about the discipline, will help you better master the obvious marketing issues in your business life, as well as integrate those techniques into other business areas. This latter strategy, especially, will give you new ways to look at things and new tools to use in pursuit of business success.

Prentice Hall's One-Day MBA in Marketing will review the topic in both theoretical and practical applications. Upcoming chapters will cover marketing basics, including product and company awareness, knowledge about current and potential audiences, the importance and elements of developing a brand, building marketing plans, writing budgets, and understanding the full marketing gestalt. The opening section on marketing principles is critical to establishing a firm foundation in the discipline.

Subsequent sections will fine-tune those principles and begin building on that foundation of knowledge. We'll talk about key criteria, such as good copywriting and design and review the basic principles of each. We'll offer tips on working with an advertising agency and how to get the most for your marketing dollars. We'll also walk through the steps of a successful product launch and how to approach, enter and, with any luck, conquer your chosen market segment.

This volume also will detour slightly to talk about two related disciplines—public relations and sales—and delve into each from both theoretical and practical levels. In fact, we've created mini texts-within-the-text to provide you with as comprehensive a guide as possible to the thoughts and applications that drive each. We'll also give the same treatment to media relations and offer ideas on ancillary marketing and advertising opportunities and channels to help you make the most of the opportunities available to you.

Finally, we'll wrap up with some next generation marketing ideas, including a comprehensive look at the new demographic and what that means to your marketing efforts. We'll talk about the media explosion and how to capitalize on one-to-one marketing strategies. We'll look at what the Internet has done to traditional marketing methods and finally attempt to peer into the future and see just what may lie beyond the new century's next cyber curve.

In the end, you will walk away from this volume with a greater understanding of marketing principles and basics, tools and applications and high level concepts with an eye toward marketing for the future. We can't afford to award you an MBA, of course, nor should you turn your back on future studies just because you've read this book. What we can promise you is a greater sense of market acuity and clarity of thought. You'll have a greater appreciation for the discipline of marketing and perhaps even an enthusiasm for the level to which its principles have woven their way into our world.

In the end, we are all marketers. *Prentice Hall's One-Day MBA in Marketing* will be the first and best step you can take to become a better one.

—Michael Muckian

The sole purpose of marketing is to sell more to more people, more often and at higher prices. There is no other reason to do it.

—Sergio Zyman, consultant and former head of marketing for the Coca-Cola Company

The Marketing Mystique

Marketing is one of the most misunderstood disciplines in business today. Ask any marketer and that's exactly what he or she will tell you. When it comes to understanding marketing, many executives and most consumers know as much about marketing as they do about nuclear thermodynamics. In fact, they may know less.

That's not to say your cohorts in the office or plant don't recognize the symptoms of marketing. They've heard about focus groups, participated in telephone surveys and are among the millions bombarded with advertising every minute of every day. To them, that's marketing and to many that's all there is to marketing. Case closed. End of story.

But as you'll discover throughout this book, there is much, much more to the marketing mystique. It's a complex construction that complicates all of our lives. But in the end it answers many of the questions it originally raised in ways that, in many instances, have made our lives that much better. Don't believe me? Please remember that you are part of the consumer culture and, as such, participate regularly in the receiving end of marketing's 50-yard promotional pass. If you weren't there, companies wouldn't market. You're just as much a part of the equation as they are. In the minds of marketers, you're the most important part.

Let's start with a definition. According to the American Marketing Association, marketing is "the process of planning and executing the conception, pricing, promotion and distribution of ideas,

SNAPSHOT

Pricing is one of the most difficult tasks a marketer faces because it must be about more than recovering costs and making the appropriate margin. It's also more than a reflection of what the competition charges. Pricing is strategy that's part of your company's overall plans and should reflect market position and product value. No more. No less.

goods and services to create exchanges that satisfy individual and organizational objectives." It's a process designed to bring buyers and sellers together, using the economic goals of one group to satisfy the personal and professional needs and wants of the other. And it does so in a way that begins with a concept, travels through development and distribution and ends with fulfilment.

Marketing at Gillette isn't just the sharp packaging or colorful ads promoting a basic piece of personal hygiene hardware. It's the recognition of the need for a close, comfortable shave and the fulfilment of that desire in the lives of its customers. At Gillette, marketing is about understanding the needs, identifying the solution and working hard to make that solution affordable, accessible and desirable for the shaving public. In marketing terms—and you'll pardon the expression—that's cutting edge thinking.

In many cases, marketing is also about alerting the public to a new idea and creating a desire for the byproducts of that idea. When Fred Smith was a student, his marketing professors challenged his idea that individuals and organizations some day might have use for a service that guaranteed overnight package and letter delivery. Wasn't that what the U.S. Postal Service was supposed to be about? Fred proved his thesis by starting Federal Express, changing the way goods are distributed and delivered worldwide forever. Now a multitude of companies offer the same service, including the U.S. Postal Service.

Whether simply responding to consumer desires or creating a need in order to fill it, it's all a part of marketing. The process can easily be broken down to a series of steps in which the foundation principles occur:

- *It begins with an unsatisfied need.* The buying public expresses a desire to have a need satisfied. Whether it's a basic need, such as food and shelter, or a more profound one, such as defining the purpose and meaning of life, it's the articulation of that need that sends signals to the seller of an opportunity to serve and profit. Marketing's key byproduct is a living illustration—or at least a practical application—of psychologist Abraham Maslow's Hierarchy of Needs.

In his research, Maslow postulated that all human beings have a hierarchy of needs, the most basic of which must be satisfied before the next will receive attention. The hierarchy begins with physical needs, such as food, water and shelter. It continues on through socialization needs and the need to be a part of a community or society. Maslow's hierarchy concludes with the need for self-esteem and, ultimately, self-actualization. Whatever the need of that buying public, it likely will be found within this hierarchy.

In a more sophisticated scenario, the seller may reach beyond the current hierarchical step and anticipate a future need with the idea of creating a product or service designed to fill that need. In either case, the goal is to satisfy a desire on the part of the buyer that fulfils an equally strong desire—increased income, revenue or market share—on the part of the seller.

- *It requires the ability and the desire to meet that need.* For the buyer, that means having the necessary wherewithal to have the need satisfied by a third party, the seller. If the need is transportation, buyers won't be able to afford a Ferrari if all they have is bus fare. Buyers must have the funds to pay for having their needs fulfilled at the level which they find satisfactory.

Likewise for the sellers. They must understand where that need falls in Maslow's hierarchy and have the ability to produce the goods and services to satisfy that need, not to mention the desire. Sellers must *want* to undertake the effort and investment necessary to fulfill that particular need or set of needs, knowing that buyers will be able to reward those efforts at the level at which they need to be rewarded. Without that desire, the ability to meet those needs has little meaning.

• *It requires further research to understand what those needs really are and to anticipate how the buyer will evolve with the satisfaction of those needs.* If the stated need is transportation, but only a Ferrari will do, then the level of need is greater than it would at first seem. There is an additional quotient of speed, luxury and the slightly exotic. There's an issue of status, wealth and exclusivity. There's even the desire for increased sex appeal that such an automobile can bring. In Maslow's hierarchy, there is something more than satisfying a basic physical need at work here. The need for a Ferrari is higher on the scale, up somewhere around self-esteem and perhaps even self-actualization. In light of all that, in fact, the transportation factor may be secondary almost to the point of insignificance.

The seller also must understand how this desire fits into the grand scheme of things in order to see it in the proper perspective. Without understanding the context of the desire—how it alters the life of the buyer, its relative importance compared to other aspects of the buyer's life, and the anticipated longevity of that need or want— the seller can't make a good decision about whether or not to satisfy that desire. Like any business arrangement, it takes a clear understanding of all particulars by both parties before it's safe to proceed.

• *It requires a means of effective communication.* This almost seems too basic to mention, but it's the failure of this link that often causes the breakdown between buyer and seller, between consumer and provider. Often that breakdown occurs, not due to a lack of understandable communication methods, but in failing to make that communication meaningful to the buyer. That involves knowing the need, understanding the audience and recognizing the intrinsic levels to which that satisfaction must go on Maslow's scale.

Specifics of communication come into play here. That includes the message itself, the context in which it's sent, the relational aspects that allow for full understanding and the desirability of the benefits the message creates. The seller must understand all it can about the buyer in order to send the right message. More often than not, that means a lot more data than height, weight and shoe size. And that's true even if shoes are what you're selling.

• *Finally, it requires a medium of exchange.* The buyer who wants the Ferrari must be able to afford one; otherwise there will be no exchange and the needs will not be met. Likewise, for the buyer who can afford such a purchase, the seller must be ready to provide it with all the trimmings. Otherwise the buyer won't be back and the chance for future business will be lost.

If all works according to plan, those seeking mere transportation will become regular riders of public transportation and the Ferrari buyer will have his or her higher-level needs met. That's marketing at its most intrinsic and its most basic. It's the process of identifying and satisfying consumer needs and wants in a way that benefits both parties involved in the transaction. There is really no more to marketing than that; and there is no less. When you think about it, that presents marketers with a formidable challenge and one we'll spend the rest of this volume addressing.

MARKETING BASICS:
THE FOUR Ps, PLUS ONE MORE

Marketing is a complex discipline with many conceptual and delivery components designed to facilitate the process. It's hard work to market and harder still to understand the subtle nuances that find their way into the process. However, there are building blocks that form the foundation of any marketing program. The sales and delivery concept about which you just read is just such a building block.

There are others that are critical for any budding or veteran marketer to master. Foremost among these foundation stones are the

MARKET RESEARCH

The perfect marketing plan integrates long- and short-term strategies into a seamless mix that helps kick-start the company's or product's campaign but lays the foundation for a long growth curve. Sound difficult? It usually is, which is why careful application of marketing principles rather than a mere overlay of slipshod promotional efforts is critical to your company's continued survival. Walk cautiously, and do big research.

Four Ps of Marketing, developed in the 1960s by Professor E. Jerome McCarthy. It's been Dr. McCarthy's shorthand that has served as a road map to many of the great marketing efforts of the last half century. The Four Ps are:

- *Product:* the goods or services that you enter the marketplace to market and sell.
- *Price:* the value applied to the goods or services in that marketplace quantified in monetary terms.
- *Promotion:* the method by which the benefits of those goods and services are communicated in an effort to justify the price.
- *Place:* the marketer's ability and strategy for exposing buyers to products and getting the products into their hands.

Twenty years later, the marketing community added a fifth P:

- *Position:* the way the product is perceived in the mind of the buyer through efforts made by the marketer to create a certain ambience or image around the product. Our Ferrari example from earlier in the chapter works well as an illustration here.

The five Ps of marketing help define the marketing mix for any product and service. They are the control factors that help attract, engage, involve and ultimately sell the consumer the brand of beer, butter or bubble bath that the marketer happens to be promoting. In any marketing effort, all the Ps must be addressed. Without that, the marketing effort will fail.

More importantly, all the Ps are intrinsically part of marketing and should be overseen by the marketing function. Some businesses still see marketing as the means to handle promotion and, perhaps, position only, leaving pricing, placement and product development in other hands. Without marketing's overall influence, each of these functions operates in a silo and the integration critical to the marketing mix does not take place.

When that's the case, the company isn't likely to be around for very long.

The flip side of the five Ps—all controllable factors—is the environment in which the marketer operates. This generally consists of uncontrollable factors, including social and demographic shifts, technological advancements, upswings or downturns in the economy, changes in regulations and other issues that will affect the preferences and habits of buyers.

When the oil embargoes of the 1970s forced a shift in automobile purchase patterns, the big-engine gas guzzlers were replaced by smaller, more economically run cars. Regardless of the auto manufacturers' capabilities, preferences and inventories, public sentiment had changed due to external, relatively uncontrollable factors, and the industry had to respond accordingly. With the growing popularity of sports utility vehicles, the pendulum has swung back in the earlier direction, but cautiously and not to the degree seen by the previous generation. With past lessons well-learned, the automotive industry will likely be better at adapting to that change should another embargo hit—or the current spike in prices, for that matter.

One of the purposes of the five Ps is to help identify adaptability strategies and, as much as possible, to address the uncontrollable elements when they occur. (Admittedly, this can be difficult, if not downright impossible.) They offer a surprising adaptability for marketers, even in the most difficult of circumstances. The five Ps applied help either accelerate companies through such situations, or brake uncontrolled progress to avoid unnecessary collisions with various issues. Some of that depends on luck, the rest on how skillful a marketer you are.

FROM FIVE Ps TO THREE QUESTIONS

Admittedly, the five Ps exist to describe the process from a marketer's point of view, and that's critical to our understanding of the marketing mystique. But that's just the first step. To successfully market and sell goods or services, you're going to have to understand the process from the buyer's point of view. The key to that understanding is this:

Buyers buy the benefit, not the product.
In old line marketese, they buy the sizzle not the steak.

This may be the most significant tenet of marketing from both a conceptual as well as a practical point of view. People buy things for the benefits they will receive from those things, not to have the things themselves. Our Ferrari buyer spends a lot of money on the world's fastest, sleekest automobile because it will make him feel good. And powerful. And wealthy. And sexy. He may appreciate automotive performance and the car's safety features, but he really wants the Ferrari because of the cachet that comes with it.

Understanding that is the first and biggest step toward becoming a successful marketer. It's also the root of desire linking all levels of Maslow's hierarchy. But there's another way to look at this concept and another way to break it down into its component parts. Once you accept the concept that it's the benefit, not the product that is the marketable commodity, there are three questions whose answers can help further refine the process.

1. *What is the form of the product and how does that enhance its function?* When Starbuck's launched its line of high quality coffees, the company knew they were combating the image of bland, stale brew served in a chipped, white-china cup. They exploded the old stereotype and built their reputation on a wide array of high-quality exotic coffees and coffee drinks served in three different sizes. The form gave an old product a new distinction and changed the nature of coffee drinking overnight.

In this case, the new style of coffee—rich, robust blends served numerous ways in sizes convenient not to the server but to the buyer—literally changed the function of the drink. Coffee in any form is still a social beverage, but the variety of the blends and ambience of the stores added an opportunity for an increased luxury element in terms of time spent with the coffee and, presumably, in discussion with friends. Under the Starbuck's flag, coffee was now more than just liquid caffeine. It became a gourmet beverage favored by the average and elite alike. It had attributes that, like fine wines, bore greater discussion among those who liked to consume it. People also spent more money on Starbuck's, which allowed them the rationale to spend more time with it.

In the end, the product's form altered its function such that it changed the market. Along with the better flavor, the higher price magnified the cachet for Starbuck's and the dozens of companies that followed it. All those combined elements propelled coffee from an average workaday beverage to a gourmet item that was as fun to talk about and experience as it was to drink.

2. *How does time and place of delivery accommodate customers' needs?* In today's time-starved, convenience-driven environment, delivery methodologies often play as much a part of customer choice as does the product itself. How and when you make your services available may make a difference in whether or not they continue to be your customers.

Consider today's financial service institutions. The most progressive ones are 24/7, providing Internet access to deposits, withdrawals and even loans on a 24-hour-a-day,

MARKET RESEARCH

Know your customers if you would sell your product. That seems so logical as not to bear mention. But the word "customer" goes far beyond the product's end-user in its definition. Your customers also include your wholesalers and distributors, who make sure the product gets into the right hands. It includes the company employees and directors, who must stand behind the product in order for it to be successful. It even includes those who would know but not use the product. You may change their minds some day. But even if you don't, having them accept the product as a part of the marketing landscape is worth making the effort.

seven-day-a-week basis. The point of purchase is as close as the nearest desktop or laptop computer and delivery comes sometimes in a matter of seconds. Services couldn't be more convenient than that. And, as far as the customer is concerned, it doesn't really matter that he or she is interacting with a database rather than a human teller. The job is completed and service provided at a time and place convenient to the customer's needs.

Let's take the time and place quotient one step further and note that there are now cyber banks that exist only online. Because of the nature by which consumers have begun to exercise their financial service options, coupled with the ease of electronic funds transfers, there simply is no need for brick-and-mortar institutions. Consumer preference has not only changed the way customers receive service, they've altered the very nature of the provider of those services. From a marketing standpoint, that's as profound a change as we can ever hope to see.

3. *Finally, what is the price of possession?* Ease of possession is as critical as the time and place equation. How hard is it for a customer to get his or her hands on your goods and services? What obstacles do you put in the way or how easy do you make it? What are your "no money down" variables?

As a member of Columbia House, the music and video club, I know that ease of possession was a major consideration in the planning and launch of this music membership product. In the old days, record clubs demanded regular sales, offering customers several free records in exchange for the promise of future purchases. In addition, the club would send monthly notices with automatically chosen selections. If the customer didn't send back a card with his or her refusal by a certain date, like it or not, the record would be shipped.

Under Columbia House's current plan, I still received my bonus CDs up front, but I am required to purchase only one more CD to complete my contract. And when I do, I will get another CD free! In addition, I am privy to specials and closeout sales that will bring me music at bargain basement prices. If I get a bad disk, I will get complete credit for it with one simple phone call. I can even create customized disks from existing tracks from various artists for the price of the average mass-produced CD. And best of all, I never have to respond if I don't want the pick of the month. It no longer is automatically shipped.

Columbia House has removed virtually all barriers to my participation and actively increased the benefits far beyond any I would have imagined. When it comes to the price of possession . . . well, it could only be lower if they paid me to be a member.

MARKETING IS AS MARKETING DOES

In the end, it all comes down to marketing. That's a broad and overly simplified definition, but truer than you might think. Marketing does not create needs, it fulfills them. It does not generate needless sales; it uncovers hidden wants and seeks to be the first to satisfy them. Marketing learns all it can about its current and prospective audiences and creates equity among those audience members by exposing their similarities and characterizing common needs through the promotion of products and services designed to meet those needs. Marketing is a service industry that's always seeking to close the sale and satisfy the need.

Businesses thrive on it, but so do we in our personal lives. Whether we're selling soap to an unwashed public or selling a vacation destination to unenthused family members, we've all taken steps that involve the classic marketing principles we talked about early in this chapter. They may not know they need to be washed or that this destination will provide more fun and relaxation than they've ever experienced in their lives, but with the right background information, a clear understanding of our audience, the proper approach and making it relatively easy for them to accept, we may just get our idea across.

Our marketing efforts may turn into a sale. And, as Coca-Cola's former marketing kingpin Sergio Zyman said in the quote that opened this chapter, selling stuff is what marketing is all about. Case closed. End of story.

To know one's self is wisdom,
but to know one's neighbor is genius.

Minna Antrim

2

Know Your Market

The basis for any decision in business—or anything, for that matter —is knowledge. Be it knowledge of a product, a situation, a constituency or group of customers, fact must be the foundation by which decisions are made. So, too, with marketing.

Nonmarketers sometimes see the marketing discipline as a seat-of-the-pants, take-your-best-shot effort in which conjecture is the only constant. The old marketing axiom, "Ready, fire, aim!" doesn't do much to help that image in the minds of those who don't understand it. And, frankly, some marketers do act that way, riding on hunches and deciding based on instinct what may be the best approach to market corn flakes, soap flakes or even snowflakes. Sometimes, it even works. Often, however, it doesn't. That's when upper management wonders what the hell it was thinking by letting some wild-eyed creative risk the company's reputation and drain the corporate coffers to follow his or her nose down the primrose path of fantasy.

Before deciding that all is lost, however, those executives might do well to check and see if those crazy schemes were based solely on gut-instinct or might have had something to do with the meticulously crafted research that most marketers pursue today as a regular part of their discipline. Knowing customers and their behavioral and buying preferences is the core of any marketing plan. Without that knowledge, one cannot do very much or proceed very far with any kind of comprehensive effort.

MARKET RESEARCH

━━━━━━━━━━

What's the biggest challenge researchers face? It's the fact that, when people know their opinion is being measured, they tend to respond differently. It doesn't matter that they're merely a statistic and you're a nameless stranger they never will see again. Rather than tell you what they do like, they often tell you what they think they should like, just so they don't look unsophisticated. In addition, those researched may not be qualified to render an opinion or may be incapable of responding accurately on a moment's notice. Such are the challenges you will have to overcome in your research efforts.

Even the best research sometimes takes unusual turns. The Ford Motor Company once had a new design on the table that it had researched carefully with consumers and dealers. All said the product had all the features they were looking for, as well as a distinctive design and appeal for the new decade the nation was entering. Certain he had a winner on his hands, Henry Ford Jr. even decided to name the product after his son. That year the firm proudly unveiled its newest entry into the automobile market, an odd-looking vehicle with the distinctive name "Edsel." The rest, as they say, is history.

Such circumstances notwithstanding, it's critical to note that, in a world increasingly cluttered with marketing and advertising messages, products not backed by research have little chance of succeeding. Take the time and do the homework. Solid research is the foundation on which any successful marketing effort is built. Without it, your marketing could tumble and fall in the first strong wind.

WHAT IS MARKET RESEARCH?

There are two schools of thought as to what constitutes a definition of market research:

• In the holistic sense, market research is the system through which a marketing problem or opportunity is defined and addressed. That system operates through the organized and systematic collection of market data, its analysis, and application of the findings based on that analysis. The net result is a study of a broader, more comprehensive nature that blends customers, conditions, and company capabilities in consensus with what your approach to the marketplace should be like.

• A less comprehensive but no less valuable description comes in the recognition of the driving factor behind that knowledge: the customer. A great deal of market research focuses solely on customers, both current and future, and their likes, preferences, wishes, hopes and dreams. Within the study of those customers, the marketer by necessity covers many of the other market conditions that fall under the auspices of the former definition.

If the first definition is a front-door approach that defines the market in terms of conditions that end in service to the customer, then the second definition comes through the back door, starting with the customer and building the environment from there. One or the other may work better for your company, but both answer the same need and can be successfully applied with good result. It all depends which way you want to enter in the research equation.

There also are two types of research that you can utilize in your marketing efforts. Direct research, also called primary research, takes you right to the source of the data, usually the customer. You may poll consumers via telephone surveys, focus groups or man-on-the-street interviews. Direct research takes you right to the source of the information you seek without the fear of interpretation by a secondary source getting in the way.

Indirect research, also known as secondary research, comes from sources other than the consumers. Trade associations often have mounds of secondary data collected for the industry they serve. Trade publications and even government bodies often have accumulated such material for their own use and are more than happy to share it, even among nonmembers. You may find valuable data such as manufacturing and sales trends, customer population information and consumer buying patterns from secondary sources at little or no cost.

In the best cases, secondary data can and should be used to augment primary information collected from consumer sources. Research can be as cheap or as expensive as you want it to be, but you can glean some very good, statistically valid information from numerous sources that are close to home and easy to access.

LOOK WITHIN

Start inside the company. Many firms forget that management and staff are themselves users of the products and should know more than the average consumer about its benefits and features. See if that's the case by surveying your own staff. You may be surprised at how much—or how little—your people know about your products, their purposes and the goals of your marketing efforts. If someone stopped them on the street and asked about the purpose and use of your key products (and your position in the market for each of them), would they be able to respond rationally and accurately?

It's important for everyone to be on the same wavelength when it comes to defining your position and understanding your marketing message. But there are employees whose exposure is more direct and whose understanding is more critical. These are the people closer to the end of the customer food chain who can provide valuable feedback that no one else can.

Your sales staff likely has the most direct access to the customers. Find out what they're hearing and seeing while they're on the street and use it to your advantage. Take special care to solicit their opinions because they can be more than just the eyes and ears of your company. A good salesperson works hard to please his or her customers and may be able to build a bridge between what the company supplies and what the customers want and need. They often will know what the overriding need is and may have some sound ideas for filling that need. If products are created to

MARKET RESEARCH

Primary research usually yields the best results if you keep the questions insightful but simple. Stay away from Yes and No answers and look for qualitative information like the following:

• What is the name of our product? What does that name mean to you?

• How often do you purchase this type of product and what is the primary reason for purchasing it?

fill a customer need—and the successful ones always are—then it's the sales staff who can provide the most accurate input because they're out on the street getting the information first hand.

Receptionists, customer service staff and other in-house people with direct customer contact are valuable in the same way. Although more reactive than proactive in their approach to the public, front-line staff hear an awful lot more from customers than the executives in the office suites. They can be an excellent resource for first-hand (primary) information. In addition, unlike outside researchers, they may be able to interpret it in ways more meaningful to the company. Listen to what these staff members tell you and respond accordingly.

Even your shipping department has value to bring to the research equation. They handle daily those items going out, as well as those being returned. They may not know your specific marketing position or have the same level of customer contact as your sales and customer service staff, but they're handling the purchases and returns of those same customers on a daily basis. They see the patterns that develop and know what sells and what doesn't. Don't underestimate the power of that observation.

HARVESTING OPINION

When you do step out to survey current and potential customers, you first will need to know whose opinion it is that you're after.

MARKET RESEARCH
(Continued)

- What are our product's strengths and weaknesses and how do they compare with those of our competitor?
- What is the primary benefit you see from our product and how does that match with your preferences?

Well-formed questions can reveal a wealth of information in a short amount of time. And that's likely all you will have with consumers you survey.

That means understanding your market segment, the niche you seek to serve and the consumers you want to capture. There are numerous measures by which you can define your market segment, but the ones that lay at the root of customer segmentation are as follows:

• Geographic measurement identifies customers by the physical region in which they live or work. You may have a product specific to a certain region of the country, city or even neighborhood, and you may be able to use geographic research to identify how best to market it. If you produce antifreeze, you can probably kiss those states south of the Mason-Dixon line goodbye as sources of potential customers. They don't have a need for it based on their location. Geography is the most basic determinant when it comes to identifying a potential market for your goods.

• Demographic research studies basic characteristics of the population in order to determine various segments' potential applicability as a market for products. Rather than look at where the market is, demographics looks at who the buyers are by measuring things like age, race, gender makeup, income, education, marital status, and occupation. Those characteristics are further balanced by population size, density and location in order to determine specific demographic profiles. Marketers of mass-produced spaghetti sauce, for example, may or may not be successful in old-line Italian neighborhoods because the families may choose to make their own. However, in a white collar Yuppie neighborhood where time is money there may be a strong market for foodstuffs that are quickly prepared and easily consumed.

• Psychographics are the least well-defined of the three and often the most telling. This is the type of information—which measures characteristics from preferences to personality traits—that really identifies potential customers and helps isolate them from the masses. Rather than choosing a market based on geographic location or physical and social attributes, psychographics seeks to identify personal characteristics in consumers that will predispose them to buying your product. Understanding personal preferences and characteristics within the buyers' minds will help you better craft advertising that appeals to those characteristics.

How do you measure psychographic preferences? Market studies today often have psychological components that question not only product preferences, but beliefs, ideologies and characteristics of the audience and then match them up with the related characteristics of current and potential products. That way, marketers can anticipate the needs of an audience and be ready with their advertising message to help consumers decide how to fill that need.

Why would Pfizer Pharmaceuticals buy three pages of advertising in *National Geographic* to promote Viagra? Because a significant portion of the magazine's readership is over 55 years old, which is the prime audience for the drug. For the same reason, the magazine might be an appealing place for General Motors to advertise its Cadillac line. Placement due to the correlation between the age of the product user and the age of the readership is a function of demographic research.

Why would General Motors run similar Cadillac ads in a magazine like *Outside,* which has a younger, more vibrant readership interested in physical activities? Because Cadillac researchers may have uncovered that *Outside* readers, like Cadillac drivers, tend to be well-educated professionals with a higher income level and more sophisticated tastes that are looking to trade up their next auto purchase but are more predisposed as they age for an American-made vehicle to replace those Beamers and Audis. By placing the ad in a more youth-oriented magazine, Cadillac may be attempting to expand its market down the age scale, or at least to set the stage for the day when those readers become more sedentary and enter the Cadillac-and-Viagra period of their lives. Those are psychographics in action.

Among the three characteristics by which research and marketing are cast, the broadest to define is also the easiest to change. Geographic variables tend to be the most fluid because people do move and, today, more frequently than ever. A case could be made that a middle-income family in Dallas shares many of the same characteristics as a middle-income family in Seattle. But the similarities are distinct enough without going into the other two research methodologies. Nevertheless, geographics are considered a fairly stable characteristic.

Demographics are firmer still, only because that same middle-income family has a better chance of staying middle-income than reaching true upper-income status. However, other demographics do change as time passes. People grow older, more sedentary and exchange their *Outside* subscriptions to subscriptions to *National Geographic*. Family members grow up and move away. Gender remains the same. (In most cases, anyway.) Overall, demographic traits offer still more stability than geographic ones.

Despite their complexity, psychographic traits, when accurately identified, offer the greatest stability of all. People can change their address, their age, and their marital status, but they rarely change who they are as individuals at an intrinsic level. Personality tests have proved time and again that our character is defined early and often carried in one form or another to the grave. It drives us and governs everything we do, no matter where we live and what age we are. Marketers able to capture those characteristics can establish a lock on a customer that could last a lifetime.

But capturing that customer means recognizing that there also are dynamic tendencies within that psychographic or demographic grouping whose needs must be addressed. One buyer may want that Cadillac because of the prestige the car brings, another because of nostalgia for an early era when wealth and affluence meant owning a large American touring car. Another may want it for the safety and comfort features.

Knowing which segments appreciate which facet and marketing accordingly to capture the appropriate dynamics could mean the difference between success and failure.

I suppose there are similar dynamics to the marketing of Viagra, but that's a discussion best left for another place and time.

THE MARKETING
DECISION PROCESS

All the attributes previously mentioned contribute to the decision-making process, steps by which research ultimately is conducted. There are various methodologies and techniques that utilize the different geographic, demographic and psychographic characteristics and there are any number of ways you can use those approaches to conduct research.

Mail surveys still are popular, with a growing application of online research opportunities available. With the advent of near incessant telemarketing efforts, phone surveys have become less tolerable for consumers. Shopping center surveys also can work, but they tend to be self-selecting based on the body language that potential subjects exhibit to the surveyor. Using the guidelines above, you can craft the appropriate questions for your purpose. The various approaches should be familiar to most readers. Time and space preclude us from belaboring the obvious here.

What will help your survey efforts is understanding the process by which marketing decisions often are made. The basic steps aren't necessarily specific to the marketing discipline. In fact, they can apply to just about any decision-making process. However, they do provide a useful analysis of the process by which you can take your marketing efforts from concept to action.

1. Define the Marketing Challenge

Know first of all what you will be up against in successfully marketing your product to customers. There may be cost factors, availability issues or simply a need for customers to better understand what you have and how you have positioned it. Having a clear take on the challenges that lay ahead is crucial. To help facilitate that process, consider the following components of the definition equation:

- Know the *objectives* that will contribute to your decision-making. These objectives may be as basic as raising revenue levels or increasing market share. They also may be more esoteric and include discovery of psychographic components of the audience and the product elements that appeal to it.

- Understand the *restrictions* placed on achieving certain solutions by the size, scope and position of the challenge at hand. This may be something as simple as a lack of market for the product; or it may be a more complex situation involving a variety of demographic and psychographic variables. Recognize those hurdles ahead of time and plan to overcome them accordingly.

- Define your *benchmarks* so that you will know when you've achieved certain levels of success. The old axiom, "That which is measured is done," applies here. Knowing when you've hit the various milestones in your processes will better enable you to mark your level of success.

2. Identify and Employ the Decision Factors

Different sets of variables will affect the outcome of your efforts. Knowing how to identify, engage and measure the impact of those variables will be critical to your success. Knowing, too, how those variables rank relative to two distinct characteristics also is critical.

- *Alternatives* are variables that oftentimes can be measured and controlled. Remember the annoyance caused by the three-year-old who continually asks, "Why?" to every explanation you give? Try that process on your product development and marketing efforts. After awhile, substitute the questions, "How?,"

"Where?" and "When?" Those are just one way to turn up controllable variables that operate at a deeper level and may give product developers and marketers new avenues to take and opportunities to pursue.

- But there also are *uncertainties,* uncontrollable decision factors that affect your efforts. And there often may appear to be no end to those uncertainties. That list can include products that don't work under certain conditions, plans that go haywire due to shifts in social climates and even natural disasters. Even political unrest and changes in public opinion can make a difference in the success or failure of a product or campaign. Alternatives can sometimes be used to control uncertainties, but only if there is sufficient opportunity and only if those alternatives are comprehensive enough to be up to the task.

3. Accumulate and Evaluate Meaningful Data

As any good marketer knows, data drives the marketing equation. Your collection of meaningful information must be complete enough to allow you to make sound decisions, and enable you to see things at a variety of levels and through all the appropriate viewpoints. Marketing decisions are never one-dimensional and careful data accumulation can be a more valuable tool than any specific strategy you may devise. In the best cases—in all cases, actually—it should be the data that drives those strategies.

There are three specific levels of data you will need to collect to have a complete understanding of the situation:

- *Concepts and hypotheses* are probably the most esoteric forms of information, yet they contribute a critical analytical perspective that provides the necessary intellectual elements to help guide the thought processes to the proper solution. By connecting two or more elements, hypotheses can lead to the type of breakthrough thinking critical to marketing. The logic games we all played in college come into play here, as

*MARKET
RESEARCH*

Different types
of buyers populate
the marketplace
and it helps to
know who they are
and what their dri-
ving motivations
may be:

• Some want to
  be the first on
  their block to
  try new things.
  They are known
  as *initiators*.

• Some see new
  products as ways
  to satisfy wants
  and needs first.
  They are the
  influencers.

do the "if-then" assumptions we have made about life in general from time to time.

• *Methodologies* are processes by which issues and situations can be and have been addressed. Some may be standard operating procedures for marketers; others may be gleaned from marketing case studies for similar products or situations. Accumulation and application of these studies to models of the issues with which you're struggling may yield an appropriate approach that either has been previously used or can be adapted to suit your needs.

• *Pure data* is the other type of information that you should be collecting to round out your process. This includes data on your product, its competitors, your customers and other things you will need to make the type of product and marketing judgements that are required. Primary and secondary data from various sources come into play here, as does probability sampling, the method by which the number of randomly sampled survey recipients are chosen and the percent of chance that they will be chosen.

4. Identify a Solution

This is the logical conclusion to all the steps that have come before, and is simply a matter of choosing the best alternative from the choices identified and putting that alternative into action. If you've done the previous steps properly, it's as simple as that.

5. Review and Evaluate the Results of Your Efforts

This step takes two processes into account: evaluating the results themselves and evaluating the process by which the results were achieved. If the results reach the goal predicted, then process evaluation is often easy and straightforward. On the other hand, if all the previous steps showed the likelihood of positive results, but the end effect was a disaster, then it's time to take a close, hard look at how you did what you did to make sure you don't make the same mistake again.

Consider the case of New Coke, the sweeter alternative to what has become known now as Coca-Cola Classic. In blind taste tests, drinkers identified the sweeter drink, which was more like competitor Pepsi-Cola's flavor, as preferred. And perhaps more drinkers really did like the new flavor simply as a flavor. But when it came time to purchase the product, buyers ignored it because it wasn't the old, familiar Coke with which they had grown up. In a classic marketing twist of fate, it was the packaging, the tradition and the image associated with Coke that brought out the brand loyalty in people. For the most part, all those elements were missing in New Coke, and those clearly were the elements that drove consumer preference.

A dismal failure? Not according to Coke marketing chief Sergio Zyman. The new product may not have taken hold, but the exercise

MARKET RESEARCH
(Continued)

• Some purchase products to be able to tell others later whether the product did or didn't satisfy their needs. These are the *evaluators*.

There are more as well, but the point is that people buy for different reasons. Knowing some of those reasons may help you predict marketing needs, sales trends and overall product acceptance.

did prove to the company the value of Coca-Cola "Classic" and cemented its importance in the minds of its drinkers, reigniting the original brand in the marketplace.

It would seem that marketers know how to find a silver lining in even the darkest cloud.

HOW THE CUSTOMER RESPONDS

While you're making sure all the steps you take in the launch and evaluation of a product happen in the right order and with proper evaluation, your customers also are going through their steps in the recognition, acceptance and purchase of your products. You can more keenly hone your marketing efforts if you can recognize the various stages of the consumer purchase cycle. Those steps include the following:

- Basic *product awareness* sits at the front end of the marketing learning curve. This is the time when customers passively gain knowledge about your product and recognize it as a new brand in its particular category.

- *Interest* on potential customers' parts is the next step after product awareness. Something has excited them about the product or made them see its unique capacity to answer their questions. As the next level beyond awareness, interest is a much more active stage as potential buyers become information seekers in response to your marketing messages.

- Once interested, customers will go through a process of *evaluation* wherein they will measure the product's worth to them as consumers. By using the pros and cons of the marketing messages and product information received, potential buyers will evaluate the worth, necessity and preferability of the purchase and decide accordingly.

- *Trial* of the product comes next. Customers test their assumptions about the product's features and benefits through use. The sales staff plays a role here, but only if the product is purchased as a result of human contact. With call centers proliferating and online shopping no longer a thing of the future, the impact of face-to-face sales efforts have become influential to an increasingly smaller market segment.

- When a customer researches your product and its value proposition, tries it and then chooses to buy it on a regular basis, they have entered the *adoption* phase. Customers use the data during the previous phases to convince themselves of the value of the product and become sporadic or regular brand users.

If your marketing efforts coincide with the last stage, then you have the classic supplier-buyer marriage made in marketing heaven. That's all there is to it.

Brand is the embodiment of the relationship between your company/product/service and your customers. In short, brand is the promise made to customers.

—Michael Knapstein, CEO, Waldbillig & Besteman Inc.

3

Understanding Position and Brand

Every product or service has an identity in the marketplace. Part of that identity is built on the qualities associated with that product or service, and part is based on price. When we think of a pickup truck from Ford Motor Company, durability and reliability are two words that come to mind, as well as a price competitive within the marketplace for similar products. When we think of a stay at the Ritz-Carlton Hotel chain, high quality service, the element of elegance and a hefty price tag (for some) come attached to that image.

All of those characteristics just named are just that—characteristics. They are product features that lead to the benefits associated with purchases of those products. They are a part of, but not the heart of the brand that both of those products carry. When it comes to identifying brand, there's more to the process than a menu of features and benefits. Branding is both as simple and as complex as any aspect within the marketing function. Successful branding has meant fame and fortune for numerous products and companies worldwide and many believe that a product's success or failure is dependent on its successful brand management.

That may be true, but there also are those who challenge an overdependence on brand imaging as the heart and soul of successful marketing. No matter which camp you're in, knowing what branding is and how it can affect the recognition and success of your product may be critical to the future of your marketing efforts.

WHAT IS BRAND?

Early in its introductory phase, a midwestern beer company held a series of blind taste tests for its product as part of a series of commercial spots. In one of the commercials, a young woman is shown testing two similar looking products. She is pleased that the one she chose was the brand she normally drank. In her laudatory comments explaining why she chose this brand, she says, quite simply: "That's my beer."

That commercial is a testimony to the power of branding and its value to marketers. The woman in the commercial didn't merely express a preference for a certain brand, she said point blank: That's my beer. It's part of my life, my identity. It's more than a purchase. I feel ownership of the brand.

As Michael Knapstein, CEO of Waldbillig & Besteman said in the quote that opened this chapter, brand is the relationship between the product, the company and the customer. It's the promise made to the customer—the promise of quality, flavor, service, whatever—and the delivery of that promise. As such, the net return is the loyalty that customer feels to the company and/or its product and the willingness to purchase the product again and again.

How much is brand loyalty worth? More than you can imagine.

Certainly there are sales volume figures for some of the nation's leading brands—note how the word "brand" substitutes for "product" in that phrase—that give testimony to the power of branding. The same can be said for share of market held by these brands. Statistics bear out a favorable position for the leaders, but the value of branding goes well beyond the obvious.

Consider the Walt Disney brand. The empire built by the one-time artist and animator has grown to be an entertainment conglomerate the scope of which its founder had never dreamed. In addition to animated shorts and features, the Disney brand has gone on to encompass other types of films, theme parks, consumer products, even cruise ships and clothing stores. Yet each and every manifestation of that brand comes with the assurance of high quality, wholesome, family-based entertainment with educationally redeeming features and top-notch service on which parents of children of all ages can rely.

Disney presents an iron-clad brand to its customers and enjoys fierce loyalty from those customers in return. That loyalty is so strong that the company is assured of a ready-made market no matter what it produces and distributes. The brand is so strong, in fact, that its wealthier customers have gone to the next level of purchasing Disney stock to help ensure that the brand lasts forever, or at least until their own children and grandchildren are grown.

Would that we all had that much emotional and economic equity within our specific marketplaces.

WHAT BRAND IS NOT

Brand may embody the relationship between the customer and the product or company, but it does not describe the understanding of how the product meets the needs of the customer and the strategy by which that relationship is developed in light of competitive offerings. That's called *positioning* and needs to take place before branding can occur.

Brand names have been around since Dr. Carter introduced his liver pills at the beginning of the 20th century. The understanding of positioning as the method by which increased brand value can be achieved is a more recent occurrence. Whereas Dr. Carter took a chance and created a product that found its market in a less competitive time, brand developers today know they need a clear understanding of the product, its fit in the marketplace and the impact of competitors on the market. That's positioning, a separate discipline that nevertheless complements branding and forms a cohesive partnership with it.

Branding is the result of a good positioning strategy, but it is not the positioning function itself. That requires a little more technical approach in order to place your product correctly and competitively in the customer's mind.

In 1982, ad men Al Ries and Jack Trout published the seminal volume, *Positioning: The Battle for Your Mind,* that changed the way marketers looked at customers. In all cases and for all products and firms, there are two types of positioning:

MARKET RESEARCH

Physical positioning, which focuses on matching products to external forces, tends to concentrate on physical characteristics, price-value comparisons, technical aspects and readily available objective data, including product size, weight and packaging.

Perceptual positioning turns the tables and attacks the problem from the customers' points of view. Rather than

• *Physical positioning* describes how products fit into the overall product mix for the industry of which they are part. Taking competitive products and firms into consideration, that positioning may be *imitative*—designed to look, sound, taste and feel like a similar product—or it may be *differentiated*—created with attributes and features that separate it from a spate of other look-a-like products. In either case, the product must be relevant and appealing to the buyer and measure up well within the context of similar products. That positioning occurs against outside elements designed to affect the appeal, acceptance and use of the product.

• *Perceptual positioning,* on the other hand, is the role and place a product occupies in the minds of consumers. It's not enough merely to understand how your brand of soft drink measures up against the competition across town. You need to understand the best possible role for that soft drink in the minds of potential drinkers. Never mind that your product is caffeine-free, costs 8 cents more per 12-ounce serving and comes in a green bottle instead of a white one. The important thing is what all that means in the mind of the person purchasing the six-pack or single serving bottle and what you can do to capture that buyer's attention and loyalty. That's perceptual positioning.

Easy? Not by a long shot. Consumers will evaluate a product based on its size, shape and relative value to their lives. (Is a soft drink what I really want right now? Maybe a light beer would be better.)

If there are a large number of characteristics or a wide array of competitors on the market, they may instead rely on composite characteristics or a situational analysis to answer their questions. (There are a lot of good features to the pickup trucks I've looked at, but I want something strong, so maybe I really need my truck Ford-tough.)

There also is an element of the abstract in our evaluation of products, in which we bypass the obvious features and characteristics of a purchase and look for an element that satisfies higher-level needs and becomes more of a life-affirming event. (Sure the house is expensive and larger than I need but, in addition to all the great features, purchasing this house would be proof positive that, after years of hard work, I have finally arrived.)

The perceptual process comes with a variety of indicators and, in the end, is a more reliable method of positioning that leads closer to the ultimate brand loyalty for which all companies strive.

FROM PERCEPTUAL MAPPING TO POSITIONING

With apologies to Confucius, every journey does begin with a first step, but one must know the point from which one is starting in order to set out with the right trajectory. When it comes to positioning your product, it's important to know where it currently stands in consumers' minds before you even

MARKET RESEARCH
(Continued)

worry about product size, selection and whether it's packaged in cardboard, glass or aluminum, perceptual positioning attempts to track what it all means in the consumers' minds based on their niche, their orientation and perceptions of similar products. The view is subjective, not objective and relies less on product data and more on market research.

attempt to move it in a preferred direction. This is what's known as *perceptual mapping.*

A perceptual map is generally drawn as a simple cross with all four arms of the cross equal in length and perpendicular to each other. Each of the four ends marks an extreme in perception for the product in question. The vertical bar, for example, might have "Price" at one end and "Prestige" at the other, signaling two primary reasons that consumers may purchase a product. If the object you are mapping is an automobile, the "Prestige" end may be littered with brands like Jaguar, Lamborghini and Mercedes Benz, while the "Price" end may feature Fords, Chevys and Hyundais. You get the idea.

In terms of the horizontal cross-bar, you may further delineate the product with the statements "Conservative" to the left and "Indulgent" to the right. That gives you four distinct quadrants into which the automobiles will naturally fall. The Lamborghini will be positioned toward the "Prestige" end as well as being far right in the "Indulgent" category, while the Mercedes will be up around the "Prestige" end, but a little closer to the center line. Basic Fords and Chevys will fall down below the center line, closer to the "Price" consideration and left of the center line, signifying a more conservative, low-end product.

Keep in mind that those are neither features nor benefits of the products. Those are market perceptions, but they are in many ways more telling about potential purchasers and where in the market this product should live than tire size, maximum speed or any of the other vehicle attributes. Once you know where your product stands, or where you might like your proposed product to stand, then you're ready to create the type of positioning that will help guarantee success in the marketplace.

Of course, your product's position on the perceptual map is not based on mere guesses. There are distinct characteristics to consider, requiring the following steps:

- Identify similar competitive products and relevant attributes that give each product the characteristics that make it stand out in the market. This is where elements of both physical and perceptual positioning come into play.

- Collect sample information and perceptions from consumers to determine a baseline of desire and acceptance. In the same vein, evaluate the consumers' passion (if any) for similar products.

- Measure the blend and balance of product attributes among the competition and note how each impacts the perceived value of that product. Customer preference will drive the attribute blend.

- Take a close look at market position and fit, not only for your product but for the competition as well, and determine if continued pursuit of this position is a viable strategy.

Once you've done all that, you're ready to pick a positioning strategy.

TAKING THE RIGHT APPROACH

There are many schools of thought about developing the right positioning strategy for a product or company. Some are broader and more attuned to industry trends, others more niche-derived and/or specific to issues uncovered in market research. We're going to take a look at both so that you have a wide array of approaches to follow.

No matter which route you take, however, make sure your positioning strategy is based on sound market research. While it's true that products can create demand—Did anyone express a desire for a fruit-flavored gelatin dessert made from processed horse hoofs before Jello hit the supermarket shelves?—that demand must be cultivated within the right market segment, one that has both an interest in and ability to support the product under development. Most product misfires occur because the marketers failed to understand the interest, abilities or interpretations expressed by the desired market niche prior to product launch. Measure all the elements and match the opportunity as closely as possible.

Defining a broad competitive strategy is one of the first steps you need to take in developing your product's or your company's position. Michael Porter, a professor of marketing at the Harvard School of Business, has studied the concept extensively, arriving at the following foundation principles behind developing a competitive strategy:

• Competitive strategy is the search for a favorable competitive position in the industry. That may come as the identification of an unfilled niche, or it may be an overall approach to consumer needs and wants that has not been effectively filled. In any event, it's a reason to enter the market and compete for customers without which a product or firm may be doomed to fail.

• Competitive strategy aims to establish a profitable and sustainable position relative to industry competitors. The key here, of course, is sustainability. If a niche appears currently unoccupied, there may be a reason for it. The ability to successfully enter a market is not reason enough to do so if the opportunity for sustained profit and financial growth doesn't warrant the time, effort and resource allocation necessary. The long-term financial return to investors is critical for successful product growth and development.

Both of those aspects are the result of sound research technique, something we covered in the previous chapter. Professor Porter argues that, in the course of that research, more aspects need to be considered than merely potential market demand. In determining competitive advantage, there's also a need to measure other impacts by the market.

There are five distinct factors that are functions of industry structure, as opposed to product characteristics, that will have an impact on the success of product entry and sustainability. Their collective impact helps define the nature of the product and its marketplace positioning as well as a product's level of long-term profitability. The following likely will have a distinct impact on what constitutes competitive positioning:

• The entry of new competitors, which measures the impact that similar products newly introduced will have on the ability of existing products to compete. This factor also helps measure whether new competitor entrants will help grow the market or merely sap a finite customer base, negatively affecting the ability of all competitors to enjoy economies of scale that lead to continued sustainability.

• The threat of substitutes impacts an established product or company's ability to compete, but it also measures the impact of competitive responses and what they will mean to sustainable profitability. How will existing products respond in terms of price reduction, revised distribution strategies and continued product line expansions that will enable more sustainable niche product development?

• The bargaining power of buyers is often an area overlooked by manufacturers and marketers in factoring profitability scenarios. However, veterans know that it can exercise powerful influences on price, positioning and profitability.

In the 1980s, the hotel industry, enjoying boom times, expanded its inventory with a multitude of new properties designed to take advantage of the growing consumer, business and convention trade. The early '90s, awash in fiscal conservatism, saw a reduction in the trade at the very time when the industry needed it to support increased capacity. Suddenly it was a buyers' market and hotels were negotiating very deep discounts, especially with the convention industry, so they would have the required "cheeks in seats" and "heads in beds," to use the industry vernacular. Clearly, buyers drove the market's ability to compete at the expense of industry profitability.

• The bargaining power of suppliers also affects a product's sustainability and long-term profitability. In some instances, time and fortunes can turn the tables on the buyer/seller equation.

That same hotel industry learned its lesson and changed its strategy when the pendulum began to swing back on consumer, business and convention travel. Rather than build more hotels to accommodate the increases in business, the industry instead stood pat and increased its rates for room nights, food and beverage functions and other amenities. The resulting increases in profitability, realized with little or no increase in expenditures, led to stronger financial growth for the industry. This time, as suppliers, the hotel chains were the ones in the position of influence and the buyers paid the price. What's more, the hotel industry will be better able to financially weather the storm when the pendulum of business once again swings the other way.

• Rivalry among existing competitors, like the threat of new competitors and industry substitutes, will do more to change the structure of the industry and its offerings than the bargaining power of suppliers or buyers. Rivalry can affect the way a product or company is positioned; how the company is marketed; the nature, structure and price of its products; and a host of other variables intrinsic to the company's identity and ability.

Please note that all of these structural components come into play when defining a strategic position for your product or company within the marketplace whether you expect them to or not. In fact, they serve as the building blocks to most successful positioning strategies because they often present the primary obstacles to overcome in order to make that strategy a success.

So what are the foundation strategies a company can pursue? Professor Porter identifies three, the last of which is really a niche-based variant of the first two strategies combined:

1. Cost Leadership Strategy

Companies that choose to compete from a cost leadership position have a simple strategy to follow: undercut the price of the competition while marketing a product of equal or better quality. Wal-Mart follows a cost leadership strategy, going so far as to tout its discounts in each and every television commercial it produces. No one doubts that Wal-Mart prices will be among the lowest in town; however even with the presence of brand names this strategy raises the specter of low merchandise quality. This specter has little or nothing to do with what Wal-Mart does or doesn't do in terms of offering quality merchandise. That perception is merely a part of human nature and is sometimes the unpleasant byproduct of being the industry's low-cost leader.

In order to compete with this strategy, a company must be perceived as *the* low cost leader, not merely one of several. It must have the economies of scale in order to sustain this position over time. It helps if the firm has a proprietary technology or preferential access to raw materials that give it a market edge. Without these elements, the company may find it hard to continue to be the cheapest game in town. In addition, under this strategy, the competition is fierce and consumer loyalty nonexistent. This can be a hard beach head to seize and hold.

2. Differentiation Strategy

Under a differentiation strategy, the tables are turned to tout the company's specific competitive advantage. This may be a differentiation based on the product itself, the company itself, or the method of product or service delivery. In any of these cases, you have something unique to offer (or so you position yourself) and are thus able to charge a premium price for that difference.

Ritz-Carlton Hotels know they are not the most economical option and they don't try to be. They don't even try to compete with other four-star hotel chains like Hilton or Hyatt. Instead, Ritz-Carlton trades on its image as a high-cost upscale hostelry that offers marvelous amenities and superior service. Of course, this approach reduces the number of potential clients, but it exacts a higher price from those it does serve. Positioned at the far end of an industry that already differentiates itself based on quality of service, Ritz-Carlton takes further steps in the direction of its image of a differentiator among differentiators. And its works.

Many companies find a differentiation strategy easier to market because it offers them something unique on which to trade. Low cost is low cost, period. Differentiation offers a more complex value equation with a greater number of variables with which to snag the interest of consumers and trade them to a service level based on value, not price.

3. Focus Strategy

Both of the aforementioned strategies are broad-band strategies; in other words, they appeal to the market for specific products and services overall. There are also narrow-band strategies of both low cost and differentiation, which come under the general heading of focus strategies. Plainly put, focus strategies attend to the same needs of the various groups, but based on the ability to occupy specific market niches within the industries they serve.

A hotel chain that specialized in serving the needs of traveling Middle Eastern oil sheiks, for example, would realize a marvelous return on investment, but from a very small niche that likely wouldn't have the power to support too many establishments for too long. Since being a low-cost leader requires significant economies of scale, a niche strategy within that industry has even less potential for success.

In all three cases, however, there is a distinct strategic platform on which the positioning efforts are constructed. Part of the issue is one of self-realization—what is your product and company and what do you want it to be? The other part comes from helping consumers arrive at the same conclusion and financially support your enterprise appropriate to its targets and goals. Do this successfully, and you will wind up much closer to your ultimate goal of sustainable financial success.

POSITIONING
SUB-STRATEGIES

Professor Porter's three approaches to the market look at positioning from a foundation perspective, which is why their impact can be so profound. There also are positioning sub-strategies designed to work with the confines of the three foundation principles:

• *Monosegment positioning* targets a narrowly defined sub-segment audience with a specific marketing message, like the Middle Eastern old sheiks we previously mentioned. Appealing exclusively to this group requires tailoring marketing and product development efforts exclusively for them.

• *Multisegment positioning,* as you might expect, expands on monosegmentation to embrace several related or unrelated audience segments with the same or similar product messages. The Ford pickup truck may appeal primarily to the hardworking farmer or rancher, but it may also contain some cachet for the ex-urban householders, young male population segment interested in developing a macho image or women interested in projecting an image of self-sufficiency. Messages crafted to expand the market and related economies of scale help support economic goals, but the approach may be subject to successful monosegmented attacks to the key market.

• In between monosegment and multisegment falls the standby strategy, used as a fall back by those multisegment positioners that may find a monosegment attack appealing. In some cases, this could alienate the various other segments already previously pursued and may cause more harm than good. The monosegment approach may be put on standby status just in case the product's multisegment market position begins to lose market share, thus sales.

• Products have become successful using *imitative positioning,* or the familiar "me too"

MARKET RESEARCH

Waldbillig & Besteman, a Madison, Wisconsin-based marketing firm, specializes in brand development. Executives there have created a 10-step approach to branding that has universal application no matter what the product, company or industry. These steps include the following:

1. Develop a brand positioning statement that describes the company/product and its benefits in language the consumer will understand.

2. Articulate a brand "vision" statement that describes how the company/product should be perceived in one, five and 10 years.

MARKET RESEARCH

(Continued)

3. Create a brand name that uniquely expresses those positioning and vision statements.

4. In the same vein, create a brand phrase or logo to express the primary customer benefit.

5. Develop a brand graphic mark or logo that visually represents these characteristics.

6. Create a brand graphic identity or standard that supports both the logo and benefit quality/message to consumers.

7. Identify a brand communications style—tone of voice, copy approach—that

strategy. When Hertz rental car company was number one, Avis made advertising history with its, "We Try Harder!" campaign, publicly acknowledging that they were number two and then telling consumers why renting from the secondary player was to their advantage. Such positioning isn't always successful, but can work if the supporting elements are approached in the right way.

• More difficult, both conceptually and operationally, is *anticipatory positioning*. That's when a company attempts to predict the market and position its product for consumer needs or desires not yet expressed. This can be enormously successful when handled with the right amount of market saturation— America On-Line virtually created the rapid growth in demand for Internet and e-mail access, far outpacing Prodigy, its nearest competitor. But it's often difficult to do successfully without adequate research and good gut instinct about the next wave in the marketplace.

• *Adaptive positioning* involves repositioning a product or company as the market it attempts to serve continues to evolve. One of the key complaints about companies like America On-Line in the beginning was the high cost of monthly online access. To combat this, AOL began sending out free CDs to anyone and everyone they could think of, first offering 25 free hours of service, followed by 50 hours, then 100 free hours and, ultimately, 500 free hours of AOL. In addition to being a marvelous value-added service, the free online time made consumer complaints over cost virtually impossible to voice.

• *Defensive posturing* can be used extremely effectively to protect market share and expand product line, all within the same fell swoop. In the retail industry, as any retail marketer knows, shelf position is critical to successful sales. Ernst and Julio Gallo proved to be masters at the art of retail shelf warfare when it came to promoting their line of wines.

Originally providers of moderately priced sub-premium wines in the 1960s, Gallo created lines of gold, pink and ruby "chablis" wines in wide-bottom bottles that spread the line down yards and yards of shelf space. The wines tended to cannibalize themselves in favor of meeting the newly growing consumer market for wines at all levels and made it difficult if not impossible for the competition to find simple breadth of space.

The winery also expanded vertically as well, offering even lower-end flavored and "pop" wines for even less-sophisticated palates while introducing a line of varietals designed to capture those who had outgrown the chablis line. In other words, by subdividing its market segment, Gallo stood a better chance of capturing consumers—and critical retail shelf space—at virtually all levels and hanging on to them as their sophistication—and, presumably, economic commitment to wine consumption—grew throughout their lives.

MARKET RESEARCH
(Continued)

does the same textually that the graphic identity does visually.

8. Develop brand equity, defined as a blend of all such components that establishes and holds a unique position within the marketplace.

9. Build a brand communications plan around these elements that can accomplish stated goals in a cost-effective manner.

10. Create a brand personality with which consumers can develop a relationship, the ultimate goal of brand development.

• Gallo's introductory line of varietals, launched in the early 1970s, also may be a good example of *stop-gap positioning*. With its name still primarily associated with sub-premium wines, Gallo's new varietals likely would do little to attract the attention of "serious" wine drinkers. But their existence did provide a stop-gap position that helped the company itself trade up to a higher level position in the wine market and give them a foothold until such time as their sub-premium drinkers traded up or the rest of the market began to appreciate what the Modesto, California, winery had to offer; and, frankly, until such time as the varietal products themselves improved to catch up with the market the winery had helped create.

Identifying the right sub-strategy, taken within the larger context of your defined foundation principles, can give you both the purpose and means to move forward with good positioning and, ultimately, successful brand development. Remember that positioning is the identification of how you want your product and/or company to be perceived in the marketplace and by whom. Branding, on the other hand, is the achievement of that goal and constant recognition of and appreciation for those principles by the audience you seek to serve.

During the 1960s, a wide array of small, economical foreign-made motorcycles and motor scooters hit the market, designed to combat the unnecessarily large and noisily intrusive presence of the quintessential American-made motorcycles produced by Harley Davidson Company. The new companies, most notably Honda and Suzuki, also sought to combat the image associated with those who rode Harleys—police officers and those whom police officers often sought to apprehend. Over time, however, improved workmanship on the product itself as well as a broad-band repositioning of the product—prompted not only by the manufacturer but by the marketplace as well—has now created a market that regularly outpaces the manufacturer's ability to produce product.

And the throaty, piston-rich sound of a Harley accelerating in the distance is as vivid and unique as any graphic logo. What once was an unpleasant manufacturing byproduct has been embraced as a distinct auditory trademark by those riders, now from all walks of life, who proudly say: "That's my bike!"

Make no little plans;
they have no magic to stir men's blood.

—Daniel Hudson Burnham

4

Making Plans

Marketing is both a discipline and a strategy, the means by which a business accomplishes its objectives and financial goals through an organized response to the obstacles and opportunities presented by the marketplace. As such, marketing is not a haphazard nor an undisciplined exercise, and those who think it is are doomed to fail. Rather, effective marketing is the result of a well developed plan that is soundly and thoroughly applied with an eye toward the development of measurable results.

In reality, a good marketing plan is a mirror of the strategic and economic goals of the company it represents. The company's overall mission and vision are supported by its marketing and development efforts. The chief executive officer and board of directors may define the nature of the firm and set the company's sights on the relative level of desired profitability. It's the marketing plan, however, that articulates how the firm will get there from here.

A daunting task? It can be, but more daunting still will be the situation a company finds itself in if it does not have a marketing plan to guide its developmental efforts. Without a solid marketing strategy committed to paper (or at least electronic imagery), one designed to guide you through the rocky shoals of both economic challenges and competitive marketplace threats, you may lose both your buoyancy and your direction. Suddenly, your firm may find itself adrift in the turbulent seas of commerce, consigned to wallow in the economic shallows or perhaps even sink to the depths of misguided direction or lost opportunity.

While that maritime imagery may be overly dramatic, the point it attempts to make is not: Develop a good marketing plan and let it guide your every action. Without it, your marketing efforts can easily fail and you could stand considerably less of a chance to succeed and reach your company's goals. It's that simple.

UNDERSTANDING MARKETING PLAN BASICS

A marketing plan, like a business plan, is unique to the company it serves. There are few hard and fast rules that guide its creation and implementation. A marketing plan needs to be as flexible as its market allows and as firm as is required to accomplish its goals. Despite all that, there are a few key components critical to the successful development and application of such a plan:

• A good marketing plan has both strategic and tactical elements designed to help identify and accomplish its goals. Despite the fact that marketing often appears to be no more than the implementation of direction from the corner office, the best ones also contain elements of strategy that reflect and enhance those principles identified at the highest level. Too often, marketing efforts are seen only as a media placement plan or advertising schedule. The best ones are much more than that and, quite frankly, need to be if they are going to succeed at more than the most episodic and rudimentary level.

• A good marketing plan is intertwined with the corporate business plan and, in fact, may actually be that plan, or at least include the business plan's goals expressed in terms of tactics. Despite what we said in the previous paragraph, the marketing plan can't exist in and of itself without intrinsic links to the company's overall strategies. They are two sides of the same coin and must be played together in order for either to succeed. Marketers who think they can operate independently of corporate goals think incorrectly and either their goals, or those of the company, will be compromised if they try.

• A good marketing plan is an active, living document designed to accomplish tasks, not a theoretical exercise destined to sit on the shelf. Marketing is a lot like dancing in that, if you don't execute the moves, it does anyone little good that you know all the steps. The best marketing plans are dog-eared documents with pencil edits and handwritten commentary that are falling apart at the seams. That shows they've been used and used well. The worst plans are pristine volumes that sit on shelves and gather dust. There are no grades for neatness when it comes to your marketing plan.

• Good marketers know that all things commercial revolve around marketing. That will sound heretical to anyone who is not a marketer, but when you get right down to it, marketing impacts virtually every aspect of commerce. As much as any other member of a company's executive team, the marketer's influence is felt throughout the enterprise and down the ranks.

Remember the five Ps of marketing identified in Chapter 1? Perhaps it's good to review them once again so you may judge for yourself the depth and breadth of marketing's impact:

- **Product:** the goods or services that you market and sell.

- **Price:** the value of those goods or services quantified in monetary terms.

- **Promotion:** how you communicate the benefits of those goods and services.

- **Place:** how you expose buyers to products and get products into their hands.

- **Position:** the way the product is perceived in the mind of the buyer.

In each of those instances, the marketer plays the most crucial role in determining value rather than, or at least in cooperation with, other executives who otherwise might be considered appropriate to the task. Take pricing, for instance. Isn't that a function of the chief financial officer? Doesn't the CFO have responsibility for the company's financial stability and profitability?

The CFO certainly does have those responsibilities, but he or she can't determine the price of a product without knowing the price at which the competition is selling its products and what the market will bear for such goods. Identifying the proper margin over the cost of production is part of price determination, but it plays a relatively small role in the pricing equation.

Good pricing and its related profitability, instead, are based on the strategic machinations of the other four Ps, as well as market conditions, buyer preferences, current market share and a host of things about which few CFOs have the time or inclination to study. The person in charge of finances and profitability has a role to play in determining price, but that discussion needs to be led by the marketer or someone else well-versed in all the areas that affect those prices and, ultimately, corporate profitability.

• A good marketing plan is both internally and externally focused in its determination of the company's appropriate competitive direction. Knowing market conditions is not enough. The marketing plan also must consider the company's abilities to meet those conditions profitably and on a sustained basis.

Knowing the market will support the sale of two million of the widgets you produce in the next two months does little good if your firm doesn't have the capacity to produce those widgets. Of course, you can always subcontract the work. But if the cost of manufacture, coupled with the necessary markup, does not produce the level of profitability desired or required, then it may be better to walk away from the business entirely. Without the proper internal focus to your marketing plan, that's an expensive lesson you could have learned the hard way.

• Finally, realize the marketing plan also provides the tools to measure the flow of your company's developmental steps and events. In the same way it offers a reflection of your company's business plan, the marketing plan creates a series of benchmarks by which to chart its developmental progress. If all goes well and your marketing succeeds beyond your wildest dreams, then the plan can stand almost as a stairway to that success, with each step identified with a component of that plan. More often than not, the plan will reflect a mix of hits and misses, each of which can be evaluated both by its success and by its role within the plan's strategic mix.

And last year's plan, warts and all, is always used, if not as the foundation, then at least as a touchstone for the next year's marketing effort.

SEVEN STEPS TO AN EFFECTIVE MARKETING PLAN

There is no hard and fast structure when it comes to the look, feel, taste, touch and smell of your marketing plan. As mentioned earlier, it can be as long or as short as it needs to be while still accomplishing the tasks required. More is not necessarily better when it comes to planning, but less may be too little if you fail to include the key components you'll need to draft a successful plan. Proceed cautiously and thoroughly; otherwise, as the old saying goes, you may find yourself planning in haste and repenting in leisure.

For our money, there are at least seven steps contained within a good marketing plan that you should consider for your plan. There are variations on these themes, and components are sometimes spun out as steps of their own. Whether or not this will happen will be up to you to decide. In the meantime, include at least the following as you chart your course toward greater marketing success.

Step 1: Look Within

This is not designed to be an esoteric or philosophical discussion of your value and worth as either a marketer or a human being. Rather, Step 1 requires that you look at the goals and objectives, the capabilities and directions of the company for which you market and do an internal analysis of strengths and weaknesses before venturing out into the cold, cruel marketing world.

If done correctly, the analysis of your business actually accomplishes two tasks. In addition to measuring the capabilities and desires of the firm in relation to its marketing goals and objectives, the analysis also can provide a context against which more objective elements can be measured. By nature of the process, for example, a company product analysis will contain assessment of the market segment that already uses the product. This provides the necessary context when it comes to identifying and analyzing future niches to serve. Think of Step 1 as the foundation of your marketing plan and proceed accordingly.

The business analysis also may serve purposes beyond the needs of marketing plan development. To that end, it helps to have all key decision makers involved in the process. Once again, this analysis does not exist in a vacuum and must reflect the true corporate picture if it's going to be useful both to the company and to its marketing efforts. One way that the marketer can assist is to prepare an outline of the areas of analysis and lead discussions as to the firm's strengths and weaknesses, goals and opportunities. Having the appropriate data at hand in an easily usable form also is helpful. The overall conclusion drawn from the analysis should be supported and endorsed by heads of all affected departments so that the marketing effort can move forward with as little hindrance as possible.

There are numerous areas to consider during the business analysis and specifics will vary based on whether the company in question is a manufacturing enterprise, service firm or any of hundreds of different types of businesses in between. Once again, flexibility of content, backed by firm commitment to the process, will be critical for success. There are a few primary areas of analysis that will benefit most, if not all firms:

• Review the corporate philosophy and take a snapshot of goals and purpose in light of that philosophy before moving ahead with any plans. Too many marketing efforts stray from the meaning and purpose of the firm they're trying to serve. That can skew marketing efforts in a direction the company can't support, which means little or no success in the long run. Review the firm's purpose, mission and goals before proceeding to avoid future misfires of efforts.

• Recognize and analyze what the company's target market segments are and how they're being served. Divide these segments into primary and secondary marketers and identify where the heaviest use of the company's product is by demographic parameters (age, gender, educational level, geographic location and other factors). Refine these measures as much as possible and look for patterns of usage as well as demographic trends. Is the customer population aging at a faster rate than new younger customers can be converted? Such a variable will tell you a lot about your firm, its products and its market.

If your firm sells to other businesses rather than to end-user consumers, you have a slightly different set of variables to consider, but the methodology is much the same. Rather than trying to measure the change in the nature of consumer-customers, you will instead need to study and evaluate as much as possible trends within the companies that buy from you and, in turn, how their markets may be changing. This becomes more complex, but you may find cooperation from those companies more forthcoming, since you're both trying ultimately to serve the same customer base.

• Analyze past and projected sales activities and watch for trends, both positive and negative. Such trend analyses may include overall sales, sales by department or enterprise center, and related market share issues. Since marketing is designed to support sales efforts, changes in sales have tremendous meaning for marketing in terms of what kind of support to provide.

• Measure brand awareness within the marketplace and determine what role your products play within the industry. If you haven't done so, this will require market research. Whether you're starting from scratch or already have such information in hand, it should be included in the mix. As we said in Chapter 3 the position your products hold in customers' minds is more important than all the features and attributes you can offer. Concurrent with this is the measurement of the purchase rates and buying habits of consumers. This is the quantification of many of those brand perceptions and also should be considered.

• Your company's distribution strategy also comes into play here because of its role in enabling products to be put in the hands of buyers. Issues like retail versus wholesale, channels of distribution, geography and the resulting market penetration within "communities" of all types will have an impact on your success, both present and future.

• Pricing, of course, is one of the most critical variables to analyze. Where do your products fit into the overall marketplace? Are you the low-cost leader or a high-priced differentiator? Are your prices perceived as competitive, or are they out of sync with the competition? Analyze both the reality and perception of your pricing models to determine if your prices are a help or hindrance to your marketing efforts.

• Finally, review past marketing efforts in terms of how well goals had been articulated and how well results had been met. For many companies, such a review becomes a wakeup call when it comes to identifying why targets were missed and products stillborn. Generally, it's not a case of poor marketing; more often, it's a case of poorly articulated goals and strategies or an overall misunderstanding of the product or its intended market. Close analysis of the marketing that has gone on before—not to mention the thinking and rationale behind it—can be an eye-opening lesson for company executives at all levels.

Contingent with the business analysis comes the need for analyzing the opportunities and challenges the company faces. Chances are you've already identified many of these in conjunction with your analysis of the business. At this point you need to categorize the various types of variables.

Corporate planners are fond of doing this under the guise of a SWOT analysis, articulating strengths, weaknesses, opportunities and threats as part of the overall planning processing. This also comes in handy for the marketer because it offers insight into where marketing efforts should be channeled and where corrective action needs to take place. It doesn't matter specifically how you categorize the issues that affect your firm. It only matters that you do so correctly and in a way that allows the marketing plan to properly address those issues as effectively as possible.

Step 2: Target Your Markets

With the final demise, once and for all, of *LIFE* magazine, the era of mass marketing and being all things to all people finally ended. Today's markets are rich in niches and, thanks especially to the Internet, virtually every individual has become his or her own market segment. Marketers Don Peppers and Martha Rogers stress the fact that one-to-one marketing, in which the marketing message is tailored not to people *like* you, but to *you* directly, is no longer the wave of the future but the practice of the present. That makes clear, concise target efforts critical to marketing survival.

When you think about it, this is pretty heady stuff and not an easy challenge to meet. That means great care should be taken to identify both current and potential primary and secondary markets and evaluate the opportunities offered by all of them. And remember that there is only one primary market. If there appear to be two, then you haven't dug deep enough to find out what the underlying characteristics are that connect them. Once you do discover that connection, however, you may open up entire new segments for your products connected at a level you hadn't heretofore realized.

This step requires the incorporation of some pretty comprehensive data both from within the company and without. Demographic and geographic measures will help bring particulars into focus, and the more details you have on your primary and secondary users, the better off you are. But remember that the data must serve as a basis for further analysis to identify linkages among users at the various levels.

It also pays to understand the difference between your primary and secondary markets. You may be targeting one without realizing that the other has a great deal more potential.

Consider the manufacturer of after-market auto parts—batteries, mufflers, tires and other items that need replacing during the normal life of a car. Those are consumer-purchased products, which makes the average driver and car owner the primary market, right? But what about car rental companies, corporate fleet managers and repair shops, all of whom undoubtedly purchase such items every day? Are they then the secondary market for such products? It all depends on the level of business they do, the pricing and distribution strategy of the manufacturer, and the manufacturer's corporate philosophy.

Microchip manufacturer Intel Inc. knew that the end-user was the key market for its product, but that contracts and purchases came through computer manufacturers such as IBM and Apple, who installed the chips in their machines. In an attempt to influence those manufacturers to purchase only Intel microchips, the company launched a vivid and memorable consumer campaign that stressed the importance of having Intel microchips powering home PCs. Presumably, most consumers weren't going to purchase and install their own microchips, but they could and did make purchasing decisions based on whether or not that PC or Macintosh had the "Intel Inside" sticker pasted to its front. The microchip manufacturer broadened the definition of its primary market, then took the necessary steps to serve both segments.

MARKET RESEARCH

In terms of strategies, marketers have a choice of whether to create their own market or beg, borrow or steal from an existing one. Market expansion often offers more permanent solutions, since the product likely will be the first of its type or first in its category, thus forever associated with the "invention" of that market. However, it is easier to steal market share because it doesn't require the initial steps of introducing

Step 3: Develop Your Positioning Strategy

The position your company or its products strive to achieve in the marketplace is the key not only to your identity, but also the direction of the company and its entire marketing effort and plans. After reading the previous chapter, however, you already know that.

What you may not know is how this piece of the puzzle fits into your marketing plan. It's one of the most important pieces, of course, but it's not the only piece. In fact, depending on the various execution strategies, it isn't always the most important piece, either. Nevertheless, it's critical that you manage this aspect of the marketing plan with equal if not greater aplomb because it has the ability to color all else that you do.

There are really two component parts to developing positioning that take place at the operational level as part of the marketing plan. Those two components are defining your marketing objectives and identifying your marketing strategies. Both work in concert, but each plays a separate role. One is more specific, while the other is more far reaching in nature. Developing each as part of a pair that requires both halves to function is critical.

To do this, your first act will be to return to Step 1 and review the strengths, weaknesses, opportunities and threats (your SWOT analysis) that the company or product faces. This is the foundation on which you will build both your objectives and strategies, providing the real life issues against which your theoretical approaches must be measured. Feel free at this stage to jot down ideas and solutions to those situations. You will need them very shortly.

The marketing objective differs from the strategy in that it tends to be quite specific in its identification of issues that need addressing and objectives that need accomplishing. It's sometimes easy to confuse objectives with strategies. It helps to remember that objectives have the following characteristics:

- An objective is *specific* to an individual challenge or goal.
- An objective is *measurable* and has *quantifiable* results.
- An objective can be accomplished within an *identifiable time period*.
- An objective often focuses on *changing target market behavior.*

Making a new brand of beer the third most popular brew in Cleveland and Cincinnati over the next nine months is a marketing objective. Developing a campaign to promote the brew at below-market prices and as a major sponsor of the Lake Erie Sailing Regatta and Ohio River Canoe Race is a marketing strategy.

Developing marketing objectives is done, like any aspect of good marketing, after reviewing the available data. That includes past sales figures (if this isn't a start-up company or product), the company's ability to support the product, the overall strategy and target market characteristics. Once you've done that and are sure that it is within your abilities to make Dog's Breath Lager Ohio's preferred summer drink, then you are ready to formulate that objective. (NOTE: Your marketing objectives must dovetail with your sales goals if they are to be achieved. We'll cover that in a moment.)

MARKET RESEARCH
(Continued)

your product and educating consumers as to its value. Building a market for a new product requires a different and perhaps more informational strategy than stealing market share, which falls more along the lines of "me, too" marketing. In the end, the nature of the product is the element most likely to determine which will be your strategy.

Your marketing strategy will take the process one step further by articulating how your objectives will be achieved. While your objectives are written as specific, quantifiable goals, the strategies tend to be more descriptive, explaining how those goals can and will be met. It is, in fact, the strategies that help define how you will position your product.

Under this rationale, a quick look at the introductory strategy for Dog's Breath Lager shows a possible inconsistency that, unless managed properly, could undermine the marketing objective. The beer enters the test market priced below the competition, yet publicly sponsors what is a higher-end water sports activity associated with middle- to upper-income people. Consumers understand low-cost introductory offers and may well try the beer, especially as its profile grows thanks to the regatta and canoe race associations. However, if the price stays too low, then Dog's Breath Lager becomes a low-end product permanently, which is of little interest to high-end consumers and weekend sailors.

The positioning, then, should focus less on price and more on the product's qualities and affiliation with the events. After a reasonable period—say 60 days—the price can creep back up to the same level as premium beers and micro brews with the Cleveland and Cincinnati markets so that the beer's manufacturers can focus on the proper permanent position for the product.

Step 4: Set Your Sales Objective

There are two schools of thought on where the setting of sales objectives falls within marketing plan development. One school believes that, by setting the sales objective first, you have identified a measurable, quantifiable goal that you then can develop strategies to support. It's not unlike setting a marketing objective, then defining strategies to reach that objective. From a certain point of view, that makes a lot of sense.

The other school takes a more holistic view of marketing and of company and product progress and success. A preset sales goal can spur a marketer to action, give him or her a clear target to shoot for and offer benchmarks of progress made along the way, it's true. But it doesn't necessarily take into account the mission and vision of the company, or the long-term strategies necessary to put it in the desired market position.

Let's use the strategy for Dog's Breath Lager developed from the previous section. If the sales goal is set first, then we as marketers may be faced with selling 2,000 cases in the next 120 days in both the Cleveland and Cincinnati markets. Our tactic to accomplish what is in reality a short-term goal may be to simply undercut the competition and offer the product at a price that assures every beer drinker in town will at least pick up a bottle and try it. We might also offer incentives to restaurants and bars to promote the product on site, further cementing the relationship with customers of a low-cost leader.

But we also know the executives at Dog's Breath want to position their lager as a premium product for the high-end market. That's why the beer is sponsoring water sports events in both cities. That's not a position generally occupied by the low-cost leader, at least not for very long. Thus, if the sales goals drive the marketing goals, the company may fail to realize the positioning strategy it hopes to achieve.

In the end, of course, it takes a balanced strategy to reach both sales goals and marketing objectives, in which case it matters little whether one or the other is developed first. Follow your instincts on that, but remember that one should support the other in order for both steps to succeed.

What you should remember is that sales objectives are like marketing objectives in that they need to identify specific, measurable variables:

- A sales goal is *specific* to an individual product or service.

- A sales goal is *measurable* and has *quantifiable* results.

- A sales goal can be accomplished within an *identifiable time period.*

- A sales goal focuses on *changing customer purchasing behavior.*

Do those characteristics sound familiar? They should because they are reflections of the development of marketing objectives. Both parts need to work in tandem while being supported by your marketing strategies.

Setting sales goals is much like setting marketing goals in that both internal and external factors need to be considered. Sales goals need to take into consideration economic and marketplace trends while, at the same time, measuring the desire and capacity of the company to achieve its goals. Past sales activity can be used to develop trend lines and expectations, and then goals can be built around those factors. Set goals that are ambitious, yet achievable. Your sales force should work to build revenues and establish market share. But make sure those goals are achievable with effort. Setting your sights too high will only frustrate your salesforce and result in less rather than greater sales activity.

We'll talk about the art and science of sales—and it does comprise some of each—at greater length in Chapters 15 and 16. For now, however, know that sales must be part of your marketing plan and develop it according to the needs of your organization.

Step 5: Identify Your Tactics

There's an old Spanish proverb that says goals without means are like bread without flour. So, too, with marketing. You've identified your product, its position and the strategies you need to establish and support a sustainable brand. But the true role of marketing is realized in its execution. Marketing without tactics is theory without practice. Those tactics should be outlined as part of the marketing plan. Include the following steps in your tactic development process:

• If you haven't already done so, establish your product objectives and supporting strategies. Whether this includes developing new products or extending existing product lines, all should be articulated as part of the planning process for, while product enhancement and improvement can be a goal, it's also a tactic to support such goals as revenue growth and market share expansion.

• Along these same lines, you'll want to articulate any packaging strategies that need articulation. The first winery to introduce its brands packaged in a cardboard box likely did so in response to consumer survey data indicating a wine tap, rather than a clumsy glass gallon jug, would make the product more appealing and increase wine consumption. Build strategies around this tactic that involve wholesaler, retailer and sales force.

• Decide on a price appropriate to the market you're trying to serve. Since this is a strategic decision, you may price your products lower, higher or on par with the market. It all depends on what your strategy might be. That price also may be determined by your distribution plans, geographic location and the timing of the entry of your product into the market. Your pricing strategies should be set in accordance to your overall corporate strategy and in support of accomplishing your marketing goal. Remember the Dog's Breath Lager discussion? It all applies to the science of pricing.

• Review and articulate your product distribution system and how you plan to put your products into the hands of your customers. Your distribution strategy should discuss how the product will be placed as well as distributed, what the preferred market penetration will be and what distribution challenges and costs lie in the way of strategic success.

• Identify and articulate your promotional strategies, including your selection of medium and message. This starts by reviewing your marketing objectives and then applying them to your promotional goals balanced against the threats and opportunities that exist to help or harm your promotional efforts. Your media choice—be it print, broadcast, outdoor or on-line—will depend on who you are trying to reach and under what conditions. Chapters 17 and 18 will look at media selection and usage in greater depth.

• Your media choice needs to be accompanied by a set of clearly stated advertising objectives to drive the message that media will carry. Coupled with that is the need for a comprehensive media plan that sets goals and strategies. The advertising objective, like the marketing and sales objectives, is measurable, quantifiable, developed to be accomplished in a specific time frame, and designed to change consumer behavior. The advertising strategies, in turn, are the more far-reaching methodologies to help accomplish those goals. The media plan contains the tools by which both goals and strategies will be reached.

• Finally, the plan should contain ancillary support activities, such as merchandising and publicity strategies that will support the sales and marketing goals articulated in the overall plan. We'll talk about each of those options a little later, too.

Step 6: Build Your Marketing Budget/Establish Time Lines

As with any business activity or discipline, a solid marketing budget is critical to success. In addition to helping you manage available resources, the budget measures your investment in each step and allows you better computation of the payback on your investment. And marketing expenditures are definitely investments, not merely expenses, in the future growth and prosperity of your company.

Like any line item budget, each activity should be matched by an expense and, if you're so inclined, the percent of total budget that expenditure represents. That way certain types of expenditures— media purchases, for example—can be classified in terms of how much of the budget they represent. Remember that the budget is not only a record of expenditure, but also a strategic management tool. The more manageable information you have to describe that strategy, the more effectively you can use the resource.

One of the key roles your budget will play is to judge the return on your marketing investment. To that end, your budget should include payback analyses for each of the major expenditures and expenditure categories. If an expense does not appear to warrant the investment based on your analysis, then expunge that activity from the plan and use those funds where they will do more good. Two types of payback analyses have proven effective:

• The contribution to fixed costs is calculated by computing gross sales, then subtracting the cost of goods sold to arrive at gross profit from which the variable costs are then subtracted. The net results accurately reflect the results of your marketing efforts and what can be expected from marketing expenditures.

• You may use the gross margin to net sales payback method. This method takes the gross margin on the product after direct expenses, then applies that percent again to that margin to cover marketing and advertising. Thus, if a product offered a gross margin of 25 percent, then 25 percent of that gross margin amount would be consigned to product marketing. We'll talk more about the science and art of budgeting in the next chapter.

Finally, once you have established your budget, it's important to develop a time line of activity. The calendar is used, obviously, to plan activities and media placement. But it also provides at a glance the scope and reach of your marketing effort. The calendar is critical, not only for helping accomplish the marketing goals you set out to accomplish, but to provide the information to those charged with executing the marketing as well as other interested and obligated parties within the company.

Step 7: Execution and Evaluation

Once your plan has been completed, all the steps worked through and the benchmarks of plan development hit, it's time to execute that plan. To borrow Nike's positioning statement, "Just do it!"

Once the plan has been executed, it's important to measure the results of the marketing efforts. Obviously, sales results based on marketing goals are critical to measure. Whether that measurement looks at overall trends or is considered on a situation-by-situation or product-by-product basis depends on the nature of the effort. Most often, measurement considers a combination of the two. Whenever possible, it's important to tie marketing, advertising and sales objectives back to the goals outlined in the plan.

Recognition of the company, the product and/or the marketing message also can be measured as an adjunct to sales measurement. Public awareness surveys, focus groups and other methodologies to measure the impact of the marketing effort can help measure the effectiveness of the marketing plan elements and set the stage for the next round of planning.

And next year's marketing plan will be coming up sooner than you may think!

*If all the economists in the world
were laid end to end,
it probably would be a good thing.*

—Anonymous

5

Building Your Marketing Budget

To most marketers, budgeting is the antithesis of their discipline. Marketing is built around the ability to forecast the future, in and of itself a pretty inexact science. The more limitations strapping those visions to the rigors of reality, the less likely it is for marketing efforts to soar. Probably the biggest millstone around any marketer's neck, most of them reason, is the marketing budget. More than anything else, it keeps them from flying too close to the sun.

But marketing is, after all, a serious business component and one that drives the engines of profitability for the firms that practice it seriously. Because of that notion and in support of that belief, marketers, by their nature, must be fiscally responsible for their actions. If marketing's role is to stimulate growth and maximize profitability, marketers also must be responsible for the flip side of the financial equation, conserving and maximizing the resources that help achieve the desired marketing outcomes.

So, like it or not, marketers must operate under the influence of a budget, just like everyone else. And like everyone else, marketers may see that budget as an accounting restraint that does little more than limit their creativity and opportunity. However, as it is for other departments, the marketing budget also is a strategic methodology by which to stretch the impact and influence of their best efforts to market the company's most important brands. In the same way Olympic gymnasts can't demonstrate their expertise without the support of their sidehorse and the constant resistance of gravity, marketers can't

SNAPSHOT

What is a budget? Webster defines it as "the cost or estimated cost of living or operating during a prescribed time period." Accountants see it as a formal statement of management's plans for the future expressed in financial terms. Both are correct, and both are budgeting.

demonstrate their skills and resourcefulness without the limitations and foundations offered by a soundly written, well-crafted marketing budget.

If that's not reason enough for you to look at the marketing budget in a new light, consider this: Understanding and applying the budgeting process will help you understand the application of other financial principles. The marketing budget serves as the link between theory and reality. And, quite honestly, it's the way most marketers and other managers link to the accounting process within their organizations.

Budgeting also is a strategic link between your marketing efforts and the goals of the company. Marketing efforts, especially, can't exist in a vacuum. They're an intrinsic part of the company's overall operation. Just as your marketing management style must coexist peacefully within the operations and guidelines of company policy, your financial strategy must make sense within the context of your company's master plan. That makes a sound marketing budget critical to operations at a variety of levels.

This chapter will consider the basics of budgeting while taking a broader, more strategic view of the process at the same time. We'll take a look at the marketing budget and how to develop one that supports, rather than hinders your efforts. Marketers who have the ability to master the concept at all levels will gain not only better financial control of their department, but also will play a more valuable role in determining their firm's destiny. And that's always a good investment in your own professional development.

THE BUDGET: DEFINING THE CONCEPT

From a business perspective, your marketing department's budget represents a blueprint of action, a statement of your plans for the future represented in financial terms. From your position as area expert, do you see a bull market ahead? Are there steps to climb before reaching that next sales plateau? Will the competition send you back to the drawing board for newer and better advertising and promotion ideas? All that information is reflected in the marketing budget, and it's all plainly accessible for those who know how to develop and use it.

Although time periods and start dates may vary, 12 months is the most common cycle and the most practical time frame for budgeting, with 24 months popular in some quarters. The annual budget covers all four quarters of a company's operating year and conveniently correlates with the tax cycle. In today's dynamic business environment, anything too much longer is wishful thinking at best. And shorter time periods lack the perspective needed to judge the rough spots in the road that may lie ahead.

However, the budget may be divided into shorter components to better manage the flow of funds or the development and launch of new products and strategies. Most companies assess budget performance on a quarterly basis and some do it weekly if funds availability or some other factor requires more frequent examination. Subdivision doesn't change the nature or need for an annual blueprint, but it does offer tighter control when it's necessary.

Most businesses operate with two budgets. The *capital budget* pertains to fixed assets and measures the worth and financial evolution of higher-ticket items such as real estate, computer systems and other major equipment, expenditures and purchases. The *operating budget* measures the actual cash flow activity of day-to-day operations. From a marketer's perspective, this is the more critical of the two budgets because this will impact your cash flow and affect your ability to do things within your department.

The operational budget also defines the nature of the average marketing budget with a direct link to cause-and-effect results. Marketing budgets exist to quantify structure and direction of marketing efforts in monetary terms. There are strategic elements germane to the life of a particular budget, whether it covers a certain time period or a string of activities. But the net effect of both is to promote action that results in sales. In that regard, the marketing budget is primarily operational in nature.

All departmental and company budgets, marketing-specific or otherwise, predict sales and investment revenue and other earnings (income) and production and operating costs (expense). The difference between the two is the estimated profit or loss of a product line, department or overall company. In addition to its strategic component, the budget is the tool by which you can predict those numbers, enhance revenues and reduce expenses. The budget mirrors the company's strategic goals, providing a clear expression of the financial effect that those strategies may cause. And it helps set the goals for either or both as well as determining accountability for meeting those goals.

Your budget is that simple in concept, and that critical in application.

KNOW YOUR BUDGETING TYPE

Budgets, as a part of the business planning process, come in several makes and models, each of which is of benefit for the marketer to understand. Long-term budgets, which evaluate and set financial goals for a longer window of five to 10 years, are considered strategic budgets and operate as part of the company's overall strategic plan. Short-term budgets of roughly one-year's duration or less reflect the financial side of operational goals and have more direct application to day-to-day activities. Most operations have both types of budgets. Smart marketers review them regularly—sometimes continuously, depending on business conditions—and adjust the view periodically as needs arise.

The short-term budget is what most marketers expect to master first because it most directly relates to their core responsibilities. Its outcome is also more easily predicted. Designed to measure a year of production and earnings, it's a key controller of the ups and downs of operations and allows for adaptations in expenditures designed to increase revenue or reduce expenses.

The fact that the budget covers a 12-month time frame gives it somewhat of a strategic nature, allowing you to take both a proactive and reactive approach toward preserving a positive bottom line, if that's your goal. But its primary purpose is to anticipate and react to business changes within the coming year.

Longer business cycles require a longer-term budget to reflect their growth and anticipate changes over time. Most basic business operations run their courses within the standard budgetary year. Most strategic initiatives unfold over a longer period of time and often are the result of several year's worth of short-term growth initiatives. The long-term or strategic budget interacts at a higher level with your company's strategic goals, tracing a much longer financial profile that reflects those long-term goals.

The strategic budget plays a very different role from the operational budget and its numbers may appear more general and less precise in their units of measure. Together the two budgets provide a necessary and more comprehensive approach to financial management critical to long-term success.

Not all companies may want or need a strategic budget. Many operate just fine budgeting from year to year, applying what they've learned to the following year's operational budget and thus creating a satisfactory strategic component within the context of their annual operational approach. Yours may be just such a company. If so, be thankful that your life just got that much simpler.

However, if your company:

- is involved in major capital acquisition strategies that result in depreciation scenarios carried out over periods of years;

- pursues extensive research and development activities that result in incurring years of expense before realizing one red cent of revenue; or

- has significant building and development plans, the results of which will be extensive capitalization scenarios and amortization of expenses over a long time frame;

then a strategic budget not only may be more appropriate, it may be critical to the successful execution of any or all of those strategies.

By its very nature, the strategic budget identifies and measures the financial impact of long-term strategies on the business' economic well-being. What's good in concept ultimately may be bad for business. The strategic budget is the barometer by which those decisions can and should be made.

BUDGETING IN PRACTICE

The act of budgeting appears to be a simple one: the marketer identifies (or is given) financial goals for his or her operation; estimates basic expenses to accomplish these goals; and puts the two opposing forces (revenue and expenses) into a spreadsheet, hoping that the first guess is the best one. Usually, it isn't.

Successful budgeting relies less on the spreadsheet exercise and more on the thought and planning that goes on prior to any numbers being crunched. It's the issues beyond the numbers, rather than the numbers themselves,

SNAPSHOT

The key to budgeting, like the key to life, is to keep all things in balance. Marketers who budget to keep costs low may not invest enough development dollars into the expense side of their budget to realize revenue goals. Cutting essential costs to have a good bottom line on paper is not an effective way to budget.

that govern the creation of a successful budget. Consider the following questions before you sit down with your calculator and/or PC spreadsheet:

• *What goals will my budget and those of the other departments reflect?* Since "profitability" is a key component to most businesses' success, that may be the single driving factor. But profitability isn't always defined as short-term capital gain. More often, it falls under the heading of current client service and future market share growth, including new product development and new customer acquisition. Expenditures this year in pursuit of higher goals next year will definitely affect short-term capital gain. But it may make better financial sense and be more in line with company goals in the long run.

• *Will company objectives be plainly visible in my budget?* Remember that a well-articulated budget contains clear representation of goals and methodologies specific to your industry. Broad-brush growth in a short-term budget does little to aid those who either need to understand or pursue that growth. If the objectives of your budget match the goals of the company, then those goals should be clearly evident, thus more easily achieved. That makes your budget more of a strategic tool and less of a mere recitation of numbers.

• *Does my budget identify tactics by which those objectives will be achieved?* If the budget is well articulated and prepared with organizational goals in mind, it will also include a financial reflection of the tactics by which you will reach those goals. If your department's goal is increased market share, then the results of that increase will be reflected in projected revenue for that business segment. It's likely, too, that there will be corresponding marketing expenses, as well as some possible R&D costs for refining or adapting products to meet the needs of that market share. Evidence of such tactics contributes to the budget's strategic nature while enhancing its role as the tool by which these objectives will be accomplished.

• *Has my budget outlined the procedures necessary to achieve the goal?* Remember that procedures are to tactics what objectives are to goals. If the overall goal is market dominance for the product you produce, the objectives likely will be to establish footholds in the various niches that comprise the market. Your tactics, then, will

MARKET TRENDS

Your budget comprises numerous components, but its physical manifestation most often is seen as the financial statement. It's also reflected in the income statement and balance sheet. Generally developed on a spreadsheet, the financial statement displays budgeted and actual revenues and expenses for one or more years and serves as a snapshot of your financial condition at any given time.

focus on ways to penetrate and ultimately dominate those niches, as well as ways to knit them together for the full market dominance you seek. And procedures will be the steps by which those tactics are executed.

If your company produces soft drinks, your goal may be to dominate a certain price or age strata of the market throughout the U.S. Your objective, then, would be initial percentage penetration in all major metropolitan areas, followed by second-and third-tier penetration based on potential consumption. The tactics would measure key components, such as quality, price and packaging, and determine the best balance of all three. Once the proper ratios have been determined, subsequent steps would include producing the product to the appropriate specification, outlining the sales and marketing strategy, and delivering the product to those markets within the time frame and via the method that provides the highest level of customer satisfaction, thus the greatest potential for income.

Can your marketing budget measure all that? It will if you take the right approach and bring the right level of awareness, information and understanding to the creation process.

BASIC BUDGET COMPONENTS

This may seem rudimentary, but it's important to note that all budgets, strategic or operational, contain two basic categories. It's your job to learn these sections fully and come to know their implications completely.

Traditional budgets first show the revenue, which includes income from sales, investments, sponsorships, licensing fees and any other sources. Sales revenue is generally the most significant and most important.

Revenue should be divided into key product lines or sources with an eye toward understanding the impact of those sources without drowning in the minutiae of listing acquisition methods. Keep your income lines clear and understandable, but divide them into logical, reasonably-sized components. In most cases, revenues will be the higher of the two bottom-line numbers, particularly if the company wants to continue operations.

Our soft drink company would show earnings primarily from basic product sales. It also might show income from franchise fees paid for distribution rights granted in certain areas of the country. If the brand were ever to become a household icon and its name and image used on other products—much like the Coca-Cola brand has become—then licensing fees for this image also would be counted in this category. The other part of the marketing budget focuses on the expense side and accounts for all the costs of all the steps and materials necessary to promote, market and distribute the product.

In the case of categories, the budget measures revenue and expense expectations—what the company thinks it will earn and what it thinks it will spend in the production and distribution of product at the level necessary to achieve its financial goals. Revenue should balance against expense with a net margin that reflects the company's earnings objectives. With rare exception, a company that doesn't budget for greater revenue than expense won't be around very long. And you can't make up a negative margin in volume, either.

TOP-DOWN BUDGETING

The art of budgeting is an exercise in logic and hope, realism and optimism. It begins with an industry analysis, market share evaluation and sales forecast. Different components can be accumulated and plugged into the appropriate spreadsheet when and where you find them. However, many companies pursue a more strategic approach to budgeting based on goals. They tend to create the following budget components in the following order, adjusting each to accommodate the needs of the other.

The following components fit into most corporate budgets. As you can see, the marketing component is part, but not all, of the overall effort.

• The *sales budget,* which comprises the lion's share of revenue for most companies, usually comes first. This is the revenue component that serves as the foundation on which other budget components are based. The sales budget usually includes the quantity of forecasted sales of each item and the price of that item. The data is then sorted and classified by sales area or representative, with past year's data included somewhere for comparative purposes. The past year's actual or projected actual sales are the starting point. Company goals, mixed with marketplace realities, drive the amount by which this number will increase or decrease. The number of back orders, competition and remaining product in the warehouse will affect this number.

• Once the sales budget has been established, the *production budget* is developed. The number of units necessary, along with the price of manufacture and the required year-end inventory all help determine the production budget. Current inventory sitting in the warehouse should be subtracted from the production budget's costs.

By establishing the sales budget first, we've designed a more strategically based system that is goal-driven rather than cost-driven. This seemingly backward way of budgeting may make meeting the bottom line a little more challenging, but in the long run it paints a better financial scenario for any company pursuing growth.

• The *direct materials purchase budget* comes next and operates much like the production budget. Estimates should include materials for the desired number of units to meet financial goals and maintain the desired year-end inventory. Again, the value of raw materials in stock should be subtracted from this amount.

• Estimating the *direct labor cost budget* to produce products comes next and operates in tandem with direct materials cost. Manpower will have to be measured in tandem with materials, inventory and sales goals for a realistic picture of actual estimated expenses.

• Along with materials and labor, you may have to create a *factory overhead costs budget*. Unlike materials and manpower, which are directly attributable and variable with the number and type of products produced, factory overhead will include related light, heat and facilities costs, supervisors' salaries, plant maintenance, insurance and property taxes and other costs that are more general in nature to the production process.

• The *cost of goods sold budget* comes next and combines the three previous expenses categories—direct materials costs, direct labor costs and factory overhead costs—to identify the cost of goods sold. Divided by the number of units produced and compared to actual sales price, this will give you a good idea of both production expenses and net margin per unit for the work you do and products you produce.

• In addition to the cost of goods sold, there's also an *operating budget* that needs to be prepared. This adds marketing, sales, distribution and any other general expenses to the mix. While not technically considered part of the cost of goods sold, it is a very real part of the expenses scenario.

Those steps define the basic operating budget for the measurement and flow of expenses and revenues. There may be the need for the development of a *capital expenditures budget,* which measures the expense of equipment and facilities, the cost of which will be amortized over a period of years. There also is a *cash budget,* which measures the anticipated revenue and expense flow. This allows for

SNAPSHOT

Traditional budgets are not without their alternatives. Some businesses engage in flexible budgeting. A flexible budget is really a series of smaller budgets strung together and designed to measure variations in activity over a given time period. This is especially valuable in manufacturing and in businesses with strong seasonal activity.

better funds management, enabling you to create cushions where you need them and invest excess liquidity when the opportunity arises.

What at first may seem a simple process can grow very complicated. But those complications enable you to exercise greater control and better manage resources in pursuit of your strategic goals. And that, after all, is what budgeting is about.

DEVELOPING THE MARKETING BUDGET

As a central part of the operating budget, the marketing budget serves a critical purpose in defining the resources available to help achieve the company's economic goals. Critical as that is, deciding how much to budget in pursuit of those goals often is a point of contention between marketers and other managers. If our product is soft drinks, we know what it costs to acquire the bottles or cans from suppliers in order to contain our product. We have an idea what it will cost to design packaging and the price of filling our containers and trucking them to our desired markets. We even know what it costs to combine syrup and water to produce the beverage inside. We can, based on volumes of purchase, accurately forecast the cost of goods sold.

But what is the proper amount to spend on marketing? How much research should we contract? What kind and how much advertising should we buy to make the market impression we need to make? What should we spend on ancillary activities, including focus groups, giveaways, sponsorships and promotional expenses to put our name in front of our potential buying public?

There's one sure and fast guideline to marketing expenditures: Make sure you spend enough to achieve your desired results. It's that easy.

KNOW YOUR PRODUCT AND ITS MARKET

Determining the correct level of marketing expenditures is a little more reliable than predicting the weather, but only if you take the time to study conditions, review past sales and marketing activities and expenditures, and make the leap of faith necessary to develop the proper forecast. It's actually a much more exact science than non-marketers give us credit for, but does contain a distinct element of risk when it comes to making predictions and assigning appropriate levels of cost.

There also are specific benchmarks depending on the nature of the product produced and market served. Business-to-business companies spend modestly by marketing standards—anywhere from three to five percent of their operating budget—while consumer commodities producers drop anywhere from 10 to 20 percent per year to keep their brand in front of an otherwise fickle crowd. Sellers of luxury items spend more or less in marketing their products than low-cost producers, depending on their current market share and corporate strategy. New products or firms entering a market spend more on marketing than established companies, unless you count those commodities producers taking the "saturation bombing" approach to media in an attempt to drive the competition out of business.

The first rule of market expenditure is there is no rule. Do your research, study your competition, look for benchmarks within your industry and review your company's or product's strategic goals. Then, armed with this information and the courage of your convictions, you're ready to take the plunge.

Here are a few considerations that may make that plunge less dramatic:

• *Budget adequately for the marketing expense at hand.* If your product is a major consumer product with national distribution to what research has identified as a sports-oriented, television-watching audience, make sure that your budget for media expenditures is adequate to the need. Space ads in area newspapers, no matter how economical, will be wasted expenses if your proper venue is through advertising on ESPN and other big name sports venues. Make sure you've got the right amount of cost covered based on the needs determined by your research, or don't even bother with placement.

• *Articulate your marketing budget to monitor expenses and direct expenditures.* If you're planning a direct mailing to promote your product, it may not be necessary to list the cost of each window envelope and "New and Improved!" sticker you plan to use. But your budget must be subdivided and explained in a way that measures the cost per item as it reflects on the whole. Without significant articulation, you won't know where to adjust costs and/or increase effort when the promotion doesn't pull the results you want. Add the level of detail that makes sense for you as marketer, but also shows those who need to know that you have considered costs accurately and completely.

• *Keep funds set aside for those extra marketing opportunities that can come along.* If your funds are stretched to the limit without the appropriate flexibility to take advantage of unexpected opportunities, then you haven't planned sufficiently or broadly enough. You may hide those funds in extra, expendable media buys or under other categories that may be sacrificed, but make sure the option is there before you proceed to lock the budget down.

• *Focus on the future.* Your budgeted amounts, like your strategic plans, should lead to more and better strategies by which you can propel your company and its products into the future. Budget proactively with an eye toward the inevitable growth of expenditures designed to keep pace with anticipated revenues. If you budget too tightly, you may find yourself in a closed loop that doesn't allow for expansion without a major expenditure increase. Of course, you understand the reason behind this, but that sometimes makes it difficult for the non-marketers in the company to swallow.

• *Budget for results.* In spite of what we just said, make sure your expenditures directly reflect increases in sales and that marketing costs are easily viewable as an investment in sales growth. If such a relationship can't be traced or explained, then either the financial allocation or the strategic positioning of your marketing plan is incorrect.

• *Realize and promote your marketing budget's investment value.* In tandem with the last item, you need to realize and promote the fact that marketing expenditures, if correctly done, should be seen not as an expense but as an investment. Your company could not accomplish its sales goals without marketing, making your costs as critical to success as those required to produce the product in the first place. Non-marketers often fail to see that. Good fiscal responsibility on your part, coupled with responsible expenditures and measurable results, will mean a higher level of understanding when it comes to supporting and increasing the marketing budget.

And, from your perspective, we're guessing that's a major consideration.

• *Evaluate results and revise your budget as necessary.* Like your marketing plan, your marketing budget should be the subject of ongoing evaluation and review. Course correct those actions that don't seem to be working and cut back on costs where the goal has been achieved and the market appears saturated. Budgets, like plans, are made to be adjusted, and that's a critical part of your marketing responsibilities.

DEVELOPING YOUR BUDGET

From an accounting standpoint, budgeting follows a required format. There may be variance in style and content within your company. Expenses and revenue may be accrued over the duration of the budget, for example, and then those accrual amounts applied throughout the year to even out the funds that flow into and out of your department. In almost every case, revenues are estimated first, followed by expenses. For most companies, it's the same exercise in subtraction (revenues − expenses = net margin) that you learned in grade school.

Budgets generally are best illustrated in a financial statement that shows the following units of measure of your financial performance:

- the *current budget,* articulated into understandable references, measures anticipated revenue and expense;
- the *previous budget or year-end actual figures,* usually from the prior year, that shows a line-by-line comparison charting business cycles represented by increases or decreases in revenue or expense. This is a critical strategic component that provides context for your goals and strategies for this year's financial performance;
- the *year-to-date performance,* as posted to the general ledger. These are actual figures that show your financial well-being

at a precise moment in time. Remember that if you're using accrued numbers rather than actual sales, your performance figures may be based more on expectation than actual performance;

- and, finally, *quarterly or annual projections,* a line-by-line comparison that measures revised anticipated performance against marketplace realities. These numbers may be the most critical from an operational perspective, especially when compared to budget. It not only shows how close your planning was to reality, but forces you to consider or accommodate performance weaknesses that could sink your ship.

Your marketing budget operates as part of the overall expense budget, with indirectly corresponding amounts relative to sales increases or decreases over the same period of time covered by the expenses. By utilizing the projections column compared to budget, the marketer can better understand and adjust expenses to meet revenue shortfalls, thus coming closer to bottom line goals. Quick comparisons between the previous year-end actuals and this year's budget will describe the soundness of the department's strategy.

And all the information necessary will be available and clearly stated for use when next year's budget cycle roles around.

FACTORING THE HUMAN EQUATION

The budget is the financial reflection of your department's and your company's overall business strategy. But a budget also reflects the strategies and desires of the department responsible for setting the sights and striving for the goals articulated in the numbers.

Management—middle or upper—that fails to factor in the human equation does a disservice to all involved in the process. That failure also compromises—perhaps significantly—the department's ability to reach the levels described in the budget and achieve department or company goals.

Your budget will work only under the following circumstances:

• *Budgets must set optimistic but realistic expectations.* Revenues that will never be reached or expenses that can't be maintained will do little more than frustrate the marketer and undermine his or her ability to reach stated goals. In the same vein, budgets that require minimal reach will waste efforts and do little to stimulate initiative and corporate growth. Budgets should set optimistic but realistic goals.

• *Budgets must be well articulated in order to be effective.* Budgets whose goals aren't specifically defined or backed up with sound development strategies are little more than numbers on paper. Their ability to influence company or departmental growth is weak at best. Budgets must be based on sound strategies designed to help reach the necessary levels of financial growth.

• *Budgets must be active tools used throughout the year.* No well-defined budget merely sits on a shelf. An effective budget is a continual resource, a barometer for the department's and the company's financial progress. It should be checked regularly and the information it provides should be noted and analyzed.

• *The unexamined budget is not worth using.* Budgets are not pristine documents carefully created for their aesthetic value. Budgets are meant to be reviewed, questioned, scrutinized, analyzed and adjusted based on market influences and strategic changes. To that end the budget as well as the thinking behind it needs sufficient levels of flexibility. Budgets are not ends in themselves; they exist to help the company reach its financial goals.

• *Above all, budgets are guidelines, not gospel.* Both budgeters and the people supervising them would do well to remember that budgets are, at best, educated guesses. They must be based on logic, research and strategic necessity, but no one budgets with pinpoint accuracy. Treat a missed margin as just that, and use the information learned in relation to that miss to make the necessary adjustments and get back on track.

Remember, the year has four quarters. There will always be another one.

If life gives you lemons, make lemonade.
It works in marketing, too.

—Something Mother would have told you
if Mother had been David Ogilvy

6

The Marketing Gestalt

Sometime after the end of World War Two, a little black car began to appear on America's highways and byways. It was a small, odd-looking thing with sloping lines, an engine in the back and the trunk space up front. It rode on skinny tires and, with four cylinders banging under the hood . . . er, trunk, it didn't even really sound like the big, boxy automobiles that post-war America had come to know.

It was called a Volkswagen—"People's Car" in its native German—and had originally been designed as cheap transportation for the pre-war German people. Now that the Fatherland's military industrial complex was no longer manufacturing munitions and armaments, the Volkswagen was back into production and washing up on American shores.

The one thing it had in common with American autos is that all those early models were black, like Henry Ford's original Model T. The import's color, its shape and the strange whirring noise its four-cylinder engine made got it the nickname, "Beetle." Not many people were interested in them at first, except maybe college students.

Then a marketing agency got hold of the Volkswagen account, and things began to change.

The hardest thing for any product to do is stand out in the market, to be more than just a face in the crowd. And Volkswagen's unusual appearance and specifications, while turning off many American motorists, gave copywriters the grist necessary for the promotional mill. There was, indeed, a Volkswagen difference. Sure, it was a little odd looking, but it offered superior workmanship, economy and reliability. Suddenly it was clear why college kids were buying them. Others started buying them, too.

The 1950s turned into the '60s and the radical counterculture, an extension of the college kids who had purchased the Beetle a decade earlier, also found themselves in Volkswagens, partly for the same reasons their predecessors were and partly as a statement against products produced by the American military industrial complex, which was currently fighting its own war in Vietnam. They also embraced the Volkswagen minibus, predecessor to today's mini vans but at the time, the only thing like it on the road. Decorated with peace stickers and American flags, it became part of a lifestyle and, for some, their home on the open road.

Volkswagen was, to use the day's vernacular, a hip car. American car companies, late to the game, tried to introduce their own, odd-looking versions, such as the American Motors Gremlin. Some of the major manufacturers, such as Ford, offered up their own economy models in "hip" colors such as Hulla Blue, Anti-establish Mint and Freudian Gilt. Fortunately, all died a quiet death.

But the counterculture wasn't the only segment that embraced the odd little German automobile. The Walt Disney Company made a movie called, *The Love Bug,* in which the lead character was Herbie, a daisy-bedecked white Volkswagen Beetle with a mind of its own. We have yet to see a full-length feature film with a Coke bottle or a Nike running shoe as the lead character.

Then in the late '70s, the beloved Beetle began to fade. Inferior versions were still manufactured in Mexico, but the car itself became lost in a sea of models and makes too numerous to mention. One day the product was gone, but it was far from forgotten. Those who still had Beetles prized them, guarding them carefully in locked garages. Volkswagen attempted to trade on its name and substitute other varieties—the Jetta, the Rabbit—but neither ever reached the level of popularity that the Beetle did.

In the last decade, the Beetle has returned. It's sleeker, with a profile that is more extraterrestrial than its forebear, but the relationship between the two is evident from the start. The new models have the same fine workmanship, but offer more luxury at a price much higher than the original would have cost. (This works, now that those Baby Boomers whose memories are inextricably linked with their original Bugs can afford a much tonier product.) The new ones even have a bud vase built into the dash, in deference, perhaps, to Herbie and his "Love Bug" days.

In hindsight, Volkswagen may not offer the quintessential marketing success story, at least not by today's standards. But it's an early example of what might be described as the marketing gestalt.

"Gestalt" is also a German word. The classic definition of gestalt, based on a school of psychology developed in Germany, says all experience consists of gestalten, defined as a series of structures or patterns that make up those experiences, and which can't be derived from individual elements of that whole. Because of this, the whole must be considered as more than the sum of its individual parts. Gestalt psychology, then, is the analysis of behavior in response to the impact of the whole as it is defined beyond the sum of its parts, and any byproducts or properties it creates.

The whole is greater than the sum of its parts. Based on that analysis, the original Volkswagen had marketing gestalt and value greater than the sum of its individual features. Unlike other cars of its day, which served either utilitarian or ornamental purposes for their owners, the Beetle was an intrinsic part of lifestyle and behavior. Like all good brands, it played a role in public consciousness, not as a series of automotive features, but as an integrated whole. When people thought of the Beetle, they didn't think of economy or workmanship. Rather, they thought of the car almost as a character that defined certain lifestyles, and to that character they responded accordingly.

Despite its original perceived drawbacks, the Volkswagen Beetle was a marketer's dream. And it did a lot to propel not only the automotive industry in new directions, but also marketing as a profession and discipline. A product whose differences were so plainly evident to even the most myopic consumers served as a living laboratory for marketers and other industry experts.

One could argue that other products have marketing gestalt. In some cases and to some degree, that argument would be correct. But with the possible exception of Harley Davidson, one would be hard pressed to find the level of lifestyle impact and change capable of hitting the stride that Volkswagen created.

General Motors' line of Saturn cars would like to have gestalt and company executives work very hard at developing the same type of consumer loyalty that Volkswagen and Harley enjoy. They have worked to change the car-buying process—one of the most hated activities in the world after root canal and public speaking— to a pleasurable, hassle-free reward in which the sales associates offer applause rather than harassment. They even hold a summer picnic for owners, many of them repeat buyers, that features big-name entertainment.

But in the end, Saturn is just a car—perhaps the best car possible to its fans and owners—but no more than a car to those who drive it to work and the grocery store. It has marginal cachet, and it meets a need, but it doesn't create a lifestyle.

That's reserved for those products with gestalt.

Gestalt is something that can't be purchased or invented, wished for or dreamed about. You can, however, create an environment that helps cultivate gestalt:

• Create a community of consumers, those who link themselves to the product and use it to define their intrinsic character and, sometimes, their basic values. Volkswagen did it almost accidentally by attracting those disenfranchised by the mainstream and in search of an alternative. Harley Davidson had the same advantages. In fact, many of their consumers had already organized themselves into "communities." It just took Harley to broaden that spectrum beyond the outlaw realm and create the Harley Owners Group (HOG, not an accidental acronym) to broaden that community in new and more respectable directions.

• Have a passion for your product that approaches religious zeal and then preach the gospel whenever possible. Such devotion adds a different aura to your marketing effort because it creates an enhanced priority that can be celebrated right on up through the executive offices. That's the role Harley Davidson executives play, riding the motorcycles they manufacture and spending time at rallies and club meetings talking to their customers and preaching the gospel of Harley quality and commitment.

• Think uncommonly and market courageously. The agency knew it had an unusual product when it won the Volkswagen account. Executives chose to approach it with creativity and a touch of humor that made it stand out from other automotive marketing. Consumers may not have been interested in the car, but they certainly noticed the advertising. Volkswagen became a familiar social icon with a variety of meanings. Cross-over buyers, now well familiar with the little car, began to appreciate the product's features and benefits. Suddenly, a little marketing celebrity was born, one that would change the face of the American automotive industry forever.

How will you know when you've achieved marketing gestalt? If you have to ask, then you probably aren't there. But if you start noticing changes in society, ones that suddenly thrust your product to the forefront not as a product to purchase but as a lifestyle icon, then there's a pretty good chance that you're on your way.

And once your customers start tattooing your product logo on their bodies, like Harley Davidson customers do, you're home free.

*If you draw a chalk line on the ground and
direct a chicken's beak to the line, that
chicken will tend not to move its beak,
convinced it is doing the right thing.*

—Old Folk Tale

*If you only do what you've always done,
you'll only get what you've always gotten.*

—A More Contemporary Folk Tale

7

From Creative Thinking to Strategic Planning

Let's begin this chapter with a few key definitions:

creative *adj.* (Middle Latin, *creativus*) productive; having or showing imagination and artistic or intellectual inventiveness; stimulating the imagination and inventive powers.

strategy *noun* (French *strategié;* Greek *stratēgia*) the act of planning or directing a large scale military operation, specifically of maneuvering forces into the most advantageous position prior to actual engagement with the enemy; a skill in managing or planning, especially by using a stratagem or artful means to some end.

Warfare references notwithstanding, marketing is about strategy. In fact, many marketers would define the two terms synonymously. As former Coca-Cola marketing chief Sergio Zyman noted in the opening chapter of this book, the purpose of marketing is to sell more things to more people at a higher price. If the achievement of those inter-related goals is the purpose of marketing, then marketing becomes the means—or, if you will, the strategy—by which those goals may be achieved. The more creative that strategy is as a means to outmaneuver the competition, then, the more successful those marketing efforts will be. Make sense?

It should. But to the non-marketers in the office, the need for creativity sounds a little like playtime at the day care center. They hear marketers lobby for more creative thinking time and space, see graphic stimulants roll up on the walls of offices in the marketing departments and catch wind of creative outings to theme parks, shopping malls and movies, activities that appear to have little connection to the day-to-day grind that the rest of the company personally experience while chained to their PCs eight hours a day. Is the accounting department going to pack a picnic lunch and trundle off for a day with Mickey, Minnie and a wet ride down Splash Mountain? Not bloody likely.

Without understanding the critical connection between creativity and strategy, one might think marketers are wasting company time and money on activities that have little relevance to the process at hand. True, there are some who may do this, taking advantage of the relative freedom they're given. But the vast majority are desperately attempting to find ways to kick-start the creative juices necessary to pull their noses up off the chalk line and define a strategy that will propel their company above and beyond the competition in the minds of customers.

Dean Amhaus, president of Forward Wisconsin, a public-private sector partnership designed to market the Badger State as a good place for companies to do business, has a desk littered with yo-yos, sleight-of-hand tricks and wind-up toys. It's not unusual for Forward's planning meetings to evolve into yo-yo contests. A waste of time and prime example of marketing's childish indulgence? Not in Amhaus's mind. It's his attempt to get the noses of his staff off the chalk line and refocus their vision on a wide array of opportunities around them that may have nothing to do with the way Wisconsin has marketed itself in the past.

And in the dynamic marketplace in which we all operate, the more creative the thought process, the better.

CULTIVATING CREATIVITY

Volumes can and have been written on the development of creativity. Consultant Roger Von Oech has made a career out of creativity with his *Whack on the Side of the Head* series, while business enterprises like *Fast Company*, the publication for emerging corporate entities and strategies, and the Disney Institute have developed learning environments that have corporate participants cooking, singing, waving flags and even fighting the elements in search of ways to cultivate creativity and stimulate strategic thought.

What such enterprises prove is that there is no one right way, nor is there a single methodology to foster creativity within corporate America, be those in question marketers, accountants or others. Instead, such a variety of stimuli clearly support the thesis that creative thought comes through many channels, all of which run counter to our day-by-day standard operating procedures. In other words, the very efforts and strategies that have put your company on the map or driven your career to its current height will do little in the future if either entity finds itself in the position of needing to change.

Creativity operates antithetically to the norm. It's supposed to; that's creativity's job. Its twin pillars of imagination and inventiveness give it the power to drive thought and action in a new direction. Yet despite what most people think, how different that direction is depends not on random threads of thoughts waving in the wind or soap bubbles filled with insight that come floating through the ether. Instead, creativity is dependent on how varied and diverse a foundation the individual or organization has in the first place and how easily that foundation of knowledge can be accessed.

Some people count themselves as naturally creative, and they may be, while others are as dull as dust and they know it. When you come right down to it, however, creativity is a matter of successfully accessing resources and reengineering thought based on a different set of subliminally understood principles. That's why marketers play with yo-yos and visit theme parks. Like most of us, the vast majority haven't been outside of their current career trajectory in so long that a return to childhood (the root of ourselves and our characteristics) may be the only way to get to a point where the subconscious resources required for a radical shift can be reached.

Bearing all that, marketers (and others) also can cultivate creative thought through the creativity equation:

Information + Incubation = Inspiration

Creative thought is the result of an alternately viewed set of information and data that forms, in the case of marketing, a new strategic

MARKET RESEARCH

Twirling yo-yos isn't the only way to cultivate creativity. More socially acceptable ways (from a business standpoint) include brainstorming sessions in which all alternatives regardless of outlandishness are considered valid. You can also apply problem-solving standards from other industries and look for cross-over alternatives. What Microsoft does to solve a marketing dilemma may stimulate new applications for Procter and Gamble. Once again, it's the application of different data sets and new ways of thinking that develop the kinds of creativity that lead to strategic development.

paradigm. The more information that is gathered, broadening the individual's base of knowledge, the more alternatives for application present themselves. Ability to access these various forms and resources may require a more facile intellect than some people possess, but then we never said just anyone could be a marketer.

Once the proper information is gathered and an effective stimuli or media is discovered, the most critical factor comes into play. That's the incubation of thoughts, ideas, concepts and strategies. Raw thinking is just that— half-formed and immature, much like a caterpillar prior to its date with the cocoon. Without incubation in the subconscious, thoughts may never leave their larval stage.

Philosophers and physicians all have noted that humans use only a small percentage of their intellectual capacity in conscious thought. The vast majority of that capacity, either willingly or unwillingly, is reserved to power our subconscious, which is the real pressure cooker of creative thinking. People who claim ideas come to them in a dream benefit directly from the powers of their subconscious to tap both the surface and subliminal databases of their minds. Most of the rest of us must be content to download an idea into the subconscious and cook it for a day, a week, or a month before anything like a finished form of thought is produced and the inspiration we seek is reached.

When marketers speak of creativity, this is really the process to which they refer. Whether that downloading takes place while they're standing on their heads in yogic posture, chuckling over a Three Stooges comedy, or practicing the around-the-world maneuver with their Duncan yo-yos, chances are their hard drives are whirring and their data is processing for digestion and regurgitation at a later time. We don't reach "Aha!" just because we want to or feel we deserve it. The only way to get there from here is to have the all proper tools at hand and know how to use them effectively. That's all.

DEVELOPING STRATEGIES

From a practical standpoint, creativity needs an outlet, not to be useful per se, but to count as part of the solution to the challenges which you as a business executive face. For the writer, there's her text, for the artist, his visuals. For the business leader and, especially, the marketer, that creativity usually finds application in the development of strategies.

Strategy's original application had to do with military issues—protecting one's homeland from invading armies or, as one of those armies, finding new, more effective ways to conquer territory. In fact, military history has become the basis for many marketing strategies and drives much of the current marketing philosophy. Titles like *Guerrilla Marketing* and *Marketing Warfare,* rife with military reference and application, bear this out. The applications themselves have become more than mere metaphor or allegory. Many military texts have become handbooks for strategic planning at the corporate level. Today, the words of General George Patton, Napoleon Bonaparte and even Genghis Khan are finding their way into corporate boardrooms. The parallels between the challenges faced by these famous military leaders and many of America's top companies are not coincidental.

We talked about the word strategy earlier as defined from the classic military perspective. From a business standpoint, you may want to consider the following definition:

> *Strategy is the coordination of the means to achieve the desired ends as they are defined by corporate policy.*

The nature of business strategy is much like that of military strategy in that it pits company against company, marketing team against marketing team, and product against product. Ultimately, however, it's a case of mind against mind. No matter how large an organization is, or how expansive its management or marketing team, it all boils down to that simple concept.

In warfare, it was the invasion strategy defined in Gen. Dwight Eisenhower's mind positioned against the strategic defenses conceived and produced by Gen. Irwin Rommel that led to an ultimately successful Allied landing at Normandy Beach. History is replete with similar examples—and so is business. Eisenhower's plan was the result of almost a year's research and development by the finest minds in the Allied armies, with a strategic launch based on the results of that effort. And that's very much like business.

Understanding the human element of strategic development— that concept of mind (your corporate goals or objectives) versus mind (your competition's objectives)—is central to understanding the concept behind strategic development. You aren't merely trying to get on the good side of consumers in hopes that they will try your product. Often that's the easy part. The hard part is fending off attacks from competitors old and new who are interested in upsetting your strategies and causing you to lose market share and drop out of the competitive race. In fact, the twin cornerstones in any strategic development focus on the following:

• Any good strategy's foundation is built on the effort to dislocate the market, both physically and psychologically, for its competitors. This may manifest itself in a surprise attack on market segment, creation of a better product distribution strategy or manufacture of a superior style of widget to that of the competition. Handled deftly, such moves can demoralize the competition and cause its efforts to stumble and fall due to mistakes in judgement or loss of the will to compete. All efforts must operate in concert in order to be effective and may, for a time, run counter to what your ultimate strategy will be.

When A&P introduced its supermarket chain in the 1950s, management positioned its stores to undercut all the existing mom-and-pop stores in price while significantly increasing volume and selection. Once the little grocers had been run out of business,

A&P raised its prices. As the only remaining game in town, it had all the business in the neighborhood because there was no one left to compete.

• As a strategy, dislocation will weaken your competition. Once the competitor has reached a point of vulnerability, you must pull all disparate elements together and concentrate your focus on that area of weakness most easily exploited. That may be a market segment not currently being served or a product classification that hasn't been fully exploited. Just like a weakness in a fortification that, once broken through, allows the invading army to infiltrate enemy territory, concentration in a marketing strategy will allow for market entry at the point of least resistance. From there, it's simply a matter of divide and conquer.

In December, 1944, retreating German forces attempted to exploit a weakness in Allied lines at the Belgian-German border in a campaign later known as the Battle of the Bulge, thanks to a weakness in the military line that "bulged" back into Allied-controlled territory. Eisenhower, along with General Omar Bradley of the Allied expeditionary force, were complacent from their steady progress toward Berlin and failed to assess the situation from Hitler's point of view.

Driving back westward through that Bulge would be a strategic mistake for the Germans, they determined, because they could not hope to hold the territory once they captured it. Unfortunately, they did not consider that Hitler's primary mission may not be to hold territory, but to keep the Allies off German soil. Failure to appreciate that point of view—a classic mind-versus-mind struggle—nearly turned the tide of the war back against the Allies and cost both sides many lives.

Despite the continuing military metaphor, the lesson is simple: Your goal as marketing manager is not to battle head-to-head with your competition. Rather, gather information and devise a strategy that catches the competition off guard and allows you to achieve the goals that you have set forth in terms of marketplace capture. In the end, it's your mind against that of the competition. Nothing else.

IDENTIFYING YOUR STRATEGY

Whether your maneuvers are military or marketing, you must first carefully assess the situation before determining your plan of attack. Sometimes you have all the resources you need and complete intelligence about the next set of moves scheduled to be made by your competition. More often than not, however, you're shy on resources, lack the necessary knowledge about your competition and don't have the time and luxury to analyze the situation and make your next move. That last sentence describes the classic battlefield scenario, but no doubt experienced marketers would recognize the same set of drawbacks.

There are standard strategic moves that you may be able to successfully implement, provided you analyze the situation as thoroughly as possible and make your strategic choices based on sound logic and instinct, not just what you think might be cool to do. Let's consider each strategy in turn, both from a positive and negative standpoint:

The Full-Frontal Direct Attack

One of the greatest surprises to the British forces at the outset of the Revolutionary War was the colonists' lack of battlefield etiquette. Seriously outmanned and outgunned, the fledgling American army did not march in formation into the withering cross-fire of their enemy, like the Redcoats did. Rather than mount a direct attack— they simply didn't have the manpower to do so—the colonists instead hid behind rocks and trees, firing their muskets into the line of British soldiers, mowing them down like harvested wheat.

The British direct attacks met with nasty consequences, a fate not surprising considering that military experts agree that the entrenched army easily has a three-to-one advantage. For those with the resources, a direct assault can be impressive and successful—consider, once again, Normandy Beach—but it is also costly in terms of resources. The same holds true in marketing. Direct assaults on firmly entrenched market positions or products exhaust the budgets, tools and resources that go into a marketing campaign. The result often is an expensive "me too" campaign that doesn't usually work. If your product is as good as the market leader and no better or different, why would I bother to switch? Marketing history, like military history, is filled with examples of full-frontal assaults. General Douglas MacArthur said that a direct assault is the sign of a mediocre commander. The same holds true for marketing.

The Indirect Assault

The direct assault tends to play into the defending army's (or company's) hands, putting the offense at a distinct disadvantage. The indirect assault, on the other hand, exploits a weakness of the opposition, identifying and penetrating a weakly defended point of entry in the marketplace, only to grow and expand from within. This indirect assault often operates as a diversionary tactic, masking a direct assault that comes after the point of entry has been exploited.

Volkswagen did not enter the U.S. market going head-to-head with big, boxy Chryslers, Packards and Hudsons. Instead, the German automobile identified an undeveloped niche for small, economical, well-made cars and slipped quietly in while the major automotive producers were trumpeting newer, larger models in the expanding post-war environment. Once the beachhead had been established and the car became a cultural presence in the U.S., prices increased befitting not the product's size, so much as its engineering superiority.

The earlier A&P example follows the same strategy. The stores worked to establish themselves as the lowest cost provider in the market, just so they could eventually become the only provider in the market. The chain's indirect, almost diversionary tactic caused smaller grocers to lower prices to match A&P's prices, allowing the competition to drive itself out of the market.

The Envelopment Strategy

Similar in design to the Indirect Attack, the envelopment strategy identifies weakly defended points of entry in order to gain a foothold. Once established, the attacker spreads out in all directions, finding other points of entry or market niches on which to capitalize, then introducing itself to those niches and eventually enveloping the target. Mass marketers of consumer goods often find such a strategy successful introducing first one product, then another, until the marketplace is littered with the company name and its related brands.

Boston Beer Company, producers of the Samuel Adams Beer brands, did that among its customers. The company first introduced it flagship brand, the lager, as an entry into the high-quality craft brewing market that was emerging in the 1980s and established a foothold among drinkers who favored a well-made, full-flavored beer. Once the brand had established a market presence, Boston Beer Company began introducing a wide variety of ales, porters and stouts and, while it didn't leave the craft beer audience, it did envelop a wider segment of that audience until it had a contender in every category. The fact that the market itself was growing significantly helped increase public preference for and sales of that brand.

Military examples of the envelopment strategy are too numerous to mention. The most obvious one would have to do with the ways the defenders of the Alamo succumbed to General Santa Ana's troops, which significantly outnumbered the Texan defenders. The Mexican soldiers eventually found weaknesses in the defenses and flooded in. And the rest, quite literally, *is* history.

That may not be the best example, but it certainly is the most obvious one.

The Bypass Strategy

Probably the most difficult and failure-prone of all plans, the bypass strategy enables attackers to bypass its chief competitors and diversify into unrelated products or markets. From a military perspective, this may work as a temporary flanking strategy, but in marketing it runs the risk of diluting the core business and central operating strategy, extending resources into areas where the company had no business being.

Pepsico diluted its core competency—the production and distribution of soft drinks—to move into the fast food market, purchasing brands such as Taco Bell and KFC. The move was well outside the influence sphere of its chief competitor, Coca-Cola. The Atlanta-based soft drink producer retrenched and stuck to its primary purpose—producing Coke. Coca-Cola was and still remains the leader of the two brands in markets worldwide.

One company that was able to diversify successfully was Virgin, the massive British-based music retailer that acquired and has made a rousing success out of Virgin Atlantic Airlines. According to entrepreneur/owner Richard Branson, if you can succeed with one company, you can succeed with them all. Branson's belief is that if you break the right rules of business, you're bound to gain ground.

Go figure.

The Guerrilla Attack

In an age of smaller, entrepreneurially driven companies, the guerrilla attack has become one of the most frequently used marketing strategies. Most of us first heard about the concept of small, strategic strikes when a group of American and English commandos trouped through the Malaysian jungles to blow up the prisoner-built bridge over the river Kwai. From a marketing perspective, it's been a popular strategy ever since.

Most often guerrilla marketing is conducted by a small company against a larger, market-dominating firm. It's characterized by periodic, strategically driven strikes, each of which has its own single objective. Taken together, guerrilla warfare can hamstring a major operation, such as it did to American forces in Vietnam, or it can result in market or military success. Castro's Cuba is one such example. Rarely does one expect big wins from a guerrilla assault, unless it's combined with another strategy. But continued attacks well-conceived can demoralize the opposition, slow progress and sometimes draw the larger opponent to a standstill.

And sometimes, whether in military action or marketing maneuvers, that's the best we can hope for.

DEVELOPING STRATEGIC APPLICATIONS

Whether you choose one of the traditional military strategies previously mentioned or something entirely different, do so with clear thought toward the market, your competition and your corporate objectives. Strategies don't exist in a vacuum. Like any other aspect of business, the strategy you embrace must be the result of careful, thought, planning and the appropriate research.

Once you have chosen your plan, however, there are factors to consider and methodologies to apply that will add to your success. Some already have been mentioned, but may bear repeating within this context.

One of your primary goals is to unbalance your competition and get them out of their comfort zone, off their power spot or in some way put them in a compromised position that will cause them to redirect a portion of their efforts inward to fix the problem. This has to be a conscious initiative and a specific plan on your part. It won't just happen as the result of your brilliant marketing prowess. Take specific steps to dislodge the competition before stepping forward with the rest of your plan and you may reach greater levels of success.

This unbalancing act may best be achieved by applying the indirect assault strategy, probing for and exploiting a weakness. Catch your opponent off guard in areas in which they can't or won't compete, using new technologies or strategies they can't access or won't understand. The basic competitor analysis that you conducted as part of your market research should give a clue as to the company's weakest points. By taking advantage of them, you can strengthen your marketing efforts.

Competitive analysis once again comes into play as you concentrate your efforts to maximize your impact. Concentration aids in the conservation and strengthening of resources while, at the same time, providing a marketing focal point for your efforts that likely will be more recognizable and more easily grasped within the marketplace.

Your analysis should uncover areas where your competitor is weak or poorly matched to the marketplace needs. Capitalizing on those weak spots, you can introduce new products, improved distribution systems and other advantages that will give you some kind of inroad into the market. Once established, you can use an envelopment strategy to branch into other areas until you saturate all the nooks and crannies of your market with your product, brand or presence.

Above all, operate with speed so your competitor doesn't have time to react. This is best achieved by a) reducing bureaucratic structure, and b) empowering managers at all levels. Both steps contract reaction time and eliminate crippling red tape that often trips up corporate progress. Make product strategy, not corporate structure, the driving wheel of your competitive efforts. This may require forming subgroups and task forces of executives and employees at a variety of levels to accomplish those goals. Or it may simply require that upper management get the hell out of the way and let the field commanders and soldiers in the trenches do the job they're being paid to do.

Finally, map alternative objectives to your plans to keep your opposition confused and to enable you to achieve your goals in a stairstep fashion if necessary. Remember that all strategies are the result of pitting one human mind or set of ideas against another. While you're planning on behalf of your company, your opposition is planning on behalf of its company. If you have several objectives in mind, you have various plan components under execution. Just when your opposition thinks it has one set of plans figured out, you can enact another and set their expectations on their ear.

While that sounds especially effective, realize, too, that it's also part of a defensive posture. Alternate plans allow you a fall back position if you run into a stone wall with your primary efforts. In either case, however, your multi-faceted efforts likely have had an unsettling effect upon your opposition. This holds true for the strategic elements we discussed earlier as well.

British Statesman, David Lloyd George once noted the most difficult thing in the world was to leap a chasm in two jumps. Make sure your strategy is firm, multifaceted and has the full blown commitment of management and staff. From that point forward, it's full speed ahead!

*Five times as many people read headlines
as read body copy. It follows that,
unless your headline sells your product,
you've wasted 90 percent of your money.*

—David Ogilvy

Brevity is the soul of wit.

—William Shakespeare

8

Copywriting Magic

One of advertising history's most famous ads was a single-page, copy-heavy ad with a line drawing illustration and a headline that read, "They laughed when I sat down to play the piano." Chances are most readers of this volume aren't even old enough to remember this ad for a music school correspondence course and wouldn't even give it a second glance today, other than perhaps as some kind of quaint museum piece.

But the ad is considered a watershed moment in the marketing field. The compelling narrative about a man who enhanced his public stature, social connections and career because he learned to play the piano and entertain friends and acquaintances was perfect for its day. People had more leisure time and fewer entertainment options. Such strides forward could make a person more desirable, thus more valuable to his social group. While it may not actually have improved people's lives, the little dramatic treatise caused more piano lessons to be sold and more music teachers to be employed than any other strategy of that day. And that, after all, is the point of good marketing, isn't it?

Just as we learned that all good marketing starts with an effective strategy founded on creative thinking—copy concept, development and writing is another manifestation of that same process. If planning is a strategy, then copy development is one of its executions because it builds a bridge between marketer and consumer, between concept and fulfillment. And no matter how inventive or unusual a

MARKET RESEARCH

There are no hard and fast profiles for being a good copywriter, and often mastery in other types of writing is not necessarily the best training. In fact, it can be a detriment. The purpose of ad copy is to sell. That may take the form of information, education, persuasion or a combination of all three. A writer who is not comfortable with that blend, or who is not capable of asking for the sale at the close, should not be writing copy.

graphic or electronic approach is that the marketing "creatives" may want to take, it all still starts with a script of some sort, often developed as the foundation of whatever copy needs to be written to support the marketing strategy and help achieve the goals.

Today's equivalent of the music school ad? It's likely something as quick and to the point as Nike's, "Just do it!" Both speak to fulfillment of personal needs in the language of their respective times, and each is as effective as the other for the market each seeks to reach. The Nike ad also illustrates a key point made by that master of all marketing, William Shakespeare, who said: Brevity is the soul of wit.

Translation: When it comes to copywriting, make it clear, concise and to the point, or risk losing your audience members within the next beat of their respective hearts. It's pretty likely such an opportunity won't come your way again.

BUILDING COPY AROUND YOUR AUDIENCE

Copywriting often is the core of concept development, the method by which ideas, strategies and goals come together in a tactical document—a brochure, an ad, a billboard, a radio commercial, a television spot, or an Internet banner. It is the step between the seller and the buyer. It is more than a string of words, but less than a tactical plan. Not much less, however, because good copy encapsulates that tactical plan and presents it in a compelling, creative and effective way to bring the reader to whatever action is required.

Copywriting isn't about the writer, it's about the reader. Let's make that perfectly clear. Writers who write to satisfy their own muse should save it for their diary or personal journal. Writing that fails to communicate thought, feeling, analysis and action isn't the type of writing that copywriting needs to be. Why do we market? To sell more things to more people at a higher price. Copywriting is *the* central tactic to fulfilling that goal.

Writing is the manifestation of strategy (and a central part of the analysis through which such strategy was reached in the first place). As such, it becomes a self-selection mechanism that segments the audience based on the groups the marketer desires to reach. Sometimes this is direct, driven deliberately by the nature of the communications, the product or the copy placements. Sometimes this is subconscious, based on the copywriter's unspoken understanding of the product, its audience and the task at hand. In both cases, it needs to be appropriate to the goals that have been established.

In other words, know for whom you are writing and respond accordingly. If you need to research the market segment before putting finger to keyboard, then do so with great enthusiasm. No time will be wasted and your life will only be easier when you try and come up with a creative hook that will draw people into your text and inspire them to do what you want them to do.

Know, too, that the time you spend on rewrites, edits and other literary exercises also will be time well spent. More is less in today's market. "Just do it!" works. "They laughed when I sat down to play the piano" does not work. Don't make the mistake, either as a writer or as someone who reviews and approves copy, of thinking that more words mean more effective copy. It's just the opposite, in fact.

Finally, know the product as well as you know the audience and look for ways to link its features and benefits to their needs and desires. Product descriptions are only valuable when they answer questions that have been or will be asked. Good copywriting creates a feeling for the product right along with an intellectual analysis. Sure, I want to know how much horsepower the new Ferrari has, how fast it will go, how well it will corner and what its safety record

MARKET RESEARCH

Knowing your audience is as important as knowing your product if not more so. A copywriter attempts to get inside the head of his readers and react to the marketing proposition in the same way they would. Failure to do so means failure to communicate. Copywriting is, first and foremost, communication and should be treated as such. If that means compromising literary intent or speaking so plainly that it hurts for the copywriter, then so be it.

and fuel efficiency ratio are. I will use that information to help decide whether or not to purchase one.

But what I really want to know is how it will make me feel to sit behind the wheel, the wind in my hair and sun glinting off my Wayfarers, sliding slowly to the stoplight, the throaty V8 engine ready to rev up to a high-pitched whine just as soon as the light changes from red to green. Do all that and you've captured your customer.

Copywriting magic doesn't exist in and of itself and it's not based on the experience and skill of the copywriter alone. The best copy is a rare blend of skill and insight on the part of its creator wrapped together with the right product at the right place at the right time. Despite the success of the ad, piano lessons would not have been sold if the population of the day didn't have a need or desire for them. Good copywriting can only bring buyer and seller so close, then the magic of the product or service has to take over. That, of course is a function of developmental strategy by the company on behalf of its product. Without that strategy, there is no copywriting magic.

A well conceived and developed product won't be killed by poor or inefficient ad copywriting, but good copywriting can only go so far to promote a product for which the market has no desire. Once again, good copywriting is critical to marketing success, but it's simply a component of a sound strategy. We've already talked about some good strategic maneuvers, the best of which match product features and benefits to corporate goals. In this chapter, we're simply going to tell you how to tell people about this in the most creative effective ways possible.

As you will soon discover, there's an awful lot to learn.

CHARACTERISTICS OF GOOD WRITING

There is a sub-group of writers out there who understand and seem to have mastered the art of advertising copy. Not every writer can do it and many don't even want to try. It takes a rare amalgam of creativity, insight and a slight sense of hucksterism, all of which balance to create, in the best possible case, a blend of the elegant and the obtuse, the homespun and the highbrow. A good copywriter is worth his or her weight in Addies, Clios and the host of other awards visited upon the ad industry.

But good copywriting skills have their foundation in plain-old good writing skills. Writing can be learned like most technical skills, but the truly gifted writers are blessed with both an insight and passion for their occupation. In addition, they have mastered a few literary basics endemic to all types of writing:

• Writing, first and foremost, is communication. As such, its meaning must be *clear* to the reader or recipient of the message. Your most brilliant prose means nothing if it is not understood or it miscommunicates your purpose. If you haven't accomplished this foundation principle, then you have not written.

• That clarity is supported by the right level of *coherence* to make it effective. That is, thoughts are arranged and delivered in a logical order so they may be better understood. Nothing propels a reader through text like a logical, coherent, cumulative structure. In the same vein, nothing grinds readers to a halt like its absence.

• It goes without saying that the writing must be *complete,* containing all the necessary elements to communicate its purpose. In addition to details, this completeness may contain layers of meaning that speak to the reader at several levels, both conscious and subconscious. This is especially true of ad copywriting.

CHIT

It's an old axiom, but when it comes to copywriting, the acronym KISS still applies: Keep it simple, stupid. And if you do keep it simple and clearly understandable, you will find that it's a strategy that is not so stupid after all.

• As you strive to make your writing clear, coherent and complete, you run the risk of also making it circuitous and cumbersome. Like the Bard said, good writing also is *concise* and to the point, muscular in its structural strength and scrupulous in its efforts to save the reader time. Good writers say more with less; often, the quality of writing is proportionate to its length. One of history's shortest documents is Lincoln's Gettysburg Address. It is also one of the most powerful.

• Good writing also is *consistent* in all aspects—its tone, voice, appearance, cadence, tense and verb structure. Writing, like thought, can build power through cumulative characteristics played against its structure. Consistency can fortify and further strengthen that foundation, or it can dress it up and flesh it out.

• Finally, writing benefits from *creativity* applied liberally but tempered critically in the mind of the writer before it reaches the eye of the reader. Each writer—poet or sign painter, copywriter or novelist—strives to present his or her own thoughts in a personal voice, one that is characteristic of the writer and his or her intellectual and emotional predilections. The best can trademark their work through this voice and help it accomplish what it needs to at levels of which more ordinary prose can only dream. We'll talk more about voice in a minute.

Helpful as these guidelines may be, they are all, in the end, no more than intellectual tools. The driving force behind good copywriting may be a need to express thought, an ability to cleverly manipulate words and ideas or, quite simply, the need for that weekly paycheck. But those writers driven by passion for the product or the process will produce better prose than those without such drive. That's the key characteristic you should be seeking.

BEYOND THE BASICS

We'll get to specific copywriting issues and ideas over the next few pages, but a good ad copywriter needs more than writing basics on which to build his or her creative foundation. Once you understand the structure and framework of writing and decide you have a passion for the process, it helps to have a few ideas at hand and literary tricks up your sleeve to make your writing effective.

Remember what we said earlier—writing is about meeting the needs of the reader first and the writer second. When those two blend together, then you have a perfect communications marriage. If they don't—and they often won't—there are tricks of the trade you can employ to help bridge that gap. Here are a few ways to build a better relationship with the reader and make your writing more vivid:

• Consider the purpose of your writing and reflect it in the tone of the work. One may be able to sell odd looking little German cars that resemble insects with humorous prose, especially when the advertising of the day tends to be more straitlaced and serious. But it's unlikely humor would be effective for ads about raising funds for disabled children. Match the actions of your audience to the outcomes you desire through proper use of tone and flavor.

• Do you write in the first, second or third person? The answer will depend on the nature, purpose and tone of your project. First-person narrative draws readers in and helps them identify with the purpose of your prose through identification with the writer. Second-person text, when used skillfully, becomes a conversation with the reader. It can be a call for action and involve the reader in the outcome advocated by the text. Third-person writing is more formal and standard in its approach. Writers who are less skilled or concepts that are less distinct are more appropriate to this approach. Whichever tack you decide to take, make sure it's right for your project and be consistent with it throughout.

• In radio patter, the announcers are told to keep things "tight and bright." That means keeping concepts crisp, concise and to the point and maintaining conversation that is upbeat and friendly. That works in ad copywriting, too.

• Use the five senses to their best advantage. This is especially important in copywriting. Readers or listeners should be able to smell the rich aroma of the coffee; taste the crisp, clean, refreshing flavor of the soft drink; feel the rumble of the road beneath their wheels and the supple softness of rich, Corinthian leather beneath their backsides; see the vivid colors brought out by the laundry detergent; and hear the power and clarity of the stereo speakers. If they can't, then your ads aren't going to sell very much merchandise.

• Good writing is intuitive in nature and answers questions before they're asked. Much resistance to advertising comes from decisions made with incomplete information. Ad copywriters for Volvo assume safety is first and foremost in consumers' minds when they consider that brand, so they stress that up front, followed by an emphasis on luxury and class second. Customers draw the necessary connections and make the buying decision appropriate to their needs based on more complete information. If a customer forms a resistance to your advertising message, chances are it's because he or she made a decision prior to receiving all the information from you. Head off that natural human tendency by offering that information before it's requested.

• Utilize structure and sentence length appropriate to the project at hand. Writing structure can be used to facilitate communication or create an effect that makes an impression on consumers. The wrong structure for the product means you've lost the customer before they've even reached the sales pitch.

Short sentences attract attention. They make points quickly. They can have a dynamic impact. But their staccato nature also creates text that is abrupt and sometimes jarring. One may be able to create verbal exclamations that remind the motorcycle-buying crowd of short engine bursts on the open road, but that same writer may lose buyers of more elegant goods who need to be romanced by the rhythm of well-crafted, near poetic prose. Match structure to the purpose of the product, the nature of the customer and the tone of the ad campaign. You'll know quickly if your writing is out of whack.

• Make sure your writing is pitched at the right level for the audience. By nature of what they do, writers often tend to be more generally learned people with a better command of vocabulary than the average readers. Showing off your level of education or writing prowess can alienate the readers and turn them off to your message. An inexperienced writer often overcompensates by overwriting, and that inexperience shows. It also may be misconstrued as insincerity, which is death to ad copy.

A more mature, experienced writer isn't afraid to use clear, simple words and sentences that make the point to the reader without unnecessarily demonstrating the writer's knowledge and skill. The best writing is nearly invisible, making that subconscious connection with readers that allows them to identify with the prose as if it were their own idea. Writing that draws attention to itself detracts from the message. And that's the last thing you want to happen.

CAPTURING VOICE

If you think back on memorable ad campaigns, you may remember some snappy graphics or arresting visuals, a jingle or a catch phrase. Most often, however, you will remember those components as part of the marketing concept behind the campaign. And you will remember that concept because of the way in which it was texturally delivered. That includes not only what was said in the ads, but also what was not said and how both sides of that same coin were delivered.

That's called "voice" and is perhaps the most critical element to successful writing. You can read an unidentified page out of an Ernest Hemingway novel and know immediately that it was the work of this author because of his profoundly distinctive voice. Regardless of whether the novel involves an old fisherman in Cuba, young libertines in Paris, or the Michigan backwoods boyhood of a man named Nick Adams, Hemingway's voice rings clear, alerting you to the fact that it is indeed his work.

CHIT

Good copywriting creates a sense of urgency in the reader, a sense that it addresses with repeated calls to action. Copywriting is never a matter of simply saying, "Here is my product." It's always "Here is my important product and this is why it's absolutely critical that you have one. Or two." Copy that fails to excite fails to sell.

The need in copywriting is even greater because consistent voice brings increased brand identification. The pride and heritage present in image ads for Anheuser Busch, makers of Budweiser, differs markedly from the funky, nearly iconoclastic 30-something-aimed ads for Miller beer. The voice present in that copywriting creates an emotional link for the audience and is evocative of that brand the moment the first few words are uttered. That voice then becomes as distinctive as the trademark or logo for those brands. In addition to maintaining and increasing sales, preserving the right tone from commercial to commercial and ad to ad is critical to maintaining that brand awareness and identification. And that's a matter of voice.

What voice you choose depends less on the writer, in this case, and more on the marketing strategy as it has been defined. That strategy, in turn, depends on characteristics of the audience with which the market seeks to connect, hence the "heritage vs. funk" dichotomy of the two similar brewed product campaigns. Like other aspects in writing, consistency in voice, more than almost anything else, is critical to continued copywriting success. But unlike elements in writing, voice can bring the single-most distinctive element to your ads, an element that can't be duplicated no matter how well you cover the five senses, how active or passive a role your prose takes and how humorous or serious you make your copy.

The voice belongs to the writer and to the writer alone. Matching elements within that voice to the right product, right audience and right position is critical to achieving strategic success. That's best done through the use of the right voice.

Internet pundits maintain that voice will, in fact, be the only way to market on the 'net. The nature of the medium—and that's assuming you consider it a medium and not a lifestyle—is informal, conversational, colloquial and even somewhat blue in its tone and vocabulary. This *vox populi* form of communications puts a new and more stringent demand on marketers who want to align themselves with the new medium. It's conversational, they say, and driven by users, special interest groups and broadly defined communities of like-minded people who make buying decisions *en masse* while constantly polling each other for opinion and information. Try and market to us, they say, and you will meet with little success.

Perhaps. On the other hand, this may be considered another group with simply a more dynamic psychographic to which the marketing message must be tailored. The fact that marketing on the World Wide Web attracts a motivated, more sophisticated and global audience may make the loss of any upstart groups a little less painful.

COPYWRITING COMPONENTS: A PRIMER

There is an entire science to copywriting, one that we've only managed to hint at here. Don't assume that your marketing assistant can do it just because she or he took some college composition courses and is one of the few people you know who can conceive thoughts and speak in complete sentences. There's a little more to it than that. However, if your budget or other considerations absolutely force your work to be done by someone who does not write copy professionally, here are some tips that may make the process less painful.

Prewriting Will Save Time and Result in More Effective Copy

Before embarking on the specific writing task—an ad, some radio copy, whatever—decide what your copy "platform" is going to be. In other words, what are the objectives of your ad or campaign?

Summarize them into a writing position statement so that you're clear on what you're trying to achieve. From there you develop your "concept," a combination of your platform wrapped up with the methodology by which your copy will achieve its goals.

Once that's done, define the approach you want to take—humorous or serious, a mere sharing of information or a call to arms—and identify the components that will help establish that approach. That will include the proper tone and style, as well as the facts and details you will need to include to reach that goal. Knowing what to include is as critical as knowing what to leave out. Copy should be clean, crisp and to the point. Good prewriting habits help the writer more easily reach those goals and objectives.

Headlines Appear First, But They Should Be Written Last

Headlines encapsulate the concept of your marketing message. They also serve as the teaser to get readers into the body text. Sometimes they ask a question, occasionally they pose a threat and they always must entice and attract. Headlines are the most important part of the copy you will write.

Despite the fact that headlines appear first, they should be written last. You may have a concept in mind that you jot in your headlines, then follow with a cogent text you believe makes sense given what you've initially announced. And it probably does, but it won't be one-tenth as effective as if you had done it the other way around. Writing the headline first may make it easier for the writer, but remember that the goal of writing is to be effective for the reader. That means you have to put in the extra effort because you know that the reader won't.

Think of your headline as the summary statement of your thesis. Think of it as the core of your sales message. Think of it as the source of the key member benefit. It's all those things tied up in a short, concise phrase that also romances the reader into the text. To that end, you'll need to back that headline out of your text and turn it around so it takes the lead role. It will be a lot of work, but it will be worth the effort.

Chances are your first pass at a headline will be several sentences long. If that's the case, then you've performed part but not all of the function. Continue to cook your words until they boil down to their essence. Move components around and look for phrases that are unnecessary. Find the core, the essence of the message and highlight that.

Nike's "Just do it!" says nothing about the company, the product, the process or even, directly, the benefits of running. It addresses the major challenge—getting out there on the road—and implies that Nike will help you overcome your personal obstacles (presumably because of the characteristics of their shoes) and the benefits will follow. Brilliant.

Body Copy Needs to Be Cumulative and Tailored to the Medium, Audience and Message

One does not put long lines of copy on billboards because motorists will a) ignore them, or b) get into accidents attempting to read them. No matter what the value of that specific medium, the nature of its relation to the reader dictates its use. If you're going to use outdoor advertising, think of your text as an extended headline with product and company identifiers and create accordingly.

Direct mail offers more options. In fact, research has proved that people who are motivated to open your direct mail will spend more time with a long enclosed letter, which often means better results, than they will with a shorter letter. Once they're in the envelope, consumers will review most of the contents, so maximize your approach accordingly. A variety of component pieces, including those requiring an interactive response ("Put the YES or NO sticker in the appropriate square and mail it back to us.") also have been shown to produce more effective results.

Space ads in publications operate as snapshots. Those communicating the benefits at a glance will likely be more memorable. That sometimes means greater dependence on graphics than text, but the goal should be brand recognition and/or a call to action. Much more than that you can't really expect.

Electronic media—radio and television primarily—require a more creative turn these days. As competition heats up, audio and visual texturing has become even more important. If anything comes close to encapsulating the concept along the lines of a headline, then

MARKET RESEARCH

Call it "tagline shooting" if you want, but one useful exercise, both for headline creation and concept conceptualization, is to create as many product taglines as you can think of using many different concepts of the product, its audience, its features or its benefits. You can involve your marketing department only, or bring in others from other areas of the company. In fact, the richer mix might result in a clearer insight into what you're trying to do. If you can involve

electronic advertising is it. Once again brand recognition and/or a call to action tend to be the twin goals of such ads. In addition, there is an underlying goal to make the ads themselves memorable so that consumers draw the attention of friends and family to them, thus serving as unwitting foils for your marketing message. ("Hey, Bobby! Watch this ad with Louie the Lizard. Man, those Budweiser people are a hoot.")

Marketing over the Internet tends to run into a combination of clever headline writing, direct mail and infomercials, depending on the product, the message, and the way the "ad" is laid out. In addition, because of the net's interactive nature, consumers can be more actively involved in product marketing. The individual book sites on Amazon.com allow for the opportunity for buyers of the books to render an opinion—to write a "review of" the book—which the company then adds to the Web site. This can evolve into further discourse and even debate, all of which can help stimulate interest in the product.

Review, Rewrite and Reduce Your Text

Experienced writers know it is easier to write something long than it is to write something short. That apparent contradiction boils down to the realization that writing is an intellectual process, the byproduct of which is words on a page. Inexperienced writers often fail to "cook" their thoughts long enough to get them down to the essence, thus ending up with text that is obtuse, indistinct and too long. Reviewing your work for accuracy is a must, of course. But reviewing it again with an eye toward reducing superfluousness and excess is the hallmark of a piece well written. It also can be a crucial step in getting to that all-important core communication level so critical to reaching and influencing the intended audience.

In the end, all works can be rewritten to preserve and enhance economy and clarity of thought. Writers who aren't taking those extra steps are not quite doing their jobs. And their work certainly suffers for it.

Without a Call to Action, Your Marketing Hasn't Marketed

All good ad copy winds up with some form of call to action. This may run the gamut from the hard sell ("Call 1-800-BUY-THIS and have your credit card ready. Operators are standing by.") to the subtle (Coca-Cola's memorable holiday season "I'd Like to Teach the World to Sing" commercial implying that the Atlanta soft drink bottler supported world peace . . . or at least a worldwide market). If the copywriter has done the job, the consumer has been softened and made pliant to the marketing message. In the best of circumstances, that consumer is ready to buy. Without a call to action, there's a good chance that sale may not take place.

FINAL THOUGHTS

Much of this should go without saying, but in writing it rarely hurts to belabor the obvious.

• Be truthful in your advertising. People will quickly find out if you are not and avoid your

MARKET RESEARCH
(Continued)

qualified individuals from outside your firm, so much the better. When it comes to tagline shooting, there are no limits or restrictions. Be as creative as you want. You just might find the key to your marketing campaign here.

A variation on this theme is to create taglines for products that otherwise didn't have them or don't need them. How would you have originally marketed fire? What about a tagline for the stealth bomber? Use your imagination. It helps.

product and company like the plague. There is an inherent belief that all sales rhetoric is built on lies to begin with, so scrupulous honesty is critical. That doesn't mean you can't spin the text in the direction you wish it to go. Consumers, ultimately, will make their own decisions. Your best hope is that you can get them to make that decision in your favor.

• Depending on the product and/or approach, testimonials can be an effective strategy. This is not the same as celebrity pitchpersons, who can lend their own cachet. Testimonials refers to real live consumers who can show how effective the diet plan was, with before and after photographs, or talk about how a certain physician or hospital saved their son's or daughter's life, which speaks well of the health plan to which they subscribe. It's much like what's going on with the Internet. Never underestimate the power of the average user to sell your product to his or her cohort group. It can and does work.

• Sell one aspect and sell it well. Human attention spans being what they are, no copywriter can hope to hold a reader's attention much beyond making his or her key sales point. Pick one product and weave the marketing message around. If you have two products, you need two ads. Three products, three ads. Coca-Cola uses its ads to sell Coke, period. Sprite gets its own marketing effort. Budweiser sells Bud or Bud Light in its ads, but never both in one ad. That confuses the consumer and is death to your marketing effort.

• For heaven's sake, make whatever you write and produce interesting. That's creativity backed by a solid strategy. You're competing with thousands of marketing messages and if yours doesn't stand out, you won't make many sales. No matter what your medium, find a way to make it pop from its pages, so to speak, and you'll have a better chance of getting noticed.

• Remember you're writing for the reader, not the writer, and what you write should not be aimed at winning you a rack full of Addies or Clios. Awards, commendations and recognition by your peers are secondary to the effect you're trying to achieve: selling more goods to more people at a higher price.

THE LITMUS TEST

If you follow through on even part of what we talked about in this chapter you will wind up with copy that is better written and more effective than before. Use the sections we discussed to measure the effectiveness of your headlines, taglines and intervening text. There are variations based on product, medium and audience, but each section can serve as a benchmark for your efforts. The real measure of copy success—the litmus test, if you will—consists of the following four components:

1. Is your ad focused on the specific product or service that it's selling? Does each and every word—not to mention the spaces in between—contribute to the sale of that product? Does the copy leave no doubt in anyone's mind what the product is, what its benefits are, who its intended users might be, and where those users may purchase that product?

2. Is the copy honest in its portrayal of features and benefits? Will purchasers walk away agreeing that they received everything you told them they would from the purchase? Do they understand what they've bought and how it should be used to the greatest benefit?

3. Does the copy create an impact that causes it to rise above the clutter? In the same way many of us still can whistle ad jingles for products decades old, will the copy create a visual and auditory impact on our psyches that will cause the product and its marketing message to pop into consumer minds with little or no provocation?

4. Finally, does the copy sell and do the results show that this is work well done?

It's going to take a little longer to answer this final question but, given the purpose of marketing and advertising, this is the most important criteria of all.

The real key to this nebulous thing
called "creativity" is the art of establishing
new and meaningful relationships
between previously unrelated things
in a manner that is relevant, believable
and in good taste but somehow presents
the product in a fresh new light

—Leo Burnett

9

The Art of Design

Industry types will tell you there is no marketing without the talent necessary to take trend analyses, customer traits, social conditions and economic implications and weave them into a creative tapestry that spins the attention of consumers in favor of the company attempting to peddle its wares. The topics we've covered thus far have gathered that information, organized and evaluated it and come up with a strategy or battle plan. In Chapter 8 we discovered how the talented copywriter gives that strategy voice. In this chapter, we're going to discuss how the designer gives it vision.

To say that there is an art to design almost seems unnecessarily redundant until we realize that graphics have been a part of marketing since the first cave dwellers scribed the walls of their abodes with tales of the hunt and images of the mastodons they tracked and musk oxen they captured and killed. These scions of early commerce weren't selling a product to their fellow tribesman per se, but they were communicating a narrative of achievement through pictures designed to illustrate as graphically as possible the value of their efforts to the group. To those who sat around the open fire gnawing the bones of those animals, the value proposition of that effort was abundantly clear. The artwork had had its impact, and that undoubtedly was the strategic design of these early hunters.

Everyone processes information differently, but the majority of us process the bulk of it visually. The old chestnut that a picture is

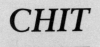

CHIT

Before letting your design take on a life of its own, make sure that you've considered both its medium and its purpose. That will help shape and conceptualize it within the space allowed. Consider all economies of space, shape and scale when developing your design. Pay attention, too, to the subject. That may make all the difference in the world.

worth a thousand words has a solid basis in scientific fact. Nearly 68 percent of the knowledge we take in comes through visually. That means all processes benefit through visual representation, and none more so than advertising and marketing. The critical nature of the designer's role in the creation of logos, ads, campaign collateral, premiums, packaging and even business cards, letterhead and corporate uniforms can't be denied.

There is an art to art and design. That goes without saying. But there is also a science to it. Graphic treatments don't happen randomly at the whim of some paint-splattered visualist perched at the crest of his or her creative bell curve. That vision, however unique, comes out of training, discipline and a common visual psyche, the foundations of which can be traced back to ancient civilizations and cultures. This chapter won't teach you how to create, but it will give you the foundations on which creatives operate so you can better understand, appreciate and perhaps guide their efforts.

CAPTURING THE CREATIVE MIND

Creative types flock to marketing and advertising like pigments to a base coat. For the artists among them, it's one of the few places where they can be paid—and often handsomely—for capturing their creative visions in print or broadcast. Of course, few of them initially have creative visions that involve detergent bottles or cereal boxes but, all other things being equal, it's often an effective and satisfying way to exercise their skills without having to subsist on rice in a cold-water walk-up. They know they could do much worse.

You'll know the creatives within an agency by the unusual workspace they occupy and invigorating company they keep. Inflatable figures hang from the ceiling and vivid graphics plaster the wall of their cubicle or studio. As long as those images aren't illegal, offensive or, worst of all, illustrate competing products or firms, then give them the opportunity to cultivate their already fertile minds. The end result might be exactly the images you seek to blow the top off the market for your product. After all, no one ever was inspired by polished wingtips and a gray flannel suit except, perhaps, a mortician. And that's not the direction you want your marketing efforts to go.

DESIGN DYNAMICS

For most of us involved in marketing, it all begins with a product and its strategic marketing and development concept. We see that product in terms of revenue and market share, of ratings points and column inches. The jug of laundry soap is no longer a utilitarian cleanser, but rather a share of shelf space. It's a means by which revenue is earned and the company grows in service to its stockholders. In the best of all worlds, that jug of soap becomes a leading brand by which the rest of the market is measured and our success and immortality are assured. The fact that it is laundry soap designed to clean clothes is often last on its list of duties.

The designer also has a unique view of the product, but one that has little to do with market share, ratings points or return to investors. The designer sees the product as a concept, all right, but one that is interpreted in graphic representation based not only on all those good things that your research has uncovered, but also his or her own innate sense of what that product communicates in light of the market it serves. That jug of laundry soap is a jug of soap, all right, but it also is something that has shape, scope and heft. It sloshes when you shake it, feels filmy to the touch when you rub it between your fingers and smells like a perfume-scented cleansing agent when sniffed.

How do artists capture that in a label design, an ad and other forms of promotion and packaging? First and foremost, it begins with the dynamics of dimension and the special relationship between the line and the shape.

The line can be vertical or horizontal, long or short, thick or thin with all variations of size and content thereafter. The line is most often the headline for the ad or the name of the product emblazoned on the package. The size, positioning and other elements that determine the line are critical to the success of the graphic because it's the headline that commands attention and, in most cases, will draw consumers into the ad and result in the purchase (see Chapter 8). The line is to be taken seriously.

But so, too, must the shape be given more than a mere passing recognition. The shape is the dominant graphic element on the display. It may be a photo, an illustration or some other form of graphic. It is the shape and its contents that often catch the eye of consumers and involve them both intellectually and emotionally in what that content represents. That, in turn, promotes involvement with and purchase of the product in the ad or behind the packaging. If the line is that important, then so is the shape. Perhaps even more so.

Basic design teaches the relationship between the line—or lines—and the shape. Sometimes the lines are blocked to mirror or complement the shape, forming another shape in and of itself. That, in turn, adds to the dynamics of the presentation and the strength of the graphic representation. How a designer manipulates those shapes may well determine whether the product is a hit or a miss, simply because people will respond to the image they received from the ad or the packaging, not from the soap within the jug, which is the true product that they purchase.

Above all, it's the line and the shape and how they relate to each other that creates the tension behind the design dynamics. It doesn't matter to the designer whether we're talking laundry soap, foreign cars or rat poison. The basic platform behind the graphic medium remains the same. It's common to see designers experiment with pure shapes without content, and blocks of letters—commonly called "greeking"—that is mere gibberish repeated over and over.

The importance is not the content but how text looks in relation to the shape(s) used. And for the designer, the importance of the area *not* filled with stuff—commonly called "white space"—aids the dynamic in a very meaningful way.

Chances are that your striking packaging and award winning ads started out first as shapes and lines, nothing more, from which your designer was able to build a commanding piece of graphic work in a way that spoke to consumers on both a subconscious and a conscious level. That's what good design does, by the way. It provides another level of communication for marketers by which they can communicate with buyers that has little to do with the product itself.

Colors work that same way. When Minute Maid began packaging its orange juice in black cartons, the industry was aghast. Black simply wasn't a color used to package food, and especially not something as bright and health-oriented as orange juice. But the black color caused Minute Maid to stand out from the competition and gave it a classier look. It wasn't long before this particular designer's brainstorm had propelled it to the front as one of the leading brands of juice.

And that forward stride had nothing to do with the quality or flavor of the juice itself and everything to do with how the designer portrayed the product. Design helps sell, and good design helps sell more products to more people at a higher price. And that, as you know, is the purpose of marketing.

CHIT

One of the most powerful tools at the designer's disposal is the negative space. That's space that doesn't have any images, words or messages in it. By viewing negative space positively, you suddenly see the dimension and shape of the "frame" around your images. You'll find it that much easier to adjust all space accordingly when you realize this white space has a positive role to play in aiding and strengthening design.

MASTERING COMPOSITION

Design can be free-form and flowing, or it can be built around the natural dramatic tension between the line and shape. But in order to create the right impact on the page, design has to follow the rules of composition, an organizational system that brings into focus new and exciting graphic ideas by applying them to the familiar rules of design. If design is the bright colors and wild shapes in your artistic flag, then composition is the rectangle that contains those colors matched with the rules of perception designed to keep those shapes from seeming to slide from the flag to the ground.

Composition is the manipulation of these elements into a graphically and aesthetically pleasing arrangement. Composition also describes the design as a satisfying whole, creating the appropriate weight, balance and poise of those elements. Many compositions are built on grids which, on the printed page, are measured in column inches. Of course, using such a grid too religiously can render designs as static or mechanical in appearance. The grid is only as effective as the dramatic tension between the elements that play off its framework. When both elements work correctly, the graphic representation can be strong and forceful, as well as dynamic and creative. Once again, the image of the gymnast and his sidehorse come into play. Neither is interesting without the pressure supplied by the other. But when the right moves are made against the stationary resistance, the performance can be pure artistry.

Design frameworks exist because they speak to a subliminal level of understanding within the composition with which all or most viewers identify. In the world of playwriting or screenwriting, it's called the three-act structure. A plot is established and conflict arises in Act 1. Additional information is uncovered and more plot twists are added as the action takes a new direction in Act 2. The action is resolved and a resolution reached in Act 3. All the classic plays and films follow this structure for a reason and those that don't run the risk of failing before they start.

Page composition has a similar set of guidelines, often referred to as the Golden Mean or Golden Section. Developed by the Roman architect Vetruvius, the Golden Mean is a mathematical equation through which the page is divided into thirds both vertically and horizontally. Picture a giant pound sign (#) straightened up and laid across the page.

The divisions form natural ribs on which the page rests and the eye follows. As a framework, high points in the graphic display—including the appropriate white space—can be aligned with one or more of the ribs. Through careful placement and deliberate interaction of the elements, the design becomes stronger and better in its capability to attract the viewer's eye and hold his or her attention. Key shapes and lines can be enhanced based on their placement along these measures, with subordinate components positioned in relation to those elements.

Like the three acts of a play, the Golden Mean provides a familiar, yet transparent frame on which the designer can hang his or her elements for maximum impact. The stronger and cleaner the design, the clearer and more powerful the message and the greater its result.

USING ART

There is an art to the use of art—illustrations and photographs—as well. Except for the fact that both art and photos fall subject to the same framework criteria that other graphic elements do when encountering the framework of the page, both tend to be used very differently. Each offers different emotions, different options and different finishes for the piece in process. The designer likely will know which works best artistically, but may need your help in deciding which is best in terms of measuring project success.

Size and shape often determine whether to use art or illustrations. If you need something to fill a square or rectangle, a photo may be a better choice. Realize that a professionally taken photograph is a design in and of itself and that the rectangle or square often is its natural shape. There are some very funny photos out there but, due to the nature of medium, photographs tend to be more dramatic, sometimes serving as an end in themselves and giving the piece a greater sense of importance than it might have with a spot illustration. As a rule, photos don't work quite as well when

MARKET RESEARCH

For a short-short course in successful advertising design, simply observe the following rules:

- Keep it simple by focusing on one person, product or image.
- Match visuals to the headline so viewers don't have to try and guess the connection.
- Show your product. Isn't that, after all, what the ad is about?
- Use visuals to arouse curiosity and demonstrate your product. With any luck, you will be able to do both.
- Use visuals that evoke emotion. Pathos is good; humor may be even better.

bursting their rectangles as illustrations do, but that is not always the case.

Unless they're highly detailed or drawn by a famous, familiar hand, illustrations generally are considered more informal, sometimes whimsical alternatives. Both forms communicate emotions but, by nature of their flexibility, illustrations can communicate a lighter, wider range that, due to its nature, doesn't fully involve the viewer the way a photo does. A viewer can picture him or herself in the context of a photo, dramatic or otherwise. That's more difficult to do in an illustration, where the subject may be a talking snow tire or the Cat in the Hat.

The art works within the same dynamic we discussed earlier and, most likely, constitutes some or all of the shapes that we discussed. The line, then, would be the ad's headline and the same rule of dynamics applies. The headline and piece of art must work together, interacting accordingly and effectively to make the marketing point that needs to be made. If it doesn't, even the most dramatic photo and cleverest headline will lack the necessary impact.

The required dynamic usually means something other than side-by-side coexistence for the line and the shape. Often the line is integrated with the art, overprinting onto the open space in a particularly appropriate photo. Sometimes the photo is a cut-out and the type wraps around the image for a particular effect. And, in the case of illustrations, the type actually can be part of the illustration, either wholly or in part, for maximum integration of images. It all depends on what the designer thinks is the most appropriate image to carry the message you're trying to send.

There is an element of art in typefaces, too. When mixing art and type, make sure to choose a face appropriate to the task at hand. There are some beautifully wrought typefaces that are as emotionally evocative as they are informative. You need to exercise the same care in choosing a typeface as you do in choosing art, because they often are one and the same. There are old fashioned faces and newer, more contemporary varieties. Choose according to your project needs and the emotion you wish to convey to the viewer. It is surprising what a typeface itself can say, regardless of its integration in the graphic context.

Color and white space also go hand in hand when making visual decisions about the ad's design. Never confuse white space with wasted space. It acts like the frame on a picture, providing context and elegance, helping dominant elements stand out. Used wisely, white space enhances the effect you are trying to achieve.

The same goes for color. It can add excitement and drama depending on how it is used. In an over-stimulated world, subtle use of color and even the use of spot color in black-and-white contexts can add an element of drama, sophistication and elegance to the design's appearance. Use color wisely and it can serve you well.

DEVELOPING VISUAL CONTEXT

The first step in the development of any ad is seeing that ad, first in rough sketch, then in finished form. It's at this stage that the training and talent of the designer takes over and most of the rest of us fall away from the mix. Up to now, all members of the marketing team may have had some say in the development of product, strategy, positioning and concept for the ad. Putting the finishing touches on the visualization of those principles falls squarely into the realm of design, something for which most of us are very glad.

The first step is developing the visual context for the ad, often done with a series of rough or thumbnail sketches. All those elements we've talked about thus far—design, composition, integration of art and type—come into play in creation of the rough. Often numerous roughs are created and approved by the appropriate marketing team members. In addition to helping visualize the concept for the team, this is also a good way for the designer to keep from firing off too many false starts.

Identifying the right visual approach for the ad is as much an issue of the product as it is of the ad concept. If the positioning and concept have been adequately developed, the right approach quite naturally should suggest itself. Often, however, it falls to the designer to finalize the concept through layout and design, providing the visual clues necessary around which the rest of the marketing effort will start to wrap itself. That may not be the best way to do business from a strategic point of view, but it still has been known to work and work well.

There are four basic types of visual contexts in which the product can be placed:

The Product May Be Shown Alone

Without the benefit—or perhaps the obstruction—of background context, the product appears suspended in time and space. This sometimes takes place in new product introductions, but more often when the product's design, color, style or overall general visual nature needs to be emphasized. Many of the original Volkswagen ads showed "The Bug" sans context in an attempt to stress its unusual design, as opposed to showing the car in traffic, where its diminutive size may have caused it to become lost in a sea of tail fins and headlights. The freestanding product shot is often considered a bold move, since there is no context to provide added dimension. But the effect is undeniable and, when done properly and with the right product, can be very powerful in its approach.

The Product Can Be Shown in Its Natural Setting

Picture an ad for a Coleman outdoor product—say a tent, a gas stove or a lantern—without the benefit of a beautiful natural outdoor setting. You may be intrigued by the design of the lantern, or by the way the tent fabric folds and lays against the aluminum frame of the structure, but the ad may rob you of the emotional satisfaction and feeling of relaxation you experience by associating the products with the camping motif in which they are used. Context of use can give the product shown an additional dimension from products that are shown alone. Sometimes it is critical to explain how and where the product may be used, while at other times it's necessary to use the setting to help viewers identify lifestyle choices with the product and its use. Your designer may decide to use a full background setting—either a natural setting or an indoor studio shot with the appropriate props. Setting can also be one or two props or support items to give the image partial context. A lot depends on the positioning statement you want to make.

The Product May Be Shown in Use

Showing the product in its setting tends to be passive. Showing a product in use is active. The difference often lies with the product itself and how best its benefits can be displayed to produce both intellectual recognition and emotional impact. The Coleman tent benefits from taking a passive stance as opposed to, say, showing campers erecting the structure. A CrisCraft boat, on the other hand, is best shown plying the waters filled with happy outdoors people as opposed to merely floating dockside tied to an ugly wooden or concrete pier. Don't make the mistake, however, of showing people standing or sitting and admiring the product. To make the most of this visual context, those people have to be using and enjoying the product. That will help viewers identify with the benefits of ownership and, presumably, send them out to the store to buy one.

The Product Benefit May Be Highlighted

This is the fourth and final step in the visual context developmental chain. If you recall, we began showing the product alone, then the product in its natural setting. From there we evolved to showing the product in action and now move to the showing the benefits of that action. This fourth and final context is significantly different and, in some ways, a more profound statement to make. But it doesn't work for all products at all times. The benefit to our CrisCraft owners is

MARKET RESEARCH

What is advertising? Industry giant Fairfax M. Cone, partner in the firm Foote, Cone & Belding, had these five rules to share:

1. The basic proposition of the ad must be immediately clear to consumers. No one will take the time to unwrap the tenets of a poorly developed ad.
2. A well-defined value proposition is critical to an ad's success.

the freedom and enjoyment they feel speeding along in the boat. That, in fact, is the product in action as well as the benefit. It's difficult to tell the difference.

The benefit to participants in a diet program from Jenny Craig International is, of course, weight loss. That can be shown in before-and-after weight loss shots, or through the use of svelte models enjoying themselves. Showing the benefit, in fact, is probably the only way to advertise weight loss programs. Showing the dieter in his or her natural setting or using the product likely will do little to support the marketing efforts.

Choose your visual context based on the product, its purpose and the marketing concept you are trying to sell. Some approaches will naturally suggest themselves, while others will offer a variety of options. Make sure the visual context chosen is appropriate to the task at hand.

DESIGN CONSIDERATIONS

Once the proper visual context has been identified, the designer is at the point of creating the ad. Within each of the contexts, there are standard formats that can be considered as the basis for the design. There are three basic types of format:

1. The picture window style uses one large illustration that dominates the ad, often taking up as much as three-fourths of the available space to make its impression. Similarly, the silhouette style utilizes only figures in the foreground, with

any or all background omitted as a way to emphasize the graphic. Both styles call on the strength and simplicity of the single image to make the necessary point. These contexts often produce the most memorable, elegant ads.

2. There also are element-heavy styles that stress content rather than design. The *copy-heavy* style is just that, with a heavy reliance on body copy often necessary to tell the product's story. The *omnibus style,* sometimes referred to as "the circus poster," shows a wide array of product and price information. Its overall sophistication and effectiveness rank near the bottom of the marketing scale.

3. The more elegant and obtuse styles may focus on type, but with a designer's rather than a copywriter's eye. The dominant symbol in the ad may be a word or phrase that becomes as much a graphic symbol as it does a word. This is a common approach for companies whose logo incorporates the product's or company's name. Since logos, no matter what their content, are first and foremost graphic representations, we tend to view them this way.

   In the 1980's, there was also an ad style called Mondrian, based on the geometric design work of Dutch artist Piet Mondrian. Generally consisting of rectangular patterns placed close together, this is distinguished from the multi-panel style that tells a story in comic-strip like fashion. In Mondrian,

MARKET RESEARCH
(Continued)

3. The ad's offer will be delivered in personal terms directly to the audience segment for whom the product and message are meant.

4. A good ad represents the personality of the company and product it represents.

5. There will be a call to action; otherwise, it should not be considered an ad.

there are no words connecting the illustration. The visual representation tells the story.

The right design will be the result of the concepts and strategy behind the ad as well as the designer's own level of sophistication. Understanding the design and purpose behind the visual context elements we previously discussed will go a long way toward making the right layout decisions at this stage.

OTHER ELEMENTS AT ISSUE

Finally, before creating the ad, the designer should ask him or herself the following questions:

- What is the proper dominance or emphasis of visual elements within the ad? Remember that the dominance of a single element draws attention to the ad.

- How will those elements flow to draw the viewer into and through the components to the ad's sales message? The ad's movement or direction needs to have eye appeal.

- What are the elements of balance and proportion that the ad will embrace? Remember that height and width of the elements should correspond to the contours of the space available and be relative in size to their value to the viewer.

- How will the ad achieve coherence of elements and unity of concept? The overall visual relationship must support the visual context as a whole

THE BOTTOM LINE

When it comes to design, it all needs to work together or none of it works at all. And more is often less.

The essence of good design, whether we're talking about ads or product packaging, about publications or promotional flyers, is a clear, clean, uncluttered presentation. The product or its benefit should dominate the imagery, and graphics should be relevant, clear and contributory to the whole of the ad and the goal of the marketing message. Good design appeals to viewers on numerous direct levels. Excellent design is capable of building that subconscious connection with viewers that speaks to them intrinsically, as well as intellectually and emotionally.

Like all other marketing, design is meant to communicate first and foremost. The motto of Metro Goldwyn Mayer Studios may be *ars gratis artis*—"art for art's sake"—but when it comes to marketing design, it's art for commerce's sake.

A good designer never, ever forgets that and responds accordingly each and every time. That, in fact, is what makes the designer good.

In the world of advertising there is no such thing as a lie, only expedient exaggeration. You ought to know that.

—Roger Thornhill (Cary Grant) in Alfred Hitchcock's North by Northwest

10

Working with an Ad Agency

Other than meteorology, advertising is the only industry in which nebulous results are the norm and no one expects to be able to measure the exact impact and return on investment for what constitutes one of the most significant cash outlays a business can make in its future. It's this very inexactness, in fact, in which the industry trades and upon which agency empires are built. If there is a place for pikers, shysters and prima donnas to not only hide out but prosper in this world, it would be in advertising.

Such is not usually the case, however, and the massive success of the brands with which we all are familiar would indicate that something good is going on during those creative sessions, many of which result in wild successes for the companies spending the billions of dollars that support the advertising industry. That advertising is often educated guesswork. Taking significant consumer research and turning it into creative—and sometimes silly—forms of persuasion is part and parcel of how the industry operates. Further, that those efforts result in sales of sometimes enormous magnitude that can make or break products, corporations and careers is grudgingly accepted by even the industry's most vociferous critics.

Finally, it is a given that virtually all firms, including yours, will call on the services of an advertising agency at some point in its existence. In today's market, you can't compete without advertising, even of the most rudimentary kind. As the world grows more and more sophisticated, only the most professional ad messages will be heard. Like it or not, that means hiring and working with an ad agency. Knowing what to expect and how to go about it is what this chapter is about.

Advertising is an unusual business to be in and one of the few where people are rewarded for daydreaming, thinking out loud and often spending long hours at expensive restaurants under the guise of "taking a meeting." Admittedly, these are stereotypes, but all of them have some basis in fact. Agencies operate more like regular businesses than they might first appear, but the relative glamor of living life on the fringes of show business causes their clients to help keep these stereotypes alive. As a marketer, you may be the most colorful, unusual character in your shop, but we're guessing that some of the agency types with whom you deal make even you seem a little like an IBM salesman. And chances are you admire and envy them for it.

Getting the most out of your agency relationship requires more than merely giving them all the money they want, although you won't find an agency that doesn't think this isn't a worthy strategy to consider. Working knowledge of agency procedures, plus a cast list of who does what, could be a valuable tool for maximizing the returns on that particular investment. That way, you'll have a better sense of what you can and can't expect in return for your retainer.

Agencies take a lot of ribbing, some of it deserved. But in most cases they play an integral role in the success of your marketing efforts, a role that should not be taken for granted nor taken lightly. Like any professional resource, the more you know about it, the greater value it will return to your marketing effort.

THE AGENCY EQUATION

Advertising agencies exist because companies need the services they provide. Those services range from advertising creation to brand consultation, from media selection and purchase to public relations and image development. As with other phases of marketing, agency services are designed to give the employing company competitive advantage in the marketplace and make that company or its products stand out from the crowd on the supermarket shelves. Marketing identifies the goal and provides the strategy to accomplish this task; advertising provides the tactical maneuvers.

In some cases, companies do develop their own in-house agencies, just like they hire staff accountants and attorneys to take care of daily business. But many of these same companies hire similar talent outside of the firm, professionals trained to accomplish the same types of projects and goals. While it often makes sense in the case of accountants and attorneys, it may seem unnecessarily duplicative in the case of agency services. However, even in companies having their own in-house ad people, outside agencies may have a significant role to play.

A good ad agency can bring a company the following advantages:

- Top-line expertise in all phases of ad creation, media development and strategic management. That's their business, after all, and they are likely to have some of the best minds in the business on their payrolls.

- A broader perspective on the market, taken not only from a customer-research perspective, but also with a clearer vision of competitor advantages and disadvantages and strategies for maximizing the situation. Even the best in-house marketing and advertising suffer from an institutional myopia brought about by the politics and mores of the workplace. An external agency is happily devoid of that excess intellectual tissue, which often makes them more capable of seeing the product and its intended market unfettered by nonessential thoughts.

- Access to a wide array of services under one creative umbrella. An agency is familiar with and can suggest alternatives and ways to market and advertise that the company otherwise might not think to employ.

- A pipeline to the top talent in the area, either through employment or in association with freelance purveyors, for everything from copywriting to voice-overs and from art and design to event planning. By virtue of the volume and diversity of the work they do, agencies will know where to find the best candidates for this job, either in your market or anywhere else, for that matter.

In addition, if the company is small, the agency serves as an extended staff that can brainstorm, kibbitz and generally help the abbreviated marketing staff solve its problems and accomplish its goals. Of course, as with any professional, these services don't come free. But, dollar for dollar, the return on that investment is often a good one and much more economical than increasing staff size, if for no other reason than the broad, outside view with which the agency personnel come equipped.

No matter what the depth and breadth of a company's relationship, the agency can and will offer a wide array of services. However, there are four core specialties in which most ad agencies excel and from which a company can benefit.

1. Developing the Appropriate Strategies to Accomplish the Required Goal

At its best, this service begins with a partnership between client and agency. The client can answer the question, "Why?" (To sell more laundry detergent, to penetrate a new market, to compete more effectively against Brand X). Together, the client and agency can determine the "Who?" (Middle class housewives, teens, aging Baby Boomers—those for whom the message should be targeted.) At that point, it's up to the agency to identify the "What" (the tactical plan that will accomplish the task); the "How" (the methods by which to execute that plan); and the "When" (the frequency with which the message shall be communicated to the target audience).

In fact, a tactical plan is one of the most important services that an agency can provide. The best ones build off the client company's strategic marketing plan which, of course, supports the business plan in the accomplishment of its goals. The agency, then, becomes both arsenal and armory for the advertising and media battles that lie ahead.

2. Developing Creative (Ads and Collateral) Designed to Accomplish the Goals

As part of that arsenal, the agency will create the necessary ads, supporting collateral and events designed to tactically achieve those goals. That's called "creative" and is a visible byproduct of the agency effort. The agency will call upon its own talents as well as those of freelance specialists to create the best possible materials, meanwhile looking for the most effective avenues of communication. The work of the agency likely will achieve a consistency at both conscious and subconscious levels, positioning the ad messages based not only on the product for sale, but also on the best strategic advantage within the market. Those messages also will maintain a consistency and at least the veneer of a higher level of professionalism than non-agency work would have. It's polish as well as the process by which the ads and external messages communicate that give agency work its edge. It's the content and purpose, jointly developed with the client company, that can make it exceptional.

3. Defining and Handling Media Scheduling

A real strength for agencies is their ability to handle effective media placement in a way designed to maximize the value of placement in terms of dollars and advertising effectiveness. Agency professionals talk the lingo of media outlets and truly understand how ratings points and pass-along readership can combine and multiply the impact of an ad's message. Because they are frequent media buyers, they also can secure better rates, although they often take the discount as part of their commission. Financial savings notwithstanding, however, the agency's real value comes in getting the client the best buy for their needs and making sure consistency of message and frequency of placement help hammer the images and the message home.

4. Serving As a Clearinghouse for All Media and Creative Services Billing

It stands to reason that those responsible for contracting for creative services and placing media buys also are the best ones to do the necessary follow up and handle billing issues and questions as they arrive. Of course, those costs are passed on to the client and some are marked up (or, at least, not marked down) to account for their administration, handling and any necessary collection steps the agency will have to make.

This is a fair and equitable way for an agency to earn part of its commission and it's the same type of service for which a company might contract another professional, such as an accounting firm handling payroll, to perform. What's more, the agency has a better sense of knowing when it has and hasn't gotten what it's paid for on your behalf. Once again, since they live in that world, they are better prepared to deal with any issues that arise while they're working in it.

Other services exist, but they all tend to fall under one or more of the previously mentioned categories. When looking at agency services, it's helpful to keep in mind that such a total package approach puts a critical component of the company's marketing efforts in the hands of professionals trained to do them effectively and efficiently. That frees up staff members to help manage other aspects of the marketing operation, as they are paid to do.

CHEAPER AVENUES

There are shortcuts to using a full service agency that may seem to make sense. A company can hire its own freelance copywriters and artists and contract for printing. In addition, media outlets like newspapers and TV stations will offer support services for an additional fee that is cheaper than the going agency rate. Plus, the media outlets will argue, the work will appear in our publication or air on our station so it will be closer to the necessary formats and requirements. That, too, may be true.

But once you remove the agency from the picture, you eliminate the coordination aspect. That means all developmental work, media placement and creative strategies will have to come from the marketer's own office without the assistance of professional advice or an outside perspective. That could severely limit the competitive effectiveness of the resulting work.

As project manager, you also become the clearinghouse for developing the proper tone or perspective in relation to the project as a whole. Creatives are notoriously, well, "creative." That can mean wild inconsistencies and occasional flops that then must be dealt with. Without the agency layer in between, dealing with those shortfalls becomes the responsibility of the marketer, who may not have the time, initiative or expertise to handle the problem.

And, when it comes to having the media outlet provide assistance, that only works for small business or on a small scale. Like the case with freelancers, quality issues enter in and media-employed creatives usually aren't the best of the breed. The best folks are all working for agencies.

Use good judgement when making such decisions and don't let the financial savings drive you to sub-level talent when really only top-line agency work will do. Your advertising tactics are an investment in the most visible part of your growth and development strategy. Make sure you invest wisely and well and the benefits of that investment will show.

AN AGENCY PROFILE

Let's assume you've decided to hire a firm as your "agency of record"—that's the agency to which you turn to help develop both the tactical and strategic sides of your communications efforts. They operate much like your attorneys do and often on a retainer. They don't have to compete for every piece of business, project or campaign that comes down the road. They're already there, so they automatically get the business. In a situation like that, it's not only helpful but downright critical to know what life inside the agency walls looks like and who the players are, both major and minor, with whom you will be dealing.

All agencies differ and many have special emphases, either in terms of a special skill or talent or based on the market or industry they serve. But all agencies of any size deal with a wide array of services. Those services may be broken down into the following areas:

• *Account Management.* This is the area in which the agency's relationship and services for the client company are managed. Account managers are the liaisons between creative people, media buyers, researchers, administrative executives and the client company. Many times the account manager is the only agency rep the client company sees on a regular basis. And he or she is always good for a free lunch because client relations is part of the job.

- *Creative Services.* This is the most visible of the areas within agencies, if only on the basis of its work. Creative services are where logos are designed, ads are created and television and radio script is written. Creative services includes writers, artists, video and audio producers and technicians, photographers and creative directors. When you see ad people with purple crewcuts, dusty jeans and strange eyewear, they usually belong in creative services.

- *Media Services.* Less artistic and more scientific, media services study viewer/reader traffic plans and recommend where ads, billboards and radio and TV spots should be placed. They negotiate space and time and they monitor media schedules so that the hard work of the Creative Services people won't go unnoticed and its impact won't be dulled by placement during a 4:00 A.M. rerun of "Sea Hunt."

- *Research.* This is perhaps one of the most unsung departments at an agency, but easily among its most important. All creative and media placement decision is based on research done on the company, its product, the audience and its preferred method of communication. Researchers also test the effect of creative material before it hits the streets, the pages or the airwaves to measure its effectiveness and make sure it's ready for public consumption.

- *Production and Traffic.* That uproarious commercial or highly effective ad may bring the next Clio or Addy to Creative Services, but how does it turn into a commercial or ad suitable for air play or print? That's the job of Production and Traffic, which does exactly that. This department schedules and keeps track of all production work to make sure that the Creatives are kept on track so that their work is ready for the Media Planners to negotiate space for and place. Production and Traffic is a critical link between the two groups and is responsible for developing the tangibles that then go into the campaign.

- *Administration and Management.* When all the work is done, all media placed, all ads run and, as a result, all goods sold and profits reaped, this is the department that sends you the bill. Like any other business, Administration and Management includes all office and financial functions, as well as the top executives responsible for the growth and development of the agency as a business. Chances are you may never meet one of these uber ad men unless you are one of the larger clients or you've chosen one of the smaller agencies.

As you might expect, the appropriate denizens occupy each of the aforementioned departments according to their creative bent or business orientation. Some of the more creative ones are not the types you'd see working at, say, an insurance company or law office. But the best agencies choose staff based on track record, skill and ability to meet deadlines and accomplish tasks. If looking a little out of the norm means creating advertising that increases your sales by 15 percent, then you'd probably agree that it's a small price to pay. And you'd be right.

SELECTING AN AGENCY

Picking the right agency to serve your account is a lot like picking a spouse. There have to be similar interests beyond money or money-savings. The agency should be in sync, at least to some degree, with either your product, your industry or both. They must be sized appropriately to your company and its needs. And they must have a genuine interest in your marketing success. In other words, they better be a pretty good match; otherwise each of you will end up wasting a great deal of time and you will spend a lot of money needlessly, which is very much like an unsuccessful marriage.

There are two ways to hire an agency. You can contract on a per-project basis, meaning that the agency is hired to do one specific campaign or promotion. Or you can hire an agency of record, providing council and guidance as well as handling the various marketing and advertising needs your company may have. Needless to say, the pay-as-you-go approach will be far cheaper in terms of cash outlays. In fact, you may pay just a fraction of what you would for an agency of record kept on retainer.

But in advertising, as in all else, you get what you pay for. The agency may do a very good job promoting that new line of bed sheets or frozen foods, but the results will be disjointed, lacking a comprehensive and cohesive feel. The agency will know everything there is to know, but only about that single product or line of products.

Because of that, their work will stand out from the rest of your marketing efforts, and not always in a good way, either.

Companies and agencies have known for a long time that creative, consistent themes promoted in a consistent graphic concept that reflects deeper levels of thinking within the company are more likely to achieve marketing success than periodic campaigns focused on one small episodic event or product. It's the difference between weaving a fabric and patching that fabric. Part of the resources the company provides the agency is a comprehensive look inside the corporate brainbox. When that look encompasses all product and development strategies, then the understanding is greater and the rate of return higher. An agency that becomes a partner, rather than merely a supplier, has the potential to make your company great.

Before getting to know an agency, you will have to get to know yourself first so you can explain your purpose and goals to the agency. Remember that the agency is shopping you just as you are shopping them. They want the relationship to be as successful as you want it to be because they know that a wrong match, no matter how lucrative it may be at first, is the recipe for disaster.

That means you must create a snapshot of your firm so the agency can get to know you better. This snapshot should include the following elements:

• *An overview of the philosophy and purpose of the firm.* Knowing where your corporate thinking is headed helps the agency better anticipate marketing needs. Without knowing who you are, right up through the vision of your top executive, the agency will not be able to help you chart the course necessary to find out who you will become.

• *Identification of past strategies, goals and objectives.* This is different from the prior item, which ends up in a discussion of strategies and goals, because it is a closer look at the tactics and objectives used to address those strategies and goals. Often these are subject to change once the agency has been signed, but knowing what they are up front will help the agency decide where to take your marketing efforts next.

Both of these strategies, in fact, also help the agency decide if they are a good match temperamentally to your firm. You will be spending and they will be earning thousands, perhaps millions of dollars. Remember the relationship analogy. There better be good personal and business chemistry; otherwise, it's better not to embark on the journey at all.

• *A catalog of marketable products and services.* The agency will want to know what you do and what you sell so they can gauge the relative ease or difficulty of the account. It seems basic, but you will want your prospective partner to know all that you do and exactly who you are if you are going to be successful together. A complete list, even of those efforts you may consider to be dogs, is required in order to get an accurate fix on the challenges ahead.

In and among that list should be laced the special or unexpected features these products have. These may be considered your competitive advantage, or they may be your greatest liabilities. Either way, the agency is going to have to deal with them so it's wise to disclose them up front.

• *Total annual billables and/or budget.* In fairness to the agency and in contribution to the success of the process, disclosure of how much you can or will spend to help accomplish your marketing goals will give the agency a more accurate feel for the account as an account. It also will tell the agency how extensively it can expect to fund its arsenal of marketing and advertising techniques. It doesn't pay for the agency to develop a plan that the company's budget won't support. Being honest up front about the funds available and what can be expected in return for those funds, again, is a lot like a relationship.

• *Special needs or services required.* If your business is seasonal, that's going to change the nature of the marketing effort. There also are distinctly different needs for a company in start-up mode versus one whose products are mature and well-entrenched in their market. In either case, early disclosure of special requirements will help further the relationship and maximize the value of the dollars spent.

• *Finally, a brief description of each of the principal officers and his or her background.* By understanding who they will be dealing with, the agency will better know what to expect in terms of demands and at what level of effort and sophistication their efforts should be made. They may also gain some sense of the sophistication and appreciation—or lack thereof—they can expect when presenting their work, allowing them to tailor it more appropriate to the required effort.

PROCEDURAL
DECISION METHODS

Once you know who or what your company is through the creation of a basic profile, it's time to start shopping for agencies. We've already identified some philosophic and operational benchmarks to consider. Here are other ways to start, continue and conclude the process.

1. Conduct a Media Review

Keep an eye out for work that catches your fancy or that you feel would sell your product. Don't rely on what you think you already know. Take the time to conduct a thorough review, as if you knew nothing about the market or the media that ply its waters. Study newspaper, magazine, billboard, television, radio and Internet advertising. Look for creative approaches that make the products advertised look exceptional. Review creative strategies that steer clear of the industry norm and make a bold new statement. Look for that ad that turns your head, that talks to a deeper you, that describes a familiar product in terms and ideas that make it all seem brand new again. Find out which agency produced that ad because that's the agency you want.

2. Narrow Down Your List of Prospects

When seeking a job candidate to fill a position on your staff, you have a fixed set of criteria in mind, as well as a distinct personality type and auxiliary skill sets, that you use to winnow likely candidates from the herd. The same is true with your agency selection process. Have a set criteria for both agency skill set and track record and begin the search for your ideal partner. Like the ideal job candidate, there probably won't be one. But going into the process with some fixed ideas will result in greater success in finding the right candidate from the list of applicants.

You may, in fact, find several comparable candidates. If that is the case, insist on meeting the principles of each and begin sizing them up in terms of history, background and personal chemistry. You may be inking a deal that will span decades and involve a lot of money. You'd better be as sure as you possibly can that the relationship is built to last before making the investment.

3. Research Your Leading Candidate Agencies

A list of companies that have done business with the agency should be the very least of your requirements. Contact them like you would a job reference and grill them, if possible, on the length and nature of the relationship with the agency, success and failure ratios, the costs of working with the agency and other factors that will lead to making the right business decision. Augment that knowledge with other research, including extensive examination of the agency's creative work and their apparent media preferences. How do their messages appear to mix with the demographics of your market and products? Better knowledge up front will soften the slope of the learning curve should you elect to work with that agency later.

This investigation needs to go beyond account reps and creative people to include upper level agency executives responsible for running the agency. More than the others, these top people—often partners and/or owners—control the fate of the agency and, with that, your marketing efforts. Their philosophy needs to be in sync with yours in order for the relationship to be a successful one.

Understand their working methodologies as well. Once the contract has been signed, will they shuffle your account off to ineffective, inexperienced people? Make sure you get what you want and that what you want appears as part of the contract. The same holds true with their media methodologies. Be certain they have experience in all the media you feel you need and then some.

4. Discuss Money Up Front and Honestly

One of the biggest bones of contention between agency and client is the cost of service. It's hard to measure the market value of a creative idea, at least until that idea begins producing sales. Good advertising isn't cheap and great advertising can be witheringly expensive. But

MARKET RESEARCH

Agencies survive based on commissions earned from the client company for work done in their shop. But they also earn income from additional sources. Media placement commission is probably the most common. Media outlets give recognized agencies a discount—usually 15 percent—which the agency keeps in lieu of charging the client a fee for media placement. The system is designed to keep that additional cost in check and allow the media outlets to work with agency professionals who understand the system and negotiate wisely on behalf of their clients.

the value returned is designed to well exceed the cost and is, occasionally, immeasurable. Understand your agency's rate and billing structure and make sure it jibes with your own accounting needs and ability to pay. Come to terms on compensation methodologies before signing any contracts and undertaking any work. Get the hard part out of the way first, then let the fun of creating a top marketing campaign begin.

As a side note, be sure to pay competing agencies for any spec work you ask them to do. It's fairer to the agency, showing that you recognize the value of their time and creativity. In addition, you'll likely get better spec work. In many ways, it's just a more professional way to deal with the agency and you'll wind up better for the small investment made.

5. Treat Contending Agencies Fairly If You Expect the Same Treatment in Return

Don't play one agency off another and keep all informed as you go through your decision process. Notify losers as well as the winner of your account, preferably with a call or a short personal note. Never let them read about it in the trades.

Once you do choose your new marketing and advertising partner, make it a point to issue a news release to the various business and trade media. Just like a wedding, both client and agency have reason to celebrate. If the partnership works, it could result in significantly increased sales for the client and award-winning advertising—along with significant revenues—for the agency. If it doesn't work, the two parties can count themselves better for the experience and go their separate ways.

YOUR RESPONSIBILITIES AS MARKETER

We've spent a great deal of time and space outlining agency responsibilities. True, it needs to be done. But there is a similar list for the company's marketing person charged with dealing with those agencies. Just like the tango, this, too, takes two.

1. Determine Your Objectives and Allocate Your Resources

The agency does not know what you want to accomplish. Only you know that. As the marketing representative for your company, you have to set that standard before any work can begin. Then the agency can help you achieve your goals within the confines of your budget. And never fear that you won't get the services you seek by telling an agency how much money you have to spend. The good ones generally exceed the budget without adding additional charges just to make sure the job is done as effectively as possible.

2. Become a Font of Company Information for Your Agency

Your agency needs to know everything about everything when it comes to your company. That includes strengths and weaknesses, strategies that succeeded and those that didn't,

MARKET RESEARCH
(Continued)

Agencies also markup services they purchase— photography, design, talent—and keep the markup as their commission for procuring these supplies or talent. These costs can range from 10 to 25 percent of the service's base cost and can help offset agency operating overhead. In both cases, the charges are warranted and justified to compensate the agency for that particular service. There is nothing shady or dishonest about it. The best agencies look out for their client's welfare and will use these costs to further the value of the advertising efforts rather than merely feathering their own nests.

changes in your product, your markets and even your CEO's mood. All information is necessary to make your marketing efforts a success, and you are the link to your agency for that information.

3. Be Your Agency's Creative Sounding Board

You have a role that goes beyond approval when it comes to developing the creative impetus behind the agency's campaign. Providing information, as mentioned above, is just part of it. The other part is interpretation of that information and how it should be reflected in your marketing efforts. Presumably, you, too, are a trained marketing professional. You should have a say in the direction taken because you possess a company understanding that even the most accomplished agency pros don't know about your firm. Put that understanding to work and pitch in on creative conceptualization. In addition to getting a better product, your money will go much farther.

4. Coordinate Marketing Efforts with Company Staff Responsibilities

Just have a major campaign break? Make sure the sales staff knows all about it and is prepared to take advantage of it. As liaison between company and agency, it's your responsibility to make sure that the appropriate staff members are kept informed all the way to the top. Your fully coordinated marketing efforts should include all appropriate elements. The agency effort is just part of that and the rest of

MARKET RESEARCH

What elements constitute a good working relationship with your agency? Continuity between your efforts and intent and those of the agency are a key to success. You can't operate at cross purposes and expect to come up with effective advertising. Short lines of communication is another key. The fewer links involved in the communications chain, the fewer links there are to break.

your organization must know what's going on so they can take full advantage of the efforts made.

5. Track and Evaluate Results and Report Back to the Agency As Well As Your Company Officials

If that which is measured is done, as the old saying goes, those measurements that are analyzed are improved upon. That, too, is your responsibility; all parties should know the success of the campaign, not its flashy color and stylish graphics, is what's most important and all should strive toward that goal.

Do all that and you'll have good control over an effective advertising effort that likely will generate good results. Stay close to the process, involve yourself intrinsically in all key steps, treat all parties professionally, and your efforts will be that far ahead of the game.

And you may wind up with a client/agency relationship that's the perfect creative and commercial match.

MARKET RESEARCH
(Continued)

As marketing director, you need direct involvement, or at least access, to those managing the creative process and equal say in the creative strategy being employed. That means teamwork between your office and the agency, as well as empathy on both sides for the rigors of the creative process and the limitations each side faces. And if both parties can keep an open mind, so much the better.

*Behind every overnight success
there are four years of hard work.*

*—Steve Jobs, Founder
Apple Computers*

11

Preparing Your Product Launch

Some time ago, a friend of ours was certain he had latched onto something that, while not guaranteed to make him a fortune, would certainly go a long way in feathering his nest for a more comfortable old age.

During the changing of ownership at a local diner he frequented, he wheedled from the outgoing proprietor the man's secret recipe for flavorful walnut pancakes. It was nothing special, mind you. Just a combination of familiar ingredients blended through trial and error in such a way as to create what our friend thought to be world-class short stacks. While people wouldn't pay a fortune for such a recipe, he reasoned, a lot of pancake lovers might be willing to pay a little for the secret to a better breakfast. And that could add up to big earnings for the holder of this precious secret.

This was prior to the Internet, so our friend paid several hundred dollars for a classified ad in a major supermarket tabloid with distribution in the millions. If only one percent were willing to pay $1 for the recipe, he reasoned, it would be worth the effort. He and his girlfriend sat up nights pasting stamps on to envelopes and talking about the ways they would spend the money.

Ten years later, our friend still had some of those envelopes left. Most of the rest of the envelopes were used to pay bills, including the one for the tabloid ad, the cost of which he never recouped. The lesson? Launching a new, untested product is difficult, if not impossible.

And that's true even when that product is as popular as a recipe for pancakes and costs as little as $1.

Every year, entrepreneurs and companies think of hundreds of thousands of new products, the majority of which remain in their creators' fevered imaginations. Some make it as far as the patent stage, others find their way into development and a small percentage even make their way through introduction and into the marketplace. But just because you've managed to build something and put it within reach of consumers doesn't mean they will come and buy it. That particular field of dreams usually only works, as they say, in the movies.

New product development is vital to the continued viability of companies both large and small. Without it, corporate momentum will falter and growth will stagnate. But creating the right product is a far more complex process than you might imagine and requires skill, research, a little derring-do and sometimes just plain old dumb luck—being in the right place at the right time with the right product.

That, in essence, is the secret to a successful product launch.

• You need the right product, one that satisfies customers' needs, meets or exceeds their expectations in terms of the price/performance ratio, and can be produced and distributed economically while still managing to turn a profit for its producer.

• You need the right audience, one that is receptive to your product, in need of its benefits and willing to pay the price you need to receive for it. In addition, that audience must go far beyond the early adopters—those who buy just because the product is new—to include the great unwashed masses in the middle who employ more common sense in making purchases and on whose support all products depend. Capturing this segment is the only way to assure success in the long run.

• Finally, you need the right time and place so that the wonderful benefits of your brand spanking new Whizzo Supreme are not lost on buyers not yet ready to receive them. This step is more critical than you might imagine and the one where a surprising number of new products stumble and fall. Online banking is finally beginning to take hold among financial services consumers, despite the fact that the technology has existed for almost 20 years. Those same financial service providers are still waiting for the smart card—the credit/debit card with a built-in microchip that has been Western Europe's preferred way of conducting transactions for more than a decade—to take hold in North America. Until that market is ready— or, better still, almost ready—for you, you're not ready for them.

Truth be told, successful product launches are about the most difficult part of the marketing business that you'll ever face. Following the right steps will help minimize the dangers; after that it will be up to your professional skills to help shoot the rapids that often lie ahead.

HOW PRODUCTS DEVELOP

Despite how we may feel, new product development is not like spontaneous combustion. It doesn't happen overnight, it never occurs in a vacuum and it's usually the result of years—sometimes decades— of trial, error, and revision before just the right mix of features, benefits and market demands come to bear on the situation and the creation at hand. Products generate from the work of development teams or the fertile minds of individuals. In either case, successful products never exist in and of themselves alone. There's a higher level connection and an overall method to the madness.

There also can be substantial input from consumer focus groups and even a company's own employees, who may have valuable input in terms of product development both as customers and as stakeholders in the firm. Your company's research and development department might have a breakthrough in discovering a material or compound that can be turned into a product. And there is always the old fashioned way: find out what's working for your competition and emulate it.

No matter what the source, new products more often than not are the result of development efforts tied to a company's business plan and in line with its development goals. A new product should reflect the organization's strategic plan and be established, not for its own sake but in order to further the economic and market development efforts of the company producing it. Remember that the business plan, a reflection of the company's strategies, should drive all marketing and development efforts. This includes the establishment and introduction of new products to the marketplace.

The first step is to identify the strategy behind the product itself. Is the goal to make a success out of the new product, or merely to pave the way for similar or, perhaps, even different products and create a market that doesn't currently exist? Either is valid if it supports the greater strategic purpose of the company. In addition, you must decide if the product is being developed as part of a proactive or reactive strategy.

• A *proactive strategy,* also defined as an offensive posture, is based on the identification and seizing of real or perceived opportunities that exist in the marketplace. Companies that create a product because they see a hole to fill or a gap in the market into which such a product may comfortably and profitably fit are exercising a proactive strategy.

• A *reactive strategy,* on the other hand, is a move taken against competitors by introducing products similar to the ones they already have in the market. If another company has a product that encroaches on your market—or perhaps you want to encroach on its market—then a similar product would be created as a reactive strategy.

Neither strategy is better than the other. It all depends on what your company's needs are at the time of product launch and how your marketing support, in turn, chooses to treat the new product.

New product ideas need testing while still in the development phase before you sink too much money into them:

• New products should be screened by an internal group, an external group and/or both to determine the likelihood of successful development and customer acceptance of the product. These should be formal exercises, not just casual questions, in which the value is judged and scored in a way that is likely to reflect the level of success the product may be able to achieve.

• You also should run the product through a pure business analysis during which the potential for economic success can be measured to the best of your abilities. New product development represents a significant investment of time and money. Your forecast of economic return, analysis of marketing strategy and review of the legal ramifications of the development and distribution of this product require a comprehensive review before you can safely make so critical an investment.

Assuming these steps have been taken and the hurdles successfully vaulted, it's time for product creation. In many cases, this results in the development of prototypes that are tested in the labs or throughout the company to see how well they perform under simulated use. You also may choose to institute a level of in-home consumer testing—if that's how your product is targeted—to measure the product's usage and success, and to make the necessary adjustments. This is the phase in which the kinks are ironed out and the product is fine-tuned and made ready for market introduction.

Prior to that, however, the product often goes through a period of testing to measure consumer acceptability. More often than not, these are what companies might call secondary sales markets, communities where an unsuccessful product can go to have its rough spots sanded down or die a quiet death. Chicago, Dallas and New York City are never test markets, but Rockford, IL, Austin, TX, and Syracuse, NY, often are. Such cities provide significant critical mass without constituting a major sales market for the product once all testing and introductory phases have been completed.

The final stage is the launch itself, often referred to as commercialization of the product. Presumably, all lab tests have been successfully completed and the product has been test marketed in a way

MARKET RESEARCH
_____

While we focus primarily on existing firms in this chapter, entrepreneurs know there is a separate set of steps they must go through to bring their products to market. Capital acquisition to support product development is a consideration facing many small and start-up companies. Preparing the proper prospectus, finding sources of capital and selling your idea to investors is an entirely different challenge.

that adequately measures its nature and features. Inequities in product or package content and design have been rectified and all opinion measured and recorded. The product is as good as it will ever be at this stage, so it's time to go national.

This is a major step for most companies, involving significant capital to support sales and marketing efforts that will place the product in front of consumers. In addition, there may be such things as slotting fees, which is the amount manufacturers pay retailers to put a new product on their shelves. There is also a failure fee for products that never quite manage to take off. But the fee is not the biggest cost of failed products, which is why most companies proceed with caution.

In fact, history is littered with the festering corpses of ill-conceived or poorly timed products too numerous to mention. Companies have lost millions of dollars attempting to compete with existing products, expand their own product lines or develop new markets. Careful adherence to steps previously mentioned may help reduce the product fatality rate in your firm. Just remember that, when it comes to courting a fickle public, there simply are no guarantees.

DEFINING PRODUCT LIFE CYCLES

All products, like all companies, have life cycles, individual phases of development and market awareness that coincide with the product's introduction, growth, maturity and decline. Each stage of that cycle has its own identifying marks and its own processes. Some stages make money for the company, other stages cost money. Knowing what phase your product(s) may be in can make all the difference between success and failure. More importantly, it can help you identify how company growth may be affected and whether you need to turn up or turn down the heat.

Each stage also has its own unique marketing needs and you can tailor your efforts according to the stage you perceive your product to be in.

All products go through four distinct phases in their product life cycle:

Stage One: Product Introduction

Every product begins with an introductory phase during which you attempt to enter the marketplace and introduce an otherwise preoccupied public to what you have to offer. As ubiquitous as it now seems, Coca-Cola was once a medicinal beverage that needed to be introduced to a turn-of-the-century public that was not only unfamiliar with the brand, but with the entire concept of soft drinks. Coke has come a long way from the pharmacy shelves to becoming the cultural icon it is today.

Depending on your industry, the introductory phase is a period of moderate to high costs, with high costs being the more likely of the two scenarios. Chances are, you will have research and development costs to pay down, along with a major investment in marketing support in order to make your product well-known. There are merchant incentives and product giveaways and introductory events as well, along with the possibility of a below-market price (if that is your introductory strategy) to stimulate sales. Remember that your marketing goal is to gain market awareness. Couple that with moderate to low revenue from a public new to your idea and you can see you're in a stage in which profits may be small while costs may be large.

One alternative to the high-cost strategy might be to employ skimming, a pricing methodology in which higher prices are charged to help recoup cost and take advantage of early adopters for whom price is not a consideration. Depending on the product and the market, skimming may put it out of reach of the average consumer. On the other hand, early success may encourage competitors to prematurely enter the market due to the product's significant profit margin. If you employ this tactic, proceed cautiously.

Stage Two: Product Growth

Once you've successfully completed the introduction phase and the public is familiar with and has accepted your product, you enter a growth phase in which you can plan on making up for lost financial time. Profits may soar while expenses decrease. With your R&D likely paid off and customers familiar with your offering, development and marketing expenses begin to tail off as sales grow. By the early 1990s, Microsoft had become a household word in terms of the software market. Sales began to ramp up without the need for media campaigns, and R&D needs tapered to a lower level—some would say too low—while profits soared.

This is the stage at which profits begin to increase. Advertising can become selective as different audiences express preference and support for the product. Repeat purchasers begin to surface, driving profits up. The original product begins to spawn variations designed to broaden the segment and stratify to better serve different audience groups. This is also the stage when distribution opportunity and channels tend to increase exponentially. Suddenly the product appears on retail shelves everywhere and, if you're lucky, demand meets or exceeds supply. Simply put, from a product development standpoint, this is hog heaven.

But the growth stage isn't all skittles and beer. Once you've proven the market exists and defined successful strategies for tapping it, competitors likely will enter the picture to trade on the spade work you've already done on their behalf with similar products designed to fill similar needs. Some may attempt to undercut your prices as part of their own introductory strategy. Although marketing expenses will be less than the major push you launched during startup, a certain level will need to be maintained to keep your name foremost among providers. Rest assured your increasing revenue and decreasing costs will cross each other on the growth chart, but you can't afford to let your guard down during this stage.

Stage Three: Product Maturity

Every growth arc eventually levels off, and it's at this point that your product will reach maturity. That's when your competitors, who also now may be firmly entrenched in the marketplace, begin to pose a serious threat. Your product strategy will change and costs may increase as you reposition yourself through increased marketing and attempt to hold your industry leader status. Marketing often takes the form of games, contests and other customer involvement devices in hopes of engaging existing and new customers in the products and winning over their loyalties.

This also may be a phase where price discounting becomes part of your battle plan. With R&D costs far, far behind you and the only thing drawing on resources other than basic production and distribution is a slight increase in marketing, you may be able to afford to offer price advantage as one of your more attractive features. Assuming your product continues with some level of success in the marketplace, those limited losses due to discounting likely will more than be made up for with the increase in volume.

But take care. Too much discounting without the requisite growth in volume could result in significant losses. Some maturity phases last a long time, so be careful how deep you dig with your discount and monitor customer response to the strategy closely. On the other hand, some mature phases come and go quickly, so you need to be flexible and reactive in whatever strategy you pursue.

Stage Four: Product Decline

No matter how popular the product you produce was at launch, it eventually will succumb to the wheels of progress and go into decline. Sometimes this is a function of the company's failure to keep pace with the times, but more often it has to do with environmental changes or changes in public tastes. Despite improvements, the buying public simply stopped needing buggy whips thanks to the introduction of the automobile, and there was little the manufacturer could do.

Depending on how the company may choose to handle this stage, it may not require high costs in terms of expenses. The possible exception is for companies attempting to bring new life into old products through repackaging, repositioning and increased marketing. As the product's flame begins to flicker, however, it will have an impact on revenues. What once was top shelf could become a back shelf product or cease to exist altogether.

Various strategies exist, including:

- *Deletion.* The company simply stops producing and distributing the product, abandoning whatever market segment it had managed to claim and closing down operations.

- *Harvesting.* The product continues to exist for those customers who want it, but the company ceases to financially support it, thus reducing the cost of maintenance and, presumably, increasing what profitability might still exist.

- *Contracting.* Sometimes brand name value exceeds the cost it takes to maintain it. That leaves some companies the option of contracting their brand to production to smaller companies for whom the net revenues are worth the effort long after they have ceased to interest the brand owner. Production time, effort and cost is freed up for more profitable items while the brand stays alive thanks to the efforts of a smaller contracted firm for whom the effort and income levels are worthwhile.

The lesson from all these steps, of course, is that different product phases require different strategies which, in turn, will result in different financial activities and impacts. How you go about defining a sustainable growth rate will vary with phases of your major product. Awareness of which stage you're in is critical to the success of those efforts.

ENTER THE PRODUCT MANAGER

No matter what the size of your organization or its product development effort, it helps to have someone with key responsibility for the success of whatever it is you produce. These individuals are called product managers and have been around ever since Procter & Gamble introduced them in 1927. All product managers are responsible for managing the growth and development of the product through its life cycle. Sometimes they are responsible for a cluster of related products. In either case, the success or failure of the product is their primary emphasis.

The product manager is involved in all aspects of product development and distribution, but especially in the marketing and branding of the product. This includes development and/or approval of marketing plans, product packaging design, ad copy and design, strategic development and implementation. In the event that the product enters stages the company doesn't want it to enter, or runs into rough spots, the product manager also has the capability to do the following:

- Modify the product or its marketing to better address real or perceived needs in the marketplace.

- Modify the market approach to spread the product's influence and/or increase its usage among currently pursued or different market segments. This can include finding new uses for the product as well as new users.

- Reposition the product to react to a competitor's entry into the market or as an attempt to reach a new market. Repositioning also may offer opportunities to capture rising consumer trends and even change the value proposition, either trading up to a higher-level market or trading down in hopes of capturing more market share through increased volume at a lower price.

The brand manager also is in charge of developing the brand, but that's a topic for a different chapter (See Chapter 3).

BUSINESS LIFE CYCLES

Let's step back for a moment and assume that your are responsible for marketing the entire business as a new product. Businesses go through phases very similar to those of product life cycles, embrace the same opportunities and run the same risks as those from the product life stages. The same level of care must be taken in order for the business to avoid those same types of traps.

• Every business has an entry stage, a time when it's new to the world of commerce and its principles are eager to gain marketplace recognition. Resources often are limited, the revenue stream may be no more than a trickle, and its needs are great. This is a very dangerous time for new businesses and the time during which most of them fail. At this point, all growth is perceived as good growth because the need levels tend to run very high. Good resource management becomes vital to survival, as does adequate capitalization to produce what's known as straight-line growth.

• The growth phase, which naturally follows, can be an exhilarating time for a company. The name is known, the products introduced and the customer base defined. Startup costs are declining and profits tend to run high. It's an exciting period that requires significant energy with which to keep pace, along with sufficient financial support.

• As a firm enters maturity, it's usually entering a period of smooth sailing. But those calm economic seas can be misleading. Costs may be level and profits sufficient for the time being, but nothing exists in stasis. Eventually the firm will enter a period of decline, making the strategy here one to maintain the mature phase—and the profits it generates—for as long a period as possible. Companies aware of the rigors of maturity can do very well. Those not paying attention may find themselves facing rough waters ahead without the necessary skills to navigate the currents.

• Corporate decline, the final phase, is a hard course correction to make. A company prepared for the inevitable may be able to maintain its decline for a long period of time with appropriate plans in place to exit the market gracefully. Those that have created an exit strategy may find a graceful way out. However, many firms stumble around attempting to breathe life into the corpse without luck. Whether there's reason to stay or it's time to go, financial planning should reflect this phase accurately and offer plans accordingly.

GOOD GROWTH OR BAD GROWTH?

Growth for its own sake is not an effective strategy for most businesses, even during its entry stage. Growth in revenues almost invariably means a growth in expenses. Depending on the ratio of that growth to capacity, a company can easily drown in its own excess without even realizing what's happening. The secret is a control plan that will result in sustainable growth for the company and the products it sells with a clear idea of the potential profit margin and what that means to the bottom line.

Believe it or not, excessive growth can be bad for a company because of the undue pressures it can put on resources. For instance:

• More orders mean more products, which can lead to more workers to support increased production and distribution. However, the revenue from those increased sales may not be sufficient or consistent enough to support the added staff, negating the value of those sales with corresponding increases in expenses. If the majority of those revenues are in accounts receivable, the situation can become downright desperate.

• The company's management structure may need to grow and develop to support new initiatives, creating an unwieldy, top-heavy environment that again may increase costs beyond the relative economic value such an increase was designed to support. The resulting environment of too many chiefs may do long-term damage to the company's growth and productivity.

• Increases in production capabilities and/or facilities not financially supported by increases in sales can result in unnecessary and underutilized capacity that will turn into a detriment rather than an asset as the company moves through its growth cycles.

Such scenarios show that not all growth is good growth and plans must be carefully monitored so the effect of that growth doesn't go south.

A SUSTAINABLE GROWTH STRATEGY

In terms of definition, sustainable growth can best be summed up in the adage, "It takes money to make money." How much money it takes depends on how much growth you plan to accommodate. But as long as growth is the result of planning, and your expenses coupled with your desired growth margin balanced against revenues—in much the same way as your books must balance, as a matter of fact—then your growth level likely will be sustained and progress made.

The growth stage of a product or company is one of the hot spots in terms of maintaining sustainable growth because it's the phase during which the company sees its most rapid change and realizes some of its greatest growth needs. Increased sales mean increased costs. Some companies resort to borrowing to sustain production or operations needs, which can be the kiss of death if done indiscriminately. Without a strategy for a revenue growth, such as the sale of common stock, serious problems could occur for the company overstepping its bounds. Sometimes sustainable growth occurs by default.

Understanding the ratios for sustainable growth isn't complicated if we understand how the balances of revenue and expense works within company operations. For the purpose of discussion, we'll assume your company is seeking as rapid a growth rate as possible, has an existing capital and dividend policy it needs to maintain and is unable or unwilling to sell shares of stock, one of the strongest ways to raise operating capital. The scenario is common for most firms in the growth stage of the life cycle.

The balance sheet model becomes the key to sustainable growth during this stage. In order to increase sales, the company must increase assets such as inventory, accounts receivable and the production capacity to meet the increased need. The cash required to pay for these assets may come from commercial lenders or, better yet, revenues due to increased sales. As equity grows, liabilities increase proportionately. Taken together, these determine the rate at which assets expand. This limits the growth rate in sales. In the end, it appears that the sustainable growth rate is determined by expansions in owner equity. Equity levels define sustainable growth.

Put another way, sustainable growth in sales is impacted directly by the profit margin and asset turnover ratio measured against both corporate growth policies and the asset-to-equity ratio. There are algebraic equations to prove this theory, but from a practical standpoint, it's enough to know that companies exceeding their sustainable growth rates need to improve operations or be prepared to alter financial policies to accommodate growth. Otherwise, the imbalance may knock them financially off-kilter. This can be true of individual products as well.

The alternative to too much growth?

• Reduce or reverse your revenue growth rate so sales slow down and you have a chance to make good on orders using current assets. In most cases you'll have a chance to recoup those sales as the cycle begins to flatten out. But if you plunge yourself into an expense well that is too deep for your firm, you may have a much harder time climbing out.

• Modify company policies to reduce capital and put more cash into circulation. This could have the same effect as wandering too heavily into debt, leaving you without adequate resources for future efforts. In this case, however, the assets you're using are yours. If and when you do trip up, you still may be able to turn to commercial lenders as a resource. Review your dividend policy and consider how much you should plow back into the firm to underwrite new production or retire operational debt.

• Look for ways to better use existing resources to meet growing needs. By making sure all plants are running at capacity and all employees have incentive to perform at higher levels, you may be able to meet demands without making significant investments for which you'll have to answer later. In that same vein, you may want to remove sales staff incentives to moderate growth cycles. In addition, rely on just-in-time inventory and labor to moderate costs and reduce the amount of asset investments into stockpiled goods and materials.

Your best option likely will be a combination of all three elements used in varying degrees. Again, the key to sustainable growth is good planning and effective management follow through. It's as critical here as it is anywhere else in your operation. And it's as important to market your company as it is to market the product you develop.

*It doesn't matter what they say about you
as long as they spell your name right.*

—Hollywood Axiom

12

Public Relations Part 1~ Purpose and Principles

In putting together a comprehensive marketing approach, public relations is no longer an option. It is a necessity. Never forget that.

In the past, much of the PR in practice was defined as publicity, a task for low level former news writers and wordsmiths to inform, entice, cajole and entreat editors and publishers to put good "news" about their clients in various publications in hopes of augmenting or replacing that client's advertising message. It was bargain basement media coverage that could help stretch those ad dollars and, with any luck, present the client in a favorable light to boot.

Sometimes, it worked. More often, however, the PR practitioner's news releases ended up in the wastebasket and good opportunities were missed through sloppy, scattershot approaches.

Contemporary public relations practitioners have repositioned themselves as informational links between the media and their clients. Make no mistake, the goal is still to create favorable public impressions and, in some cases, stem the tide of negative publicity by practicing damage control over bad news reports. (After all, bad news constitutes most of what we know as news; few people other than employees and stockholders are interested in hearing that things are going well at a company.) Positive media coverage also is still considered a budget stretcher to help maximize advertising dollars and increase media reach.

More recently, practitioners have looked beyond the short term gain to realize that public relations is the foundation for building what some PR professionals call *public relationships*—that ongoing and consistent impression consumers have about the nature of a company that causes a subliminal positive reaction every time an advertising message comes across. It's the logical extension of brand marketing that not only helps convince consumers that they want what the company has to offer, but that they also feel good about doing business with that company.

McDonald's restaurants, which sell some of the most highly caloric and fat-laden sandwiches in the country—and by the millions, to be sure—have this all figured out.

Early on, to differentiate themselves as a family restaurant rather than some mere hamburger joint or teen hangout, they created the persona of Ronald McDonald and his cast of colorful characters. It was Ronald's job, as the company's PR spokesclown, to communicate the image that McDonald's was a magical place that was family friendly and, most important to harried parents, entertaining to young children. Families could come there for an economical meal that parents were relatively sure their fussy kids would eat. By buying one of the restaurant's Happy Meals, the kids also could go home with a small toy, a reward for giving mom and dad a respite from the drudgery of cooking and coaxing. Such strategies are a large part of the corporation's overwhelming success.

In more recent years, McDonald's has parlayed Ronald's role as children's entertainer to that of children's savior. Ronald McDonald House is a nationwide network of homes away from home for parents of children requiring extended hospital stays. What's more, Ronald has managed to incorporate customer contributions to help build such houses and fund their operation.

It's important to note that, while the clown figure was originally part of the company's advertising and brand development strategy, Ronald's role in promoting Ronald McDonald House became one of public relations icon, in much the same way that Smoky the Bear is the persona associated with forest fire prevention. However, Smoky evolved from a public service background, not one of product promotion. Successful transitions such as the one made by Ronald McDonald are, as they say, as rare as rocking horse droppings.

Ronald McDonald House is an exceptional example of community relations and public service at its finest. But it also creates a highly positive impression in the minds of consumers, first of all by providing a service for families—the restaurant's designated market niche—and involving them in the project through contributions of nickels, dimes and quarters that are no more than the pocket change from their purchases collected at the point of sale. It's a perfect closed loop for those who want to become part of this public good deed. For less than a dollar, anyone who buys a Happy Meal or other McDonald's product can become a fast food Good Samaritan. Ingesting all those calories and fat grams is a small price to pay for feeling that good.

The real lesson learned here is that corporate good deeds alone are not enough. They have to be positioned, packaged and presented in a way that captures public attention and involves them at some intrinsic level in order to be effective. Often this works; but equally often the strategy behind the effort—and we're talking about communications of the good deed, not the motivation behind the good deed itself—fails for lack of strategic forethought.

John D. Rockefeller Sr. was one of history's greatest philanthropists, but has gone down in history as the villainous robber baron and founder of Standard Oil who was at one time the world's wealthiest individual. Few remember that John Sr. contributed what would be by today's standards more than $1 billion and years of effort to establish and build the University of Chicago as a midwestern competitor to the east's Ivy League schools. Or that the head of the world's largest oil conglomerate also was responsible for funding the eradication of ringworm and several other diseases debilitating the nation at the end of the 19th century.

To stave off the attacks of muckraking journalist Ida Tarbell, the growing interest of legislators and, especially, self-styled "trust buster" Theodore Roosevelt, Rockefeller hired the services of Ivy Lee, considered one of the industry's earliest PR practitioners. Lee did his best to fight negative publicity, at the same time taking the public relations concept into the new century and legitimizing the role of media relations specialist. But he was unable to undo the efforts already in place that ultimately broke Standard Oil up into numerous smaller companies.

As Lee found out, the task was simply too big for an end-around effort or quick fix during the eleventh hour. Had Lee been brought in a decade earlier to set a strategic development plan with a strong communications component that emphasized Rockefeller's philanthropy and public service, the net result might have been very different.

And who's to say that a clown's orange wig and red rubber nose might not also have helped.

PUBLIC RELATIONSHIPS

In its most generic sense, public relations is seen by many as the garnering of good publicity, free press and the positive public response that results. It's the false handshake and oversize check for the charitable contribution, the chrome-plated hardhat worn and shovel used by the chagrined executive "breaking ground" for a new office center, and the costumed characters marching in hometown parades to promote products and businesses. It's the truth seen through smoke and mirrors and the spin doctors' work at turning a major catastrophe into "strategic redirection."

For the true practitioner, however, the publicity aspect of public relations is merely the tip of an iceberg that should have been solidifying long before the photographer ever loaded his camera and the news release writer ever sat down at her keyboard. Public relations is exactly that: a relationship with a wide variety of publics designed to develop a more positive environment in which to do business. For as easy as it sounds, however, it can be devilishly difficult to accomplish.

All public relations efforts trade on the same thesis—to build the impression of positive environment in the mind of the targeted public, minimize negatives found either within or without the efforts of the company itself, and communicate those efforts as effectively as possible. The tools and delivery mechanisms vary with conditions, but the general goal of creating positive energy is always the same.

Not all publics are created equal, however, and good practitioners know the difference in role, purpose and strategy as it relates to the company's needs and the publics served. Each organization has its own set of "publics" with which it must build relationships, and they vary from industry to industry. Here are some of the more common ones with which many firms must deal.

Stockholders

Because of its emphasis on finance, this one doesn't always fall within the purview of just the public relations officer. Since stockholders are owners of shares in the company, courting this particular group is critical to the continued success of a company and its administration. Without stockholder support, the company would not have the finances to continue operations. Without this group's faith and trust, company executives would not be able to continue in the execution of their strategies or, perhaps, their jobs.

Unlike other publics, however, this group trades on facts and hard data in formulating its impressions. Smoke-and-mirrors doesn't work when it comes to communicating the numbers and, for as much positive spin as can be applied to an ailing bottom line, stockholders will still form opinions based on the color of the ink, not the tone of the rhetoric. Solid facts easily understood with little or no obfuscation is the best way to build good stockholder relationships.

But care should be taken to communicate consistently, frequently and pro-actively in order to keep the relationship alive and the trust level high. There is need for efforts before and after annual report season. The annual report is the keystone of any effort and the legal document required by government regulatory agencies. But efforts should be made to communicate on a more frequent basis. That way, any financial setbacks will at least be anticipated.

Customer/Member Relationships

Customers who purchase products and/or members who pay dues also have a very real financial relationship with the organizations with which they deal, too many of which fail to see this critical group as a public that needs cultivating. Make an error that costs you a customer and it likely will go unnoticed in the upper ranks. But if that same error costs you 100,000 customers . . . well, that relationship that you have not bothered developing deprives you of what could have been a safety net of customer loyalty. And you know what can happen to those who fly without a net.

United Airlines, like all commercial carriers, understands the value of good customer relations. The airline's Mileage Plus program is a perfect example of a foundation effort designed to reward frequent flyers with greater value for their ticket price. The fact that the program is tiered to reward customer performance levels allows them flexibility and leverage with which to address unpleasant situations. And there were few situations more unpleasant to air travelers than a season of delayed and cancelled flights and consistent snafus in the wake of a threatened pilots' strike along with stumbling merger efforts between United and U.S. Airways. Even the major national media took notice, prominently featuring stories about air travel problems as front page news and almost always with a picture of a United Airlines jet.

In response, letters went out to Mileage Plus members from United's chairman/CEO James E. Goodwin personally apologizing for problems and offering greater flexibility for holders of nonrefundable tickets in changing flights if necessary. More to the point, Goodwin's mea culpa also included the offer of increased frequent flyer miles to the program's top travelers. Upper tier members got as much as double the normal miles, a significant bonus since they already received double the actual miles flown. Under this scenario, a flight of 1,000 actual miles that already received an additional 1,000 miles as a bonus would have another 1,000 miles tacked on, resulting in mileage "credit" of 3,000 miles for use toward a free airline ticket.

It doesn't take a rocket scientist, or even an airline flight mechanic, to figure out what nearly all frequent United flyers did in the wake of delays and cancellations with such an offer pending.

Community Relations

No man is an island, entire of itself, as the poet John Donne said. Likewise, no company operates in a vacuum, but is part of the greater community in which its employees and executives live and operate. Because of that role as corporate citizen, community relations become critical to its continued survival and well-being. Cultivating community relations—even if no one in the community buys or uses the products or services the firm produces and distributes— can result in favorable tax and zoning incentives, reduced opposition in times of labor disputes and greater patronage of the support businesses large industries often generate.

And, for the record, it's also often just the right thing to do, manifesting as positive attitude and increased self esteem for the people who work and do business with the firm.

Community relations takes many forms, including support of local youth and/or senior programs, United Way participation, urban renewal efforts, fundraising, and donated labor to groups such as Habitat for Humanity. Executives may be loaned to non-profit community service agencies and staff members may deliver Meals on Wheels to housebound invalids. In most communities, there is no end of need. And that means no end of opportunities for a company's community relations efforts.

One good example is the CUNA Mutual Group, which provides insurance and financial products to credit unions worldwide. Despite the fact that the percentage of its billion-dollar business done in its home town of Madison, Wisconsin, is minimal to the point of being nonexistent, the company maintains its role as the top corporate contributor to the local United Way office, the top corporate blood donor to the local American Red Cross chapter, and encourages employees to participate in charitable work on personal and company time. That encouragement has resulted in some 75,000 hours annually contributed by CUNA Mutual staff to a wide array of charitable efforts and community programs.

"We take our role as corporate citizen very seriously," CUNA Mutual CEO Mike Kitchen told the local city magazine, which honored the company as Madison's top community service provider. "We are committed to making Madison the best place possible for our employees to live and work."

Such an award doesn't go unnoticed within its industry. And sometimes good karma alone adds up to good business.

Employee Relations

We referenced it several times throughout the past sections so we won't dwell on it here. But it is critical for companies to realize that relationships with employees extend beyond the paycheck.

As mentioned earlier, employees are part of the "community" in which a company resides and should be considered among its most important members. A good relationship can help a firm avoid excessive staff problems during times of labor dispute and financial hardship. Moreover, it can foster a positive environment that will lead to increased productivity, corporate financial growth and greater staff development opportunities and initiatives which, in turn, can reduce recruitment costs as employees—more loyal because of the positive way in which they are handled—stay at the firm and chart their personal and professional growth through its ranks.

Plus, it's just the right thing to do.

Media Relations

When it comes to public relations, most of the attention people pay focuses on the discipline's media relations subset. That is the most visible and can be highly influential, affecting the impact of all the other relationships based on the severity of the situation and the way in which the media handles it. Unlike the other relationships, media relations most often deals with bad news, requiring swift reaction and significant damage control. This is where the PR officer must be the most diplomatic, dextrous and definitive. How a problem is handled can make or break a product's or a company's success.

It's been decades since people died due to the unsolved poisoning of several bottles of Tylenol pain reliever capsules in a Chicago pharmacy. What saved pharmaceutical manufacturer Johnson & Johnson was its swift action. Rather than attempt to cover up the situation or minimize the damage, the company pulled all of its Tylenol products off the shelf and encouraged consumers to return for full refund any bottles they might have at home. The media, used to seeing corporate cover up as the *modus operandi* in such cases, supported Johnson & Johnson, spreading the word and helping support the company's "white hat" image.

The company lost millions in product that had to be destroyed. But it gained immeasurably in terms of greater credibility and public trust in a highly competitive field. The situation also helped usher in tamper-proof packaging that we all take for granted today, making Tylenol and its sponsor a part of marketing and packaging history. And that's marketplace positioning that is simply not for sale at any price.

We'll discuss courting the media and cultivating good relationships in the next chapter. Suffice to say they can prove to be your organization's greatest ally or worst nightmare. Much of that depends on how you manage that relationship in the first place.

THE PR EVOLUTION

As a discipline, public relations is really a 20th century phenomenon, getting its start during the Industrial Revolution and moving forward as businesses grew and the country moved further away from an isolated, agrarian economy. It's been a long time since Ivy Lee counseled John D. Rockefeller to carry dimes in his pocket and hand them out to children he met on the street as a way to help dispel his sinister, curmudgeonly image. Few realize the inroads PR has made and the impact it's had.

Lee, for example, was the first to advocate an open policy in dealing with issues and the public like the approach used in the Tylenol scare. He helped mobilize public opinion in support of the U.S. entry into World War I and he helped grow the American Red Cross from 486,000 to 20 million members and raise $200 million by the time the war ended. Lee finally fell from grace when work done for the German Dye Trust in 1934 to improve U.S.-German relations led to public accusation of Lee as a Nazi spy and propagandist.

Lee's fall coincided with the rise of Edward L. Bernays, a Viennese-born nephew of Sigmund Freud and advocate of the psychoanalyst's teachings in the U.S. Whereas Lee called on his background as a former newspaperman, Bernays was the first to call on psychology and social sciences in his efforts to sway public opinion. His efforts to "engineer" public opinion and consent form the basis of modern public relations. In his book, *Propaganda,* Bernays argued that scientific manipulation of public opinion was the only way to overcome society's chaos and confusion. The influence of Uncle Sigmund was never far from Bernays' position.

Neither was irony. In a rare turn of events that completes the circle started with the false accusation of Ivy Lee, it is reported that Nazi propaganda minister Joseph Goebbels used Bernays' book

MARKET RESEARCH

Good public relations people do not have the same characteristics often associated with the classic salesperson's profile. They are not backslapping, joketelling entertainers, despite what Hollywood stereotypes may show us.

Good PR people focus on communication of facts, information and interpretation. They are knowledgeable about the ways of mass psychology and understand in detail how their company and its products fit into the fabric of the societies they serve. They think strategically and execute completely, careful to always monitor the effect of the PR message. They are flexible and adaptable in their ability to adjust to changing attitudes and reactions.

Crystallizing Public Opinion as the foundation for his campaign to destroy Europe's Jews. Needless to say, that went a long way to give PR the sometimes bad name it has today.

Such extreme examples notwithstanding, public relations and its influence have grown through the last 100 years to the point where businesses of all sizes must have at least some awareness of the discipline and its issues. Knowing the concepts behind public relations—that its goal is to build relationships—and knowing the various publics with which to build those relationships (as well as adding any additional publics of your own based on the product or service you produce and the industry you serve) is the foundation on which any and all PR efforts are built. But in order to accomplish your goals, you will have to evolve into a public relations-minded organization whose goals are tied to the image it represents and whose image has a positive impact on the achievement of its corporate goals.

Let's look at that again, but in a different way. In today's highly competitive market, the companies and products that succeed are the ones that have built more than just a buyer-seller relationship with their customers. Highly successful products and services become an active part of their consumers' lives. Without that role, a company can only hope for modest success.

That's the thinking behind brand development and awareness. If Coke is the real thing, then it has to be an active part of its consumers' lives in order to be real. Brand development through marketing and advertising is one-half of the circle that revolves toward this goal. Public relationship development closes the loop. That means your company has to evolve into a PR-driven organization if it isn't already there.

How does your firm accomplish that goal?

1. *Public relations starts at the top.* The days when a team of flacks protected the CEO from public scrutiny and the media's prying eyes are over. Today, the CEO has to be the chief marketing and public relations officer, representing the best interests and intentions of his or her firm. That doesn't mean the CEO answers every media phone call or consumer complaint. But that does mean that he or she is a highly visible representative of the firm and that the administration's strategic emphasis is a proactive, public-minded attempt to build better relationships with constituencies at all levels in order to improve public image, increase market share and boost both credibility and sales within the marketplace.

Four-term former Republican governor Tommy Thompson—who went on to be Secretary of Health and Human Services in the George W. Bush Administration—succeeded largely because he was Wisconsin's leading cheerleader when it came to boosting the state's image and selling its wares. Thompson personally led trade missions all over the globe, was highly visible at public events and proactive in seeking new programs to improve the Dairy State's commerce and presence. He has instituted some progressive programs and has succeeded in helping evolve the state from an agrarian and manufacturing stronghold into a more high-tech driven environment, even if not quite to the same degree as that of other, larger states. However, he succeeded because of his public relations orientation and visibility on behalf of the voters he represented. The fact that he was the state's longest-serving governor means Wisconsin voters must have liked that.

2. *Communications becomes a more critical element in the company's strategic profile.* Relationship building, by its nature, requires increased communications. A PR-oriented company looks for opportunities to increase communications and involve the public at new levels that foster relationship development. The next time you're scanning the entertainment section of your newspaper looking for a movie to go see, notice that all the display ads for new releases have

Web addresses. Why? So that those who are interested in more information can visit and perhaps interact with a Web site designed to make the picture even more attractive to attend. In many cases, such Web sites are irrelevant to the nature or even promotion of the picture, but exist primarily to give those who access the site the feeling they have an inside track on the film, thus a better relationship with the studio releasing it.

Fast Company magazine, devoted to the new, fast-changing economy and the wired generation that soon will populate it (or may already populate it depending on the industry in question), goes one step further, both with its Web site and in its attempts to build relationships with customers. *Fast Company* hosts a number of Web-based Communities of Friends, where like-minded individuals from all walks of life may chat online, sharing ideas, information and thoughts through various geographically distributed listservs that the site sponsors.

There's no cost to access the listservs. In fact, you don't even have to subscribe to *Fast Company*. However, by providing this public service, the magazine has built its image as one of the most significant resources in the new millennium. Revenues from subscriptions and ad-page sales are growing phenomenally as a result. Participants have proved not only to be fierce *Fast Company* loyalists, but also a wealth of article resources and ideas.

3. *Develop a PR strategy, make sure it's right for your company and your industry, and incorporate it as part of your overall business strategy.* Earlier we noted that your company's marketing plan should be the tactical layer of your company's business strategy, a tight weave that links marketing efforts to corporate goals and defines the methodology by which to achieve those goals. Your PR strategy is another thread in this weave, and one of the most significant.

Like the overall marketing strategy, the PR strategy needs to be proactive as well as reflective of marketing's goals. Unlike marketing, the goals of which are to increase revenue through increased sales, PR is designed to increase influence through image building and development, information sharing and image cultivation. When done right, PR is a more subtle science, but with the same emphasis on long-term effect as brand development. In the end, you want consumers to think of your company and/or product first whenever the need that either can answer arises. Part of that is marketing, but more of it than you might think is the direct result of successful public relations.

4. *Supply your public relations efforts with the tactical resources it needs.* When it comes to overhead, PR doesn't require nearly as much as marketing and advertising, which may spend in the millions on media placement alone, much less creative development and administration.

What PR needs is a staff of capable practitioners and strategic thinkers who can examine goals and opportunities side by side and take advantage of situations that come along, as well as create their own. PR needs less in terms of hard dollars and more in terms of support from executive level staff who embrace the concept, make them available as needed and realize that PR is more than merely typing out news releases.

5. *Give PR the respect it needs and the influence it deserves.* Like anything else, a plan of action that doesn't receive sincere support is no plan at all. Public Relations is an investment, not an expense, and in times of financial duress, it must be the last, not the first, function to be cut. Failure to realize that could be the death knell of your efforts and their effect on building positive relationships for your company.

And when all of that is done, you are on your way to creating an effective PR engine to help enhance your company's image in the marketplace and build relationships with key publics so that, when the time comes, that safety net of good relations is there to break your fall.

News is any overt act that juts out of routine circumstances. A good public relations man advises his client to carry out an overt act, interrupting the continuity of life in some way to bring about a response.

—Edward L. Bernays

13

Public Relations Part 2~ Media Relations

In the previous chapter, we talked about the history and thesis behind public relations, particularly as it relates to building relationships with the various publics that have influence and impact on your company, its strategies and its products.

We considered the issues surrounding relationships with stockholders and customers, employees and the community in which your firm lives, works and operates. Although we didn't get into it in great detail, much of what you do will suggest itself once you accept the fact that something should be done. In the case of community relations, for example, opportunities will present themselves and necessities come forward once you identify the communities with whom you want to build those relationships. Regarding customers, it's the value-added programs you offer and feedback you seek that will make a difference. In the case of stockholders, increased communications and solicitation of feedback may work wonders in the perceived value of your firm and its offerings.

One area that requires more careful scrutiny and significant attention is media relations and the concept of developing publicity. The media have been many companies' friends, but foes to an equal or greater number of firms. Knowing how to use the media as the information channel it is, while minimizing its skeptical instincts and keen desire to uncover news at your firm's expense is an art and science in and of itself that requires specialization, if not an actual specialist, to make sure your organization's story is told the way you want it to be told.

That takes hard work, instinct, intelligence, a sixth sense and, yes, honesty. It also takes a clear understanding of what the media's purposes and mission are in society today.

UNDERSTANDING MEDIA PRINCIPLES

The commercial media—let's define that as newspapers, magazines, television, radio and any other outlet that actively and vigorously pursues news stories—is a highly competitive industry that deals in information that exists at the edge. The root word of "news" is new. If the information isn't new, then it isn't of interest to most media outlets. In their line of work, print and electronic journalists need to come up with new information or new angles on old facts every working day of their lives. They have to fill column inches or broadcast minutes with stuff that is not only factually sound but achingly fresh. Otherwise, to use an oxymoron that has become a telling bit of the English lexicon, it's "old news."

What would your life be like if you had to develop a brand new product or capture new market share every single work day or your business would fold? Understanding that may give you some sense of the pressure under which journalists operate.

But wait, there's more. Add to that the critical nature of that new information—that it has to have a meaningful impact on the life of a majority of readers, listeners or viewers—and the pressure increases. News of your new product launch does not have impact enough unless it will save thousands of lives or actually takes a few lives. Then it takes on that ubiquitous quality that is known as "news." Wrap this all up in a deadline that is a week, a day or an hour long and the pressure becomes almost unbearable. Unless you happen to be a journalist, of course. Then that deadline pressure becomes the fire bell that gets the horses up, out of their stalls and running.

It's into this high pressure, deadline-driven, truth-seeking, highly skeptical world that many newly hatched media relations specialists are thrust. They do what they're told at headquarters, spending days polishing and having approved that news release about the new bread slicer their company has manufactured and then wonder why the local media outlets aren't calling for photos, more information and a sample of the bread. In the newsroom, life doesn't work quite that way. As for that well-polished news release . . . well, it's probably already in the landfill.

There are two ways to generate news coverage in most media—and keep in mind the more prestigious the media outlet or the larger the community it serves, the more difficult it is to penetrate. Those ways are:

1. Offer reporters genuine news items that will be of significant interest to their readers. Products touting a cure or relief for any kind of disease or condition, from AIDS to zinc poisoning, will automatically be picked up. The business press will view executive change-overs at major corporations the same way. Steve Jobs' firing from Apple Computers, a company he founded and then lost control of when it went public, was big news not only among technology media outlets, but the business and general media as well because Jobs was well known and the story of Apple Computers a Cinderella fable. A less visible executive in a more mundane industry or firm would not get the same treatment.

2. Cultivate relationships with reporters appropriate to your industry and position yourself and your company as a reliable source. Provide them with background information and be willing to serve as a quotable source on appropriate issues, regardless of whether or not your company is directly involved. Take them to lunch and help them interpret issues affecting your industry, even if it doesn't result in an article. Build credibility so that, comes the day that same reporter is facing a tight deadline and needs a source he or she can count on, your name will immediately come to mind.

Richard Hartley, the former senior vice president of marketing for Mission Federal Credit Union in San Diego, was a master at relationship building. As credit unions go, Mission was a formidable institution with a concentrated and extensive field of membership to serve. Hartley parlayed that strength and public recognition, positioning himself and Mission as reliable sources to be called on when needed. Because of that, Mission received more media coverage than almost any other financial institution in what is a large and highly competitive metropolitan area, including many large banks.

It wasn't so much that Hartley's news was better than that of the competition; it was just that the reporters knew him as a helpful, trustworthy source who understood the challenges they faced. And that little bit of knowledge often turned what might have been an opponent into an ally.

The most important thing to remember about reporters and the media is that the vast majority are out to provide truthful information that will help improve the lives of their readers. If your company is ethical and honest, then your goals on behalf of serving your customers are probably very similar. Taking the time to show the media that you have common audiences and common goals will be an effort well worth making for parties on both sides of the fence.

PREPARING FOR THE MEDIA

Too many companies believe the media to be a benign force that can be ignored or dismissed at will. Too many companies have found out the hard way just how wrong that assumption is. The media is a powerful, influential force that can have a dramatic impact on the fate of your company, its position in the marketplace and the products you produce. While that's certainly not true of all media, you would do well to keep that in mind. It never hurts to be prepared.

Developing the media relations side of your business is fairly straightforward and built on several key foundation strategies. The hardest part often is getting upper management to understand and accept the advantages and potential threat that can arise from media involvement. As noted in the last chapter, public relations begins from the top down. Media relations is no different. Preparing your top management for media encounters is one of the most valuable things that can be done, both on behalf of the individual involved and the company he or she represents.

Once again, what the media wants from your company is:

- Clear, honest news and easy access to someone who under-stands their needs. They need a source who can gather com-plete information and can help them find the sources they need throughout the duration of the story.

- An articulate, intelligent spokesperson who can answer ques-tions and provide information without falling back on com-pany rhetoric and corporate speak. An executive that clouds the message or obfuscates, whether intentionally or not, will be seen as someone who has something to hide. A high-rank-ing executive who can respond honestly and clearly to their questions will make friends of reporters who, after all, are only doing their jobs.

To that end, your chief executive spokesman should be coun-seled in the ways of the press and learn to be intellectually nimble on his or her feet. Executives who don't come off well will embarrass the company, while those who appear hostile or nervous will only cause reporters to assume the worst and dig deeper. Taking the time to cultivate this person's interview skills is critical to your company's success with the media.

DEVELOPING YOUR SPOKESPERSON

Many consultants make a very good living teaching corporate exec-utives to be media savvy. It's not always easy and some need more help than others. But there are a few key criteria that will help even the smoothest and most experienced spokespersons:

• *Know in Advance What Can and Can't Be Said.* Is there breaking news at your company, either good or bad, that you can ad-dress during the interview? Be clear about what you can and can't say and stick to that scenario, regardless of the direction in which the in-terviewer tries to drive the discussion. Letting the wrong information slip just because you find the reporter pleasant or attractive can and will come back to haunt you. Realize why the reporter is there and respond professionally and carefully.

• *Be Prepared to Steer the Interview in the Direction You'd Like It to Go.* Politicians are master craftspeople in not quite answering the questions they've been asked. They come close enough to the answer to give the interviewer a sense of comfort, but then they redirect the interview to address the point they want to make. Accomplished interviewers understand what's going on immediately, but they often follow the subject's thread in hope of uncovering new information they hadn't thought of asking. Sometimes it works and both parties are happy with the result. It doesn't always work, however, and never when you're trying to avoid talking about bad news. But it's enough to know that the subject can have his or her own agenda going into the interview and, in most cases, expect to have those information-sharing needs met, much like those the interviewer is trying to satisfy.

• *Be Substantial in Your Answers.* Nothing kills an interview quicker than empty rhetoric and pointless platitudes. Journalists, either print or broadcast, are looking for the good interview, one that brings color and dimension to the commentary and, quite frankly, makes for good copy. If you can do that while still accomplishing your own goals, then the time you spend answering questions and providing comments can be beneficial for both parties. Short, curt answers may keep you out of trouble, but they may also keep you out of the media altogether.

• *Be Honest to the Point of Saying, "I Don't Know."* Subjects that try to bluff their way through interviews almost always make bad impressions. Reporters are not on the company payroll and they come in with a healthy dose of skepticism. They can smell insincerity and don't appreciate dishonesty. The spokesman that doesn't know or won't share the answer should say so when the question is asked. It will go down with the media much better than if they don't.

• ***Be Prepared for the Worst.*** That includes off-the-wall questions, false accusations and ignorant or spiteful reporters. Be wary, too, of set-up questions and how answers might be interpreted outside the context of the discussion. Most often, cooperative interview subjects will be treated fairly. But not always, which means having resources at the ready to combat the bullying, insensitive and ignorant interviewer. It may not be needed, but, as we said earlier, it never hurts to be ready.

CREATING YOUR MEDIA MATERIALS

Media relations materials are simple to create. So simple, in fact, that companies spend most of their time pulling together news releases, press kits and background papers in hopes they will get the pick-up they feel they deserve. Some do; most don't.

Among those that don't, the chief cause tends to be that they don't include a level of news significant enough to warrant publishing. Other releases suffer from being overwritten, or from going beyond the news "peg"—that nugget that may be actual news—to include puffery, editorializing, sales and other facets that are of no interest to news people. The media relations specialist that learns how to recognize news and share just that will save himself or herself quite a bit of time and trouble.

A good news release includes the following information:

- A descriptive slug or headline that communicates immediately the nature of the news item.

- Solid body copy that reports the news nugget, with a little added information for those publications that have a little more space to fill. That includes following the journalistic credo of reporting who, what, when, where, why and how.

- The name and phone number of a reliable contact for more information.

- Attached photos, if appropriate.

Most news releases also will contain a short, boilerplate paragraph about the company they're representing that describes the firm, its mission and the audience it serves.

Background papers and press kits are a little more comprehensive in scope. Background papers should be as complete as possible in the information they contain and presented without bias or influence. They should focus on one topic pertinent to the industry and present as comprehensive a piece in layperson's terms as possible. Media kits can be constructed as appropriate to the needs of the firm or the products it sells. It won't matter because the reporter will save what he or she wants and discard the rest.

IDENTIFYING OPPORTUNITIES

We've talked at length about what constitutes news and what doesn't. Since media coverage is an augment to advertising, companies will want as much free press as they can get. If you're not creating news, however, it's likely that you won't get any press. However, news can pop up in the most likely places.

During the 2000 Summer Olympics in Sydney, Australia, Nike running shoes ran a commercial in which U.S. track star Suzy Favor-Hamilton was pursued by a hockey mask-clad chain-saw-wielding killer who eventually runs out of breath and starts wheezing and coughing when he can't catch her. Although played for laughs, critics decried the commercial as promoting violence toward women and it was yanked off the air. Even though the majority of the public never saw the ad, most of them read about the resulting fracas in local and national newspapers or saw the reports on TV. The public relations value of that pulled commercial to Nike was immeasurable. It also supported Nike's position in the marketplace as being different, unique and risk-taking. The running shoe manufacturer couldn't have asked for more.

If your company makes news by its actions, then you won't have a problem attracting media attention. If your firm must create news through events, stunts and other artificial means, you'll have a harder time getting noticed. Whatever efforts you undertake, make sure they are in keeping with the image you want to project in the marketplace. Funeral homes rarely market themselves by putting their names on the sides of hot air balloons, but other businesses find it very effective. Know what your company is capable of and what your community of product users finds acceptable. You can and should always stretch the bounds of propriety slightly. But stretch it too much, and you lose your audience.

Some companies create their own news by sponsoring studies pertinent to their industry and/or the products they produce. If these are legitimate, scientifically sound studies, then their results have news value and the company can ride on the coattails of the research. It's a profitable situation in which both parties benefit.

Be wary, however, of sponsoring studies that appear self-serving and designed to sell more of your products. A pharmaceutical company that manufactures aspirin and sponsors a study of cold-sufferers only to report that the best pain reliever is aspirin—no matter how true or legitimate that claim and treatment may be—will be viewed with skepticism by a cynical public. Find, instead, a study related to your product that would appear to be of interest to the company as well as the public. If that same company reported that hot water and citrus had a proven chemical impact on colds, their information would be viewed with much greater acceptance because they don't manufacture water or citrus, and thus won't benefit from increased sales. Credibility would increase and, along with it, related product sales.

That's called serving the greater public need, and companies can accomplish much the same thing through charitable work and corporate support of charities related to their industry, their product or the audience it serves. Remember the earlier example of Ronald McDonald House? Despite the enormous good it does for families with hospitalized children, its development is wrapped with tremendous public relations potential. It's to the company's credit, in fact, that it works to keep the charity's profile low and in keeping with its primary purpose of serving public need.

If all else fails, there is the media "event." These include press conferences and product launches, ground breaking and public antics designed to attract attention and, with any luck, gather press coverage. Individuals who walk, run, dance or crawl across the country, especially those who do so to raise money for charity, are conducting their own media events. The rock and pop musicians who gathered a decade ago to record "We Are the World" to raise money to fight world hunger turned their recording session into a media event in an attempt to sell more recordings, thus raising more funds for world hunger. Temporary staff that walk around dressed as animals, cartoon characters or inanimate objects and hand out samples or marketing materials are also staging their own media events, although it's unlikely they will get much media attention.

Press conferences, as a way to release legitimate news to many members of the media at the same time, are a little different. Providing you have legitimate news of a significant nature to share and that your firm has enough clout to gain the media's attention, you will have no trouble attracting the media to a press conference. But all things are relative. The Department of Defense can be assured of ample coverage when it calls a press conference to announce military action in the Middle East. Lou's Neighborhood Grocery will have less success unless Lou himself has discovered a cure for cancer among the fresh melons. It's all relative to size, scope and overall importance. Know your marketplace advantages, measure them against your limitations and act accordingly.

QUANTIFYING YOUR RESULTS

Most companies that devote time, energy and resources toward developing a good public relations program want to see results. It's easy to measure newspaper column inches, broadcast minutes, pickup frequency and loads of other circumstantial evidence. And, in fact, that's what most PR practitioners do to satisfy the demands of non-media executives who simply need to have a quantifiable measure of success.

But there is a greater dimension to it than that and companies that look no further than the PR director's clips file to tout their success are missing the real importance. Public relations, remember, is about building relationships with the various publics your firm serves. Proof of publication is nice, but if it doesn't change consumer behavior patterns and help build a positive relationship between you and the public, then column inches matter little.

Johnson & Johnson's quick and proper action in the wake of the Tylenol disaster built greater credibility between itself and its customers than it ever had before. Conversely, Firestone Tires' failure to take quicker action than it did in recalling the thousands of tires suspected of possible tread failure, along with its subsequent battle with Ford Motor Company over ultimate responsibility for the series of fatal crashes that prompted the recall, has hurt the company's market credibility in the long run. Only time and the company's continued actions will tell if that credibility will return.

MANAGING CRISIS COMMUNICATIONS

There's one way most companies can assure themselves plenty of news coverage—create a public crisis that affects the lives and well-being of a vast number of public citizens and the media most assuredly will come knocking at the door, and at a time when you least want them there. With more and more media outlets competing for fresh news, there is a greater and greater threat that, comes the day the unthinkable happens and a product fails, resulting in injury or death to users—much like the Firestone Tire debacle—the media will be at the door, through the window and down the chimney looking for more information it can expose to protect the public interest from your firm's continued and heinous crime.

Today, no company can afford to be caught unprepared. Even the smallest firm, no matter how benign its market or product, can suffer from labor problems, personal tragedy, natural or manmade disaster or some other problem that draws the eye of the public and, subsequently, curious members of the media. That means preparation of a crisis communication plan is critical as a basis to help keep things under control.

Obviously, the best crisis communication plans are ones prepared ahead of time. Crises vary in nature, severity and duration, but your response to them has similarities that cross all lines. Your public relations officer's role as key communicator is pivotal in making this plan operational, functional and successful

Your first step must be to ascertain the strengths and weaknesses of the company, its staff and the environment in which it operates. These often are where crises strike. If you can strengthen those weakened areas, do so. If not, make special provisions to shore them up and pay attention to them at all times.

Develop a response manual that clearly outlines steps for all employees to take for the different types of crises that may strike. In most communities, martial law takes over when major crises hit, and the same should hold true for your company. Everyone, from senior staff to employees, must understand his or her role should such events occur.

As part of that plan, develop a crisis team made up of employees and executives from across all disciplines, each with his or her own set of responsibilities during the crisis designed to stabilize the situation and begin repairing the damage. For some crises, such as fire or disaster, those tasks may be formidable. For others—say the CEO was caught embezzling funds from the company retirement account—there may be little for the crisis team to do but answer employee questions and support the official media spokesperson in responding to inquiries. Nevertheless, that team should be well-trained and practiced in dealing with whatever foreseeable crisis might occur.

It's critical that, as part of that team, an articulate and intelligent spokesperson be identified to deal with media inquiries and arrange the right executive interviews. As the most visible member of the crisis team, this easily also may be the team's most important member because this is who the public will see and/or hear from. It takes someone with consummate communications skills, a cool head, a professional image and confident leadership skills to manage the situation. A media spokesperson who appears panicked, nervous or uninformed invites skepticism, speculation, and mistrust. And such things can only add further to your woes.

One of the most important things to remember is to review the plan and run through the procedures on a regular basis. You will need to update procedures from time to time and improve them when possible.

WHEN DISASTER STRIKES

When the unthinkable happens and disaster strikes, remember to pull out the plan, rally the crisis team and follow the procedures that have been developed. In addition, keep the following thoughts in mind:

• *Don't Panic.* Collect your thoughts, consider the information you have in hand, what still needs to be found out and where support networks lie. The plan isn't ready to execute until the leader of the crisis team has things under control internally and can proceed with the confidence and leadership skills necessary to the job.

• *Define the Problem and Broaden the Perspective.* Consider the situation exactly as it exists and don't assume anything in your assessment. It may not be as bad as you first think, or it could be infinitely worse. Once you've brought the whole thing into focus, broaden the perspective and look for ways to address at least some of the issues in a positive manner.

• *Assign Duties.* In addition to those outlined in the plan, make sure staff and volunteers cover all bases and address all crisis-related issues. And, if there is nothing positive for employees to contribute in addressing whatever the disaster might be, send them home for their own safety as well as increased operational efficiency at a time when it's needed most.

• *Develop a Response Statement and Centralize Your Information Function.* Your company needs to have one consistent response to whatever the crisis is and it should be repeated with clarity and without deviation or elucidation. This is the job of your media spokesperson. No other staff member should be talking to

MARKET RESEARCH

Publicity is an elusive goal that most media relations experts spend most of their time pursuing. Successful achievement of that goal does not come without the creation and execution of a specific publicity plan, the tenets of which include the following:

- *Knowing your goals.* What do you want this effort/activity/stunt to achieve in its execution?

- *Marshaling your resources.* Is there a cost factor involved or specific resource allocation required of the company, its staff or outside paid professionals?

reporters. The risk of mixing signals and supplying false or misleading information is much too great.

- ***Communicate Fact, Not Opinion, Honestly and Completely.*** Except on rare occasions, saying "no comment" is worse than saying nothing at all because of what it might imply to skeptical or ignorant minds. The spokesperson's job is to communicate the facts of the crisis with a full perspective on the situation. That means making general information about the business available to reporters, keeping the media on track with their comments and questions and helping them get the facts and information they need in time to meet their deadlines.

- ***Sound the "All Clear" When the Crisis Has Passed.*** The best crises are the ones that are solvable and to which you can bring closure. Make sure all interested parties—your staff, your customers, the media and the community—know when the crisis has passed. Depending on its severity, how it was perceived and how it was handled, it may do little to mitigate the overall damage.

But at least it will get the media off your back. What's more, they can serve as your conduit to the various publics you serve, providing the information they, too, need to know about the situation. The media will report on any significant disaster or crisis, regardless of whether you cooperate or not. By working with them and helping them find the information they need, you have a better chance to control the flow of that information, minimize the damage and communicate the efforts being made to people who need to know.

In addition, it's the best opportunity imaginable to build greater credibility with an influential group of professionals who will walk away from this experience considering you and your company either friend or foe of the truth. And since these professionals have the means and the ability to share this opinion with millions of consumers worldwide, it's well worth the effort.

MARKET RESEARCH
(Continued)

- *Understanding your market.* How will this effort blend into the overall news fabric of the local media outlets and daily activities of the consumers you wish to reach?

- *Creating a time-line.* When will this event take place? How will you manage the elements up to that point?

- *Taking action.* Will you be ready when the time comes?

- *Measuring results.* How will you know if your publicity effort has succeeded?

Having a plan in place and being able to answer those questions can go a long way in assuring a successful publicity effort that achieves the results you seek.

There are as many born salesmen as there are born neurosurgeons—about two percent of the total. The rest of us have to learn the trade.

—*Jerry Vass, author of*
Soft Selling in a Hard World

14
Serious Sales Part 1~ We All Sell

Most marketers scoff at the idea that there is a connection between what they do and what their company's sales team does. After all, they are pursuing the scientifically based discipline of marketing, the strategic overlay that governs the fate of their business and its industry. They are no mere Willy Lomans schlepping from account to account, smiling furtively in hopes of bringing home an order. Theirs is a more exalted profession grounded in the knowledge that drives all the Willys, as well as everyone else in the company, to succeed.

But there is another side to it all. Many marketers are secretly afraid that when all is said and done, they really are no more than glorified Willy Lomans themselves or, more likely, will be perceived as such by other management team members. The best of the breed, however, realize there is a strong link between marketing and sales, just as there is between product design and production. That link completes a loop begun in marketing's offices, and culminates when the customer signs on the dotted line.

Marketing's research and strategic efforts help the company know itself, its market and, most of all, its customers. Through related advertising efforts, this knowledge is shared in creative and articulate ways designed to appeal to those customers on a variety of levels, building awareness and setting the stage for the next level of action. At this point, the sales team moves forward, using the knowledge generated by that marketing and capitalizing on the impressions made by that advertising to convince customers to buy

201

the product, service, image or idea the company is trying to sell. It is that moment of closure, in fact, that is most companies' raison d'etre.

That's a pretty heady concept for most salespeople to embrace. Due to human nature, they need to know that what they do is important and, by their own vanity, want to believe that their efforts have significant impact on the company's bottom line and its overall financial success. In the grand scheme of things, however, few realize that their ability to close those sales, more than any other aspect of company or product development, best realizes the purpose behind why their enterprise exists in the first place. When the customer places an order, it is the climax of a commercial venture that began way back in the product concept and design stage, or perhaps even with the founding of the company, because it puts a product or service into the hands of its user. Other staff, no matter the level at which they operate, would do well to remember this.

Other staff also would do well to realize that, no matter who they are, all have sales as a part of their job. The designer has to sell his or her ideas to production, which then has to justify costs and time of that production to executives who want it faster, better and cheaper. Marketing, most certainly, has to sell the creative concept behind its efforts to an often skeptical audience, both internally and, with its advertising, externally. Even upper level executives have to make the effort to convince staff that their concepts and ideas are the best possible ones for the good of the enterprise; otherwise productivity and morale will suffer.

In the end, we all sell our ideas, which should make us sympathetic to those on staff who find lonely hotel rooms, cold calls and cancelled appointments part and parcel of each and every day. Sales is part of all our jobs, done in conjunction with the technical or executive stuff for which our job descriptions say we get paid. More often than not, that personal sales effort consumes the better part of our days as well.

The same can be said in reverse, however, about effective salespeople. To sell effectively, they must know in some detail what the company does and how the products it produces function. In fact, as the firm's front line of defense, salespeople need to know more in a general way than most of the rest of the staff does so they can answer questions, thus building confidence with current and potential customers.

Sales is built on a foundation of trust. Knowledge and information are the cornerstones of that foundation. A salesperson not able to answer questions weakens the foundation. Those unable to provide critical information to help the customer make an intelligent buying decision can do little more sometimes than stand by and watch that foundation crumble.

In the end, sales is an important part of the team effort, not just an appendage that exists to make sure that those wonderful products you've created will be put into the hands of the people and businesses that can use them to fullest advantage. The world will not beat a path to your door just because your design and manufacturing departments have created the proverbial better mousetrap. It's marketing's job, of course, to determine if that mousetrap was needed or wanted in the first place and to alert the world that it now exists to serve its needs.

But it's the job of sales to make sure that mousetrap is out there catching the mice it was designed to catch. And that is the culmination of everyone's efforts.

THE SALES CONCEPT AND PERSONALITY

To coin a phrase, sales is the world's oldest profession, conducted whenever one object of value was exchanged for another. Primitive man hunted and gathered his own food, ultimately trading food and goods for items of similar value. If he was really good, he traded them for items of greater value and those are the genetic seeds from which today's salespeople have sprung.

Sales is a critical element that fuels society's economic fires, but often is perceived differently by different people. One wag we knew saw sales as "unskilled white collar labor." A sales manager we once met described salespeople as "business catalysts." In effect, both were right. Often bright young people with no particular training are thrust into the marketplace like so much commercial cannon fodder. Those that do succeed will, in fact, be business catalysts for future sales. Commercial survival of those individuals depends on opportunity and attitude and the personal and corporate need that drives both. There are distinct human traits that color this characteristic.

But, before we go any further, let's explode a common myth: There is no one definitive sales type. No one is born to the profession, no matter how gregarious or outgoing. No one can sell ice to Eskimos based on personality alone. The job has become just too complex in its nature and execution to allow success or failure to be determined by the brightness of a smile and firmness of a handshake. A good sales personality contains a combination of elements, all of which can be learned if so desired.

Granted, some people start with a stronger platform, which helps get their sales careers off the ground. Outgoing personality types—the ones described as "extroverts" in any number of personality tests—tend to have better luck in the beginning because the social nature of sales feeds not only their economic needs, but their personality desires as well. True extroverts, as defined by psychological principles, gain their energy from other people. They not only enjoy talking, they need to talk because their personal strength grows based on human interaction. As that "feed" increases and their comfort level grows, they come from a place of greater strength socially to maneuver their conversational partners closer to a receptiveness of their sales message.

The opposite can be true for what psychologists describe as "introverts," those who get their personal strength from within. Unlike the extrovert, who feeds on social interaction and thereby realizes greater energy from such exchanges, such interaction tends to run down the introvert's fuel supply, forcing that person to return within in order to renew those critical personal resources. Introverts are less outgoing, thus less accessible to others, something that can compromise the social strength often required for successful sales. The fact that the vast majority of American society tends to exhibit extrovert tendencies can further isolate these individuals, sometimes creating a barrier to the perception on both sides of their abilities.

Does that make the introvert an ineffective salesperson? If we agree that sales is the art of persuasion and that some of the most effective persuaders are those individuals leading today's corporations, then realize that 60 percent of today's CEOs come from a subset of the introvert population that comprises barely one percent of society. As one psychological tester said, "The secret to good persuasion comes from the desire, outlook and intellectual processes that operate below the personality's surface. As for all that extrovert stuff . . . hell, you can learn that."

What does good sales ability take?

- An abiding intellectual curiosity about the nature of society and its applications of solutions to problems, at least one of which your company provides.

- The desire to see those applications applied successfully and the willingness to go out of the way to make sure those problem solvers understand the advantages your company offers.

- The intelligence and commitment to understand and apply both unique and uniform solutions to those applications.

- The ability and desire to communicate those applications in a way that achieves success. And you'll see shortly that talking is merely a small part of that equation.

- The desire to exceed expectations when possible and with the understanding that a salesperson is only as good as his or her last product sale or service call.

- The recognition that every market offers fierce competition and effective selling goes well beyond making sales calls and taking orders.

- The capability and commitment to follow through on actions and troubleshoot situations to achieve a goal that's common both to company and customer.

A tall order? There's no doubt that sales today is a fiercely competitive business fraught with hazards and littered with corporate casualties. But it wouldn't be that way unless the rewards justified the effort. And since that cost is economic survival both for the individual salesperson and the company he or she represents, most who play the game can more than justify the cost.

THE COMMUNICATIONS GAME

One of the classic images of the salesman to come out during the last century was that of the actor Burt Lancaster in the film version of American author Sinclair Lewis' "Elmer Gantry." As a small town hustler turned sham revivalist for the sake of the dollar, Gantry was the epitome of the self-assured, fast talking salesman.

Lancaster's natural charm dressed the character up in a confident manner, while his broad, toothy smile, vivacity and fake familiarity appealed both to men or women too ignorant or uninformed to see through the polished veneer. Gantry ultimately was undone by his own corruption and deceit, as well as his inability to continue the deception once he began believing in what he was preaching.

There have always been a lot of Elmer Gantrys in the sales world, those extroverts we talked about earlier for whom style exceeds substance and a fast-talking, smooth patois takes the place of true communications. Some parlay that tactic throughout their careers, but most fall by the wayside because they fail to understand that sales is persuasion wrapped in communications. And many simply don't know what communications truly is. There's a lot more to it than merely having the gift of gab.

Webster defines *communication* as "a giving or exchanging of information, signals or messages by talk, gestures or writing." The key word in that phrase is "exchanging" because it implies that there is more to true communications than merely information transmission. Too many salespeople deliver the sales message and then stand back and wait for the order. They assume that because they have put their cards on the table using the most compelling argument they know, that they have done their job. They couldn't be more wrong.

At the risk of turning this into a social science text, communications by its nature refers not only to the transmission of information and data, but also its reception and understanding by the listener. True communications is not active-passive in terms of defining its roles of communicator and receiver, respectively. By its nature, it is active-active in that, for communications to take place, the message must be received and understood in the way it was intended.

Think of the communications stream as an arc, held at each end by one of two parties managing the communications process. The communicator can only proceed so far up the arc without the aid of the receiver, who must accept, digest and understand the message being sent. Once that message has been accepted and understood in the manner in which it was sent, communication has been achieved and, presumably, the sales message has gotten through.

What does that mean for the salesperson? It means that no amount of talking will be effective if the requisite amount of listening does not also take place. If I want you to buy my product, then I better have a clear idea about where you stand in terms of receptivity and understanding of my message. That means I will have to listen and analyze the situation before proceeding with my sales approach so I will know what is and isn't working.

Elmer Gantry rarely listened to the congregation gathered under his tent. He didn't have to because they were there due to what they thought was a higher purpose, of which he was merely the entertainment factor. When the warning signs came of his ultimate demise, however, he didn't listen to that closely enough, either. He assumed that natural charm and technique would enable him to bull his way through. Like many salespeople who try this approach, he was wrong.

Communications is built of three components:

- The ability to communicate through speech, writing and gesture the desired message in a way that is understood as it was intended to be.

- The receptivity of the listener—and that includes the person taking the lead in communications, which may be the seller— to understand and appreciate the message and its main points.

- The capacity of both parties to analyze and adjust the content and style of the message to achieve an outcome that is satisfactory to all.

Remove any of those elements and, like a three-legged stool, that effort will topple and the desired effect—a sale or sales—will end up flat on the floor.

DEVELOPING THE SALES SKILL SET

If what we've said earlier is true—that there are no born salespeople, only people whose personality types lend themselves to sales success—that means we accept the fact that sales is a learned profession. The hazard comes when we believe that those personality characteristics that make a person charming, dynamic or charismatic are enough to carry the load. That's the quickest route to failure or mediocrity as a salesperson.

The good salesperson, as we've said, is a problem solver, someone who offers a solution in terms of a product or service to businesses or consumers. To do so requires two key components:

• The first is a clear understanding of the product, the market and the customer. We talked a little about that earlier and it needs to be repeated here. Salespeople who don't know intimately what they're selling to whom and in what kind of environment have very little to offer in terms of value. Often they become time wasters and, at best, may be considered order takers. Those that assume anything else are kidding only themselves.

• The second component is good business management practices. Sales is a business, and one that exists in a dynamic, changing environment. It's also highly competitive and often driven by price, service or both. No matter what arrangement may exist with the employer, a good salesperson is less of an employee and more of an entrepreneur. By the very nature of the job, this has to be. For those who exist on commission, this is truly a reality. And salespeople who don't exist on commission probably aren't much good in the first place. Either that, or the company employing them doesn't understand much about sales.

All salespeople see themselves as potential superstars; they attend seminars filled with cheerleading motivational speakers, and they watch for techniques and strategies that will give them an edge in their chosen market. In reality, however, virtually all sales boils down to a numbers game. The percentage of effectiveness will fluctuate with the level of expertise and value the salesperson brings to current and potential customers, but not much is going to happen if the salesperson is not out actively seeking new accounts or cultivating those that already exist.

In order to succeed, salespeople need to sell. Period. And those sales opportunities will depend on the number of contacts made. There are no shortcuts and salespeople who think there are won't be salespeople very long.

So what are the habits of a superstar salesperson? There are many and the list grows longer every day.

• Superstar sellers, first and foremost, have an understanding of the industry they serve. They take their role as problem-solver quite seriously and look for ways that their products and firms can help. Of course, they want to earn high commissions and build greater market share. But they also know that the best way to do that is to provide true value to their clients. That way, there's an easy answer to the inevitable question, "Why should I buy from you?"

• The superstar also takes time to find out as much as possible about the target audience or firm. In the case of direct-to-consumer sales, this means understanding what current tastes and preferences require and not spending time promoting last year's models or anything else that has little value.

In the case of business-to-business sales, the equation gets a little more complex, but so do the advantages. Those selling larger, more expensive commodities—say computer systems, for example— need to fully understand the nature of potential clients. That includes their financial situation, their unique needs, their personal and management issues and anything else they can uncover. Part of this is due to the need to gain competitive advantage, of course. But an equal or greater amount has to do with the role of true problem-solver. No matter what your opinion of the approach, this type of research will be time well spent.

• Most of all, the superstar knows himself or herself and compensates for personal or professional shortfalls. For the extrovert, these may come in the form of too much reliance on style over substance, while the introvert may have just the opposite problem. A superstar works hard to overcome personal shortcomings and create a selling persona that is as well-rounded and as comprehensive as possible.

• The superstar never treats sales as anything other than a profession and strives to manage that profession in the way it needs to run. Whether working out of home, car, office or hotel room, the superstar embraces all the characteristics of good personal management: punctuality, reliability, self-control, professional demeanor, dedication to mission, complete and consistent follow-through and a hundred other traits of a professional. More time spent managing personal shortcomings and bad habits simply means less time spent managing the business process. And that means less opportunity to make sales.

• Superstars are goal-oriented and do what's necessary to produce business. Theirs is not a passive position. Rather, they're active members of their company's workforce, front-line people who advance the charge, not those who merely react to conditions. Otherwise, the job isn't getting done and all those other departments that depend on their success—and that's the entire balance of the company—will be let down.

• In order to keep their competitive edge honed to razor sharpness, superstars are innovators always in search of new opportunities and the next industry trend. Their strategies must involve new opportunities they find or create, often on behalf of other departments in their companies. Remember that, as front-line people, superstars often are the first to hear the desires of the marketplace and the first to sense, based on current activity, what new products or services might be a welcome addition to their portfolios.

• Superstars often have business and personality traits that help them stand out from their peers. They tend to be loners because they know there is only room for one at the top. They would rather lead than follow because they don't want opportunities and their own skills to be hampered by the shortfalls of another. They often think and see things a little differently because it can be the best way to gain competitive advantage. They innovate because that is the path to new products. They motivate because they need to build confidence within themselves and among their clients. And they represent effectively the interests of their company to clients and their clients to the company.

When all is said and done, superstars are superstars because they sell, not the other way around. If sales is a numbers game, then superstar sellers need to make as many calls as they need to make in order to achieve that status. That may be many or few depending on how far along that superstar has progressed in his or her own career. The nice thing about it is that, like the miracle of compound interest, each call allows the superstar to practice skills and gain market knowledge, bringing that person closer to the status sought.

Superstars know that each sales call, successful or not, is an investment in the future of his or her business. Like anything else, the more you invest now, the more those efforts will earn down the road.

THE SALES/MARKETING MIX

As we mentioned earlier, marketers who don't see sales as an intrinsic part of their discipline and who fail to view themselves as sales professionals are missing the big picture. Each advances the goals of the other and each benefits from the other's efforts. And the more each understands about the other's discipline, the better it will be for everyone.

In this chapter we've talked a little about the nature of sales and the successful salesperson. In the next chapter, we'll find out how to get there from here.

Chapter 14

KNOW YOUR MARKET
AS YOU WOULD YOURSELF

Successful sales is based on hard work and lots of it. But it's also based on a clear understanding of the market you serve. This is especially true in business-to-business sales, the more sophisticated of the two sales scenarios.

To succeed in this lucrative, but highly competitive environment, the sales superstar must identify industry leaders and target those he or she feels can be turned into clients. Getting your arms around an entire industry can be daunting in scope and sometimes impossible to achieve. But doing so through an intimate understanding of client, or a company you would like to turn into a client, is not only achievable, but can reap rewards in increased sales and market knowledge.

Here are some ways to accomplish that goal:

Get to know your target company's financial profile. The most direct route is through acquisition of the firm's annual report, available for any public company and many regulated enterprises. Most firms will simply mail you one if you call up and ask, even though the information is prepared primarily for stockholders. (Who's to say that you're not a potential stockholder shopping around?) The annual report contains a variety of financial snapshots that can give you an idea of strengths and weaknesses and company philosophy. All of these come in handy during the getting-to-know-you phase.

Industry analysts, such as Standard & Poor's, also can give you vital information. This is a more objective source, of course, and often with less information to share. Still, you can be confident that what you're seeing is an accurate representation not clouded or colored by rhetoric.

Get to know company principals as well as competitors and balance what they say against one another. Each comes from a different point of view, of course, and has different vested interest. What they say will need to be taken with one or more grains of salt, but those perceptions still may provide valuable information.

In a similar vein, former employees also provide a perspective that will shed light on the company. Depending on why they're *former* employees may color their point of view unfairly, but remember that in every opinion, no matter how one-sided it might be, there exists a kernel of truth that is valuable to know.

Seek out independent industry research that talks about the firm, its products or the industry it serves. Information is only valuable if understood in greater context, and you will need that to get a true picture of the situation. Trade associations often can provide such data, even if it doesn't have specific information about the firm(s) in question. By comparing industry performance ratios to those financial trends indicated within annual reports and other ratings mechanisms, fairly accurate conclusions may be drawn about the target company's performance levels and desirability as a client.

Company newsletters and other information and public relations vehicles can provide the firm's slant on itself and presentation to society. Is it reactive or proactive? Is there a 500-pound-gorilla of an issue that everyone is doing his or her best to ignore? Understanding the nature of the company's communications will aid in your overall knowledge of management styles and purpose. And that is often the most compelling factor driving the firm's success or failure.

Another facet of that same level of information can be found in trade publication articles about the company and its principles. This is not the trade pubs produced by the firm itself, but independent media that invariably exist in virtually every industry. More candid, objective pieces by outsiders can shed light not only on realities within the company, but also how the company chooses to position itself in light of those realities. Taken together, such information can be invaluable in understanding potential clients.

Finally—and this is something few salespeople have the time or inclination to do—go back through the archives of the industry, wherever you may find them and try and discern trends that have brought the company to where it is today. Oftentimes there is as much knowledge buried in past information about what the firm was as there is in current literature about what the firm is now. Once again, the broader your perspective on the firm, the greater your knowledge of what is and isn't acceptable in terms of products, services and sales approaches.

For a salesman, there is no rock bottom to the life. He don't put a bolt to a nut, he don't tell you the law or give you medicine. He's a man way out there in the blue, riding on a smile and a shoeshine. And when they start not smiling back—that's an earthquake.

—Arthur Miller,
author of Death of a Salesman

15

Serious Sales
Part 2~Mastering
Educated Selling

It was Calvin Coolidge who said that the business of America is business. That makes salespeople the nation's foot soldiers in the war of commerce. And there isn't a salesperson on the street who doesn't feel that he or she has been shelled more than once during those battles for market share. It's a tough business in a tough world, but there is still no truth to the rumor that successful salespeople eat their young.

Good salespeople have strength, stamina, optimism, a strong sense of self, determination and follow-through, to be sure. But they never sell off the cuff, never rely on Willy Loman's "smile and shoeshine" to help them succeed. They're prepared in their presentation, they've researched their product and client, and they have an arsenal of sales weapons and a wealth of informational ammunition to help them break down buyers' resistance and advance the commercial and economic goals of their company.

Different salespeople have different styles on which they rely. Each has to identify and master his or her own approach. In fact, the only constants in the art of successful selling are those models that no longer work:

- The backslapping, gladhanding salesman of the past has become a caricature of the discipline, a human cartoon that no longer packs any punch when it comes to moving merchandise.

Even used car lots know better than to employ those people these days.

- The fast-talking hard seller has lost ground in the face of more savvy consumers who have better product knowledge at their fingertips and are rightfully suspicious of anyone attempting to give them the bum's rush when it comes to making a purchase.

- The same holds true with the good-time Charlie (or Charlene) who buys the drinks, sends the gifts and never quite gets around to filling in the details of the sale until after the deal is inked. Most buyers know that those who fall for these tricks get the kind of sales terms they deserve.

Today's buyers—both businesses and consumers—have more education and greater access to information than any generation that has come before. The demands on all kinds of business are greater than they have ever been, and that includes the demands on the sales forces of these businesses. Competition is fierce, making it harder to make a sale. On the other hand, those very market conditions can put the intelligent salesperson willing to work to meet his or her customers' needs in an excellent position to serve as a partner with buyers, help them solve business problems, address issues and become part of the team. This doesn't work in all industries, or with all salespeople. But those who make a successful transition from merchandise peddler to problem-solver to operational "partner" stand to make a fortune.

THE ART OF EDUCATED SELLING

By its very nature, an educated and informed buying population requires an educated and informed sales force. People, no matter who they are, are most comfortable doing business in their own language. And if that language happens to be an articulate, informed one chock full of facts and information, the salesperson better be able to talk the talk before there is any hope at all of making the sale.

The sales effort starts long before the first handshake and salutation, and lasts long after the order is delivered and payment received. It relies on the development of strategies that will over-come resistance and bring the buyer to Yes without the full-frontal attack normally associated with sales. That's one of the reasons that old-fashioned selling techniques no longer work. Customers are nat-urally braced for a frontal assault because that's what their percep-tion of sales is. In fact, too much of selling relies on a type of verbal martial arts designed to counterblock obstacles and overthrow rejec-tion. Most intelligent buyers are tuned in to that strategy and imme-diately tune the salesperson out.

Successful sales today is a blend of psychology and consulta-tion, of gentle coercion and subtle persuasion mixed with a true de-sire to help. That requires sales people to have strategies and struc-tures that rely on a more refined set of intellectual tools. The more mastery a salesperson exhibits with these tools, the more successful that person is going to be.

THREE WAYS TO PREPARE YOURSELF

The first thing a good salesperson needs is a statement of purpose. You might also refer to it as a *mission statement* or, if you are partic-ularly erudite, a *raison d'être*—French for "reason for being." This is the statement the salesperson uses during the introductions with a prospective customer. Within two sentences, the salesperson should be able to identify himself or herself, the company and the product that is being sold. There is no pretense or artifice here. Both buyer and seller know the purpose of the business and it is up to either to decide whether to continue the conversation or move on.

In writing this volume, my own *raison d'être,* or mission state-ment, might be as follows:

> *"Hi, my name is Michael Muckian and I'm the author of*
> The Prentice Hall One Day MBA in Marketing. *The*
> *purpose of this book is to provide professional-level*
> *readers with a comprehensive overview of all the*
> *information we think you'll need to become the*
> *consummate business marketer."*

There was nothing particularly cryptic or profound about that statement. But it's clear, concise and contains the basic information you will need to decide whether or not you have an interest in this book. If you don't, our conversation is over. But if the short description intrigues you or makes you think that this is the volume you've been looking for all your professional life, then it's only taken a few seconds for you to make that decision. In either case, it was limited time well spent by both of us as the information-giving and receiving parties.

That should be the basis behind any successful sales presentation. The salesperson who can't make a statement similar in length and content shouldn't even consider leaving the house in the morning.

The second thing is presentation, both of yourself and your product. This is where we expand on the aforementioned "smile and shoeshine" to encompass the physical, intellectual, emotional and empathetic characteristics necessary to be successful. You still need to shine your shoes, and a smile, unless it's worn at the wrong time, always helps. But there is more to it than that—much, much more.

Believe it or not, the easiest alignment between salesman and products and between salesman and audience is the physical one. In years past, IBM always required its sales and business staff to wear similarly shaded blue or gray suits, white shirts and subdued, contrasting ties. It became the IBM uniform as well as the butt of numerous jokes.

But Big Blue knew what it was up to. Personal computers, from mainframe to mini to micro, as the parlance went, were used primarily by businesses for accounting and management functions. The people that IBM salesmen dealt with tended both to dress like that and trust people who looked like them. That had less to do with personal chauvinism and more to do with the fact that these business leaders were transferring big dollars and felt more comfortable with a company that presented itself with suitable conservatism. In fact, when Apple got started, it positioned itself in counterpoint to the overly conservative IBM image, looking for a market segment that was tired of marching in Corporate America's lockstep. In both cases, the sales reps became part of the company's image campaign and value structure. And businesses responded accordingly.

Your appearance should develop in sync with the product and audience with whom you are dealing, just like IBM's sales force did. If you show up at the local music store in your IBM suit trying to sell Fender Stratocasters to a rock-and-roll audience, you are not going to make the impression you want.

Assuming you've aligned successfully in your appearance with your audience and product and represent the perceived nature of your company, the third preparation step will be to align yourself intellectually, emotionally and empathetically with your audience by learning the nature, science and culture of their industry.

In many ways, Big Blue reps had it easy. Early competition was light and the only hurdle they had to overcome were the questions of how much and how big. As long as they presented themselves in sympatico with their audience and spoke knowledgeably about the data processing basics necessary to meet the challenges of the construction trades, retail market or whatever industry they were addressing, they gained an interested ear. If they presented themselves with enough product and system knowledge to serve as effective consultants (without being perceived as total computer geeks) and enough leadership skills to illustrate their grasp of the market (without appearing to be pushy salespeople), then they gained the edge they sought. Once they were able to understand and get in line with the challenges facing that particular company or its product lines, they gained empathetic alignment and likely made the first of a long line of sales.

That's how the IBM reps probably got to Yes, and that will help your efforts as well. Fail to master any of those three steps and you will rob yourself of some significant ammunition; you may stumble and fall in your effort to outgun the competition and become the business partner you want to be with your clients.

ACT I: PREPARING FOR THE SALES CALL

We all have strengths and weaknesses, and that goes double for the successful salesperson. In fact, people are successful in sales—or any endeavor, for that matter—because they know how to maximize those strengths and control those weaknesses. And despite its rather single-minded goal, sales offers a wealth of variables on which the salesperson can build a presentation that will succeed, despite any personal shortfalls or challenges he or she may have.

The first step of any sales presentation, of course, is to prepare for the meeting. This starts with the setting of an appointment convenient to the buyer, but will be more successful if it can also be scheduled in a context that will showcase the product, the company or the salesperson in a favorable light. Remember that much of sales, especially the value of the sales proposition, is based on buyer perception. The context you seek to create does not have to be a physical environment; rather, it can and should be a perceptual one that both buyer and seller can occupy in their minds during the sales call.

A strange concept? Consider the automobile salesperson who sells the car that was just named the safest, the fastest, the best value (pick one) by *Road and Track* or some other prestigious automotive industry publication. The car lot hasn't taken on a new physical dimension and the salesperson hasn't put on a new suit or suddenly grown smarter or better looking, but the perception of value has been enhanced in the mind of the buyer—or will be just as soon as the salesperson bubbles forth the good news. That act creates a new perceptual context on which the buyer-seller axis has turned slightly in favor of the seller. That doesn't necessarily mean more money or more customers for this particular car, at least not immediately. But it may mean an easier or at least more satisfying sales experience for both parties that will lead to a longer-term relationship and more business in the future.

The same can hold true, perhaps to a lesser degree, for the context surrounding the salesperson or the company itself. If the firm has just won an award from the Chamber of Commerce, that honor may give it greater cachet than the nearest competitor. This is especially true if the honor has been gained for something unrelated to the company's line of business, such as being the top contributor to the local United Way campaign. This shows that the firm's interests stretch beyond mere profits, and may be the kind of thing that will sway some of the more community-minded buyers.

Real estate companies spend thousands of dollars every year rewarding their top producing salespeople. And then spend thousands of dollars more telling the community who the members of their

Million Dollar Club are. Why? The public perception is that these people hustle and make a lot of sales. In real estate, effective selling is critical to gaining market share and attracting new business from the community, the members of which always feel like they never get what their home is worth. By employing a member of the elite sales corps, the reasoning goes, the house will sell faster at closer to asking price than if you employ some mere sales schlub.

For some salespeople, this is even better than a top rating from *Road and Track*.

ACT II: THE APPOINTMENT

Now that you've set the stage, you're ready to meet with your prospective buyer. Before you get in your car, hop on the airplane or venture out to the sales floor, inventory your resources and make sure you are armed and ready.

• Your background knowledge of the product is impeccable. You know all there is to know—or at least all you need to know—to make the sale to today's intelligent buyers. You also have anticipated questions and prepared answers ahead of time. You know where the soft spots are in the product or its application and you're ready to help the customer understand why those soft spots don't really affect performance or value.

• You know the market in which you're selling and what it means to the purchase and use of your product. This includes how your price stacks up against the competition; how the economy of your particular industry matches to your product and whether it is a must-have or an accessory; how changes in the market will impact the long-term use of your product or this model; and how customers have reacted to this product and its uses in the past.

• You have a clear vision of the average customer for this product. You understand to the best of your ability the geographic, demographic and even psychographic characteristics that drive your customer to purchase this product and you're ready with features and benefits that address the customers at all levels. You know what they can and will buy, and how much you are able to sell them.

• In that same way, you've aligned yourself characteristically with those customers so you can develop the rapport necessary to make them comfortable in their purchase. That includes the necessary traits that show you can both complement and contrast their needs so they can trust you but also feel they can learn from you in this matter. Handled effectively, this can give you a major advantage.

• You've developed your mission statement so you can quickly and easily identify yourself, your affiliation and the purpose of the product and company. This shows respect to potential customers by recognizing the value of their time and allowing them to make a quick decision about continuing the sales visit or moving on.

• You've developed or will maximize whatever perceptual context you can to put the product and company in a favorable light and the buyer in a more receptive mode. This includes any market advantage that sets your firm apart for good reasons. And do make sure they are good reasons. Ralph Nader made his name with the publication of Unsafe at Any Speed, the book that drove the Chevrolet Corvair from the market place. Nader certainly created a perceptual context, but not to the benefit of that particular automobile.

• You've got the mental, physical and emotional resources to sell today. We haven't talked much about this, but that inner strength is critical. In the movie, American Beauty, a real estate agent played by Annette Bening starts her day by announcing loudly and enthusiastically to an empty property she's showing, "I am going to sell this house today!" She ends her day in tears, not having made the sale. Bening did not pay attention to this particular lesson.

Once you can answer those demands affirmatively, it's time to keep the appointment. Remember that today's customers are educated, have ready access to information, are faced with many similar and competitively priced alternatives, and have little time to spare and none to waste. Because of all that, you come prepared to make the most of the encounter. Here are some intellectual tools you can use during your sales dialogue—and we hope it's a dialogue because, if it's a monologue, you're in trouble—to make the most effective use of the time to accomplish *your* goals.

• Use your mission statement to get your foot in the door and set the stage for future discussion. Put your cards on the table early and it will make better use both of your time and that of the customer.

• Avoid asking questions that call for short, declarative answers or Yes and No responses. Neither lead to further developmental discussions and rarely enable you to steer the conversation in the direction you need it to go. Instead, ask open-ended, probing questions that require the customer to expound more fully on the need for the benefits your product offers. Such questioning steers the conservation away from the direct, confrontational approach, employing a more subtle tactic that usually results in better sales.

A wine salesman we knew sold the marketplace before he sold his product. Exploding interest in the field created a boom market, right along with an overload of competitors. The wine salesman probed the customer's perceptions and needs, helping that customer articulate what previously had been a few vague notions and nagging fears. By carefully guiding the customer through that articulation, the wine salesman was able to spin its alignment with his product line. When an "accurate" description of the market was gained by both and the time came to talk product line, the wine salesman simply suggested products he carried that met each of the stated needs in some unique way. Often the customer was eager to buy, hoping this new product would help him raise his business profile.

• The wine salesman in the previous example also worked very hard to develop a relationship with his customers. That's a longer process and doesn't always mean a sale with every visit. But it does mean that the salesman moved closer to that coveted position of relationship with every sales call, the point where the product is no longer a matter of price, and sales are no longer a struggle. At that point the salesman enters that hallowed place where re-orders are givens and new additions to the line have automatic takers because the salesman certainly wouldn't jeapordize his position by suggesting something that wasn't right for the customer.

• Break down resistance to your message by learning flanking maneuvers that steer the conversation in the direction you'd like it to go. Sales consists of four basic phases through which the seller and buyer pass:

1. Introducing the product or service to the buyer. That's your mission statement.

2. Understanding the product or service usage and its value proposition in the buyer's mind.

3. Coming to agreement that there is a need or want on the part of that buyer to take advantage of that value proposition.

4. Arriving at Yes. This also is known as closing the sale.

Each of those phases offers its own set of flanking maneuvers, many of which manifest themselves in the form of value statements that answer buyer questions before they're asked and probe issues that get to the root of various forms of resistance prior to their manifestation. Flanking maneuvers are similar to chess moves, most of which take place in the minds of the players far in advance of the actual move on the board. Each should be made as part of the overall sales strategy and designed to set the stage for the close.

If your goal is to sell a line of clothing to a department store, flanking maneuvers might include the following:

- An impromptu market analysis that discusses the nature of fashions and the directions they've gone in the past few years, followed by a mini analysis of the line being represented and how that was created in response to current trends.

- A question about the decision-making team and the history of the fashion lines the store has previously offered. Through that question, follow-up queries could focus on the store's own fashion "mission statement" and how the represented line helps meet that need.

- Questions about the volume and prices normally run through the store and how the represented line meets or beats those pre-established parameters.

- A discussion about the marketing assistance that the line offers and how it might dovetail with what the store has done in the past. Fashion shows might be one way, celebrity tie-ins another. The reverse move would be to probe about such things prior to tying them back to the represented line. In addition to being less predatory, you might learn something that can be used with another client.

Such maneuvers, designed first to be informational, then sales-oriented, can help reduce buyer resistance, as well as answer objections before they are raised. It's a more subtle approach that better blends with buyer desires and preferences and more quietly heads toward the close.

• You're prepared to listen to what's been said and respond to the statement, rather than from a pre-arranged script. We talked about listening in the last chapter, so you know it's a critical component of sales. The greatest need for listening comes during this stage, especially if you're looking for flanking maneuvers. The buyer's statements will be filled with clues and directions for this maneuver and it often is only from these statements that the most effective flanking maneuvers derive.

Since thought operates roughly five times faster than speech, you can utilize the time the buyer spends talking to frame answers that subtly move the conversation in the direction you want it to go. But listen actively and completely. Salespeople who let their minds stray to other things often fail to detect critical clues and may even lose the thread of the conversation to the point where the buyer becomes annoyed or suddenly is moved to a position of control over the salesperson.

• You know the difference between features and benefits and can articulate each clearly. It's the difference between the sizzle and the steak. The automobile may feature anti-lock brakes, but the benefit is easier handling and greater safety. The widescreen TV may have "picture within a picture" technology, but the benefit is being able to catch two programs at the same time. You get the idea.

Remember, buyers are interested in the benefits, not the features. They ultimately want the hole, not the drill bit that makes the hole. Sell them what they want, not what you have.

• Part of educated selling is building a relationship and that demands empathy and agreement between buyer and seller. Whether you feel that way or not is less important than appearing to feel that way. You're creating a perceptual framework; thus, all that matters is the buyer's perception of how you feel. Empathetic statements ("I completely understand your concern about the safety of the product, Ms. Stone . . .") can result in opportunities to lead the conversation in the direction it needs to go. (. . . and I'm glad you brought it up. The latest issue of *Consumer Reports* rated our product the safest in its class. I made a copy of the article for you.")

As part of that, you should be prepared to isolate and counter objections. If those objections are broad or ill-defined by the buyer, they must be sharpened or reduced to their lowest common denominators. Unless you know the true nature of the objection, you won't be able to address it effectively. Shared empathy can help you get to that point more quickly and honestly. As part of your prior preparation, you should have answers to many of those questions already in mind. For the others, the work you've done developing that relationship along with other flanking maneuvers should give you what you need to counter all but the most obscure issues.

Do all this and you will be in better shape to cross the threshold into the next act.

ACT III: GOING FOR THE CLOSE

Entire books have been written around the art of closing the sale, also known as "asking for the order." Engineering a satisfactory close, one in which the customer enthusiastically responds Yes to the question, is the most difficult part of the sale. A lot of this has to do with the fact that, as human beings, we dislike and sometimes fear rejection. Ever say, "I love you" to someone and not have it said back to you? It's embarrassing and, if you deeply love the person, it hurts not to have that love requited. Asking for buyer commitment and not receiving it isn't quite as painful, but it still causes problems.

Another reason salespeople fear asking for the close is because it may sound forced to the buyer and may fly in the face of the relationship they spent the last hour, day, week, month or year building. If that's the case, then one of two things has happened:

1. The proper steps weren't taken and the proper preparation wasn't done to come to that point to make the close flow naturally. And that's a function of a bad job of selling.

2. The salesperson truly isn't interested in helping the buyer solve a problem. They are not acting as a business catalyst, as we discussed earlier, and truly are unskilled white collar labor simply out for the bucks that come from the sale. That's a bad job of sales agent preparation which, of course, results in a bad job of selling.

Closing isn't easy, to be sure. But it isn't anything to be feared, either. Careful preparation beforehand and correct handling during the closing process will result in more successes than failures. And since sales is, indeed, a numbers game, that may be the best for which any of us can hope.

Skilled salespeople seem to have a sixth sense when it comes to closing. Nothing could be further from the truth. What skilled salespeople have is not a special power, but the knowledge that results from the hard work of walking a customer through the sales presentation, handling objections and building appreciation for the product, cultivating a relationship and probing for additional information, then knowing when the customer is brought to the point where there are no more objections left. It is at that point, no matter where it is during the presentation, that a skilled salesperson can ask for the order.

That may seem a bit bold to unskilled salespeople who want a written commitment in blood before they'll believe that they have achieved this oh, so difficult goal. In fact, many salespeople undo the good they've done by pressing for more information and attempting to verify that commitment. In such a case, all they're doing is raising doubt in the buyer's mind that he or she may have made the wrong decision. Salespeople routinely give orders back to buyers because they can't shut up. Don't you be the next one to do this.

Inexperienced salespeople also think that they need a close for every occasion, a trick card to fall back on that will assure them success. While it's true that every sale demands a slightly different closing technique, all of them are more alike than they are different. And they all require a good sales effort correctly executed to be successful. But no matter if you're selling used cars, hot tubs, a jet aircraft or an idea to the United States Senate, the close breaks down into two parts:

1. *The Assumption of Success.* A good salesperson knows he or she is in business to help customers solve problems. That problem may be anything from a cure for a common disease to a new line of plastic novelties that will bring a few more coins to the bottom line of a local gag shop. Once you have successfully answered all questions and toppled all obstacles, you and the buyer can agree that you have solved the problem. Sometimes this agreement is subtle, other times it's direct. But that was the goal—often unstated but nevertheless present—of both of you during the sales presentation and it's critical to making the sale.

2. *Ask for the order.* A surprising number of salespeople never ask for the order, then wonder why they never make any sales. Some customers will take that role for you and simply tell you what to send them. If they're frequent buyers at all, they know the game and know this is the next logical step.

Others need that final shove to buy. They need to be asked to the dance, sometimes even before they themselves know they want to go. This is the hard part for many salespeople to swallow but, in reality, it is the easiest part of the presentation. The answer will be "Yes," "No," or "I need more information." All of them can be handled.

The proper way to ask for the order, however, is not to ask directly. Once again, direct, confrontational selling tends to put people on guard and threaten their perceptual safety. Using the same logic you employed in your flanking maneuver, look for ways to ask for the order that are indirect. Examples include:

- "These lines are available at different prices with or without designer labels. Since you indicated you serve an upscale clientele, let me send you the designer-labeled line first and we'll see how it sells."

- "I only have a few cases of this brand left in the warehouse, so let me call right now and make sure they put them on tomorrow's truck for you. I know I have three and I may have as

many as five, and then that's it. If I do, can I send you all
five?"

- "Would you like the entire order delivered here, or would you
like some to go to your branch stores?"

- "I have this model in red . . . I'm sorry, *bordeaux*, ebony or
sycamore. How many of each would you like?"

THE DENOUEMENT:
SERVING THE CUSTOMER IS JOB ONE

As you can see, the close is the turning point, the moment to which
all your sales efforts have led. However, closing the sale isn't that
difficult. You will either succeed or fail based on how well you have
prepared yourself and the customer before and during the encounter.
If you succeed, you can learn from your success and apply it to the
next sale. If you fail . . . well, you can learn even more.

Remember that, while no one likes to be hustled, everyone
needs to be served. Selling is a difficult profession to master. Do so,
and you will be seen as an asset to your company, your industry and
the customers you serve. Successful selling takes hard work, but the
work itself is not hard to master if you make an effort. And, in the
end, it's well worth that effort.

Just ask any Million Dollar Club member.

*Media buyers need an analytical mind,
an ability with numbers that manifests
in a non-numeric way, stability under
pressure and a taste for negotiation.*

—David Ogilvy

16

The Media Explosion

When Marshall McLuan noted that the "medium is message," he referred to the growing influence of the media itself and the impact it had as an entity, not merely as a carrier of information. That was in the 1960s, when television, specifically of the network variety, carried more clout than any other form of media. If you were on TV, man, you had hit the big time.

Television is still a critical medium, and grows more pervasive in its reach and the variations it offers all the time. That message has been split, however, among hundreds of cable channels and thousands of programming hours. There still are big ticket slots—the Super Bowl is one, special episodes of popular series are another—in which your marketing message commands top dollar. Below that, it can be a grab bag of broadcast options, forcing you to be smarter and more strategically inclined in your choices.

One thing McLuan's phrase did connote—and it has come to full flower in today's wired environment—is that the medium itself is an entity and an effective representation of the people it serves. Tastes and interests have become more divergent because the media has begun offering new options, making cost effective niche service not only possible but profitable. Conversely, the media has developed more delivery mechanisms because of that growing divergence in interest areas. One phenomenon feeds the other *ad nauseam* until there simply are too many options of which to keep track. The fact that cat owners and knife enthusiasts each have several magazines

CHIT

With the prolif-
eration of media
comes a prolifera-
tion of marketing
messages, literally
hundreds a day to
which we are ex-
posed both wit-
tingly and unwit-
tingly, subtly and
directly. Strategic
media choices can
help you narrow
the options and
make a deeper im-
pression on people
interested in your
product.

from which to choose and that there are such
things as The Food Network and C-Span says
it all.

Media experts point with longing to
simpler days when your choice boiled down
to *Life* or *Look* magazines, the NBC, ABC or
CBS television networks, assorted local radio
stations and your daily newspaper as vehicles
for advertising. Those options have multi-
plied beyond imagination and continue to do
so at an alarming rate. There are no longer
any slam-dunk media options—not in today's
information-sodden environment.

Once again, it's a manifestation of a
growing egalitarianism among people of all
interests and types. At the risk of sounding
like a social science text, society has made
way for a wide array of influences that reach
far beyond the former white, Anglo-Saxon
Protestant power structure, and the media
has learned to court those other audiences
profitably. That doesn't mean all of us live
on equal terms with each other; quite the opposite, in fact, and some of those social and
economic gaps continue to widen.

What it does mean, however, is that
marketers have learned that all groups representing any kind of critical mass are a potential market for some product somewhere. As
profit margins continue to slice more thinly,
companies are willing to pursue smaller segments in hopes of establishing a service base
that will eventually lead to a steady income
stream. The proliferation of media types and
market niches have given those efforts an
enormous boost.

These days the medium has stretched beyond the message to become the definition

and measurement of the various social groups and lifestyles it serves. And, as many marketers know, once you control the media, you control the way the audience thinks. If a well-defined segment hears only your point of view, it can become their reality. And that, in turn, offers you the maximum influence you seek to sell your products or services.

ADDRESSING MARKET NICHES

The media has done a very good job of proliferating, to be sure. It's also done a very good job of articulating the needs and identity of the groups it serves. Media buyers face a more difficult task simply because of the number of choices. Services that measure the effectiveness and reach of advertising in any media are doing a booming business because of the need to justify what can be a very pricey set of purchases.

Despite the complications now manifest, however, the proliferation of media has created a number of specific advantages:

• Buyers now have a greater ability to target specific audience segments. Certainly, a knife manufacturer knows that a magazine specifically targeted at knife enthusiasts is the best possible vertical buy in a market cluttered with ad messages. Virtually everyone who lays eyes on an ad in one of those publications has an interest in knives, or knows someone who does. The cost per thousand may be higher than, say, your average daily newspaper. But the value return is outstanding by comparison.

• Marketers have the ability to more effectively develop affinity groups and launch separate marketing efforts on their behalf. The mailing list for those knife magazine readers undoubtedly is for sale, which makes all kinds of additional marketing possible. Create a group that capitalizes on the readers' specific cutlery interest and the marketer may be rewarded with greater sales and, ultimately, influence over that particular group.

• Ultimately, the proliferation of choices becomes a very narrow set of options because of the extreme specialization. Despite its outdoor orientation, an ad in *Field and Stream* probably costs more and

MARKET RESEARCH

Media buyers—and all marketers for that matter—should understand the difference between a vertical market and a horizontal market. A vertical market refers to an audience segment strongly linked by similar personal and professional interests. Physician subscribers to the *Journal of the American Medical Association* represent a strong vertical market.

A horizontal market is a broadly defined market across a variety of strata. Those same physician subscribers all may read *Newsweek,* but the concentration is diluted by a wide variety of other types of readers interested in news, thus the desire to advertise a highly clinical product to them is less appealing and the results less effective.

makes less of an impression than an ad in a knife publication because the audience for the former is more broadly spread over a wider range of reader interest.

The bottom line? When it comes to media—especially, it seems, in the magazine world—the markets are clearly defined and the choices are endless. In the end, everyone becomes his or her own market. Look at the progression of magazine titles over the last 50 years. We've gone from *Life,* which is all encompassing, to *People,* which is specifically about one species (albeit, the one that reads magazines). From there we moved to *Us,* which is about a specific kind of people and speaks to personal self-interest. Finally, we end up with *Self,* which is only about one person, who likely is the most important person in each of our lives.

Unless you happen to be Mother Teresa, of course. But even Nobel prize winning nuns pending sainthood probably have their own publication. Or soon will.

MEASURING MEDIA CHOICES

With all the changes in the marketplace and proliferation of choices, the best person to buy media space for your marketing efforts is someone well versed in your industry. Someone who understands the strengths and weaknesses of each option and can purchase both for maximum impact as part of a greater strategic plan. However, it helps to understand the basics of the purchase process, as well as the advantages of each of the major types of media.

Let's start with the latter issue first, focusing only on familiar mass media here. We'll consider marketing on the Internet in Chapters 19 and 20. In this chapter, we'll take a look at some familiar media culprits and measure the advantages and challenges of using each. After that, we'll walk through the basics of the media buy to familiarize you with the process so you can make wise choices.

Let's look at the media choices from a top-down approach as advertisers perceive value.

Television

It's still the prestige medium for virtually all advertisers and an unattainable goal for some products like tobacco, alcohol and other goods not considered family friendly. An ad on a nationally televised program, even in this day of remote controls, video recorders and cable proliferation, still commands excellent reach. And like anything else, you pay for what you get.

Advantages: We articulated a few of them above, but there are more. Good TV advertising is often memorable and tends to be intrusive by its nature. That means if the viewer is in the room, it's difficult to avoid, especially if it is entertaining, compelling or visually arresting.

TV ads command attention from two senses—those addressing sight and sound—and can be tailored to specific audience segments. In fact, placement in programs with an audience cohort that has strong ties to the product can be a very effective way of reaching a key market. Add to that the commercial's memorability, as well as flexibility to size it time-wise to a variety of formats, and you can wind up with a very effective piece of marketing.

Disadvantages: You also can wind up with a very expensive piece of marketing. On a minute-by-minute basis, TV commercials cost 10 times as much to make as any other broadcast program. The production values have to be high if they're going to be noticed, and that means more cost, effort and time in production. Add to that the high cost of media placement, even in niche or smaller markets, and you wind up with some very expensive spots.

In addition, TV commercials are increasingly getting lost in the video clutter on most TV stations as more firms opt to pay a little less for shorter spots. It's not unusual to see as many as half a dozen quick hits strung together between program segments, making the expensive image you labored to produce less memorable. The prevalence to tape and skip forward, or to zap with a remote to another station until the commercial collage has passed can also rob the spot of its value.

Radio

Since the advent of television, radio has been the great unsung media, primarily because it appeals only to one sense, that of sound. However, radio has distinct advantages in today's market and continues to do so no matter how high-tech the other options become.

Advantages: As promoters of the medium like to say, radio is everywhere. We have it on in our cars and in the workplace. It serenades us while we shave and eat breakfast, even while we sit on hold waiting for someone to take our telephone calls. Radio has its limits as a medium but it can be limitless in its presence in our lives.

Radio also is a flexible and cost-efficient medium, allowing commercial spots to be prepared at a fraction of what a comparable slot on television would cost. In addition, it can be equally or more effective, depending on the product, the audience and/or the purpose of your message. That's because tuning in the radio is even less deliberate than turning on the television. For most of us, the radio goes on the minute we turn the key in the ignition in our cars. I can't say the same for my television when I walk through the front door of my house.

Disadvantages: The biggest problem with radio is the fragmentation of its market. There are close to 10,000 radio stations in the country, each fighting for survival with its own distinctive format. There is significantly lower start-up costs for a radio station compared to a television station, which means it's easier to get into the business. Deciding which station to go with sometimes takes strong analytical skills and a quantum leap of faith.

Radio stations have been known to change from country to heavy metal and back again in a matter of months. That means you may lose your target audience at a moment's notice and still have contractual obligations to fulfill. Identifying and pursuing that target group with the right number of impressions also could become a costly affair. And, if television has maximum impact and credibility, radio has less.

Print

As the first form of advertising, print still carries significant weight in the marketplace. The term "print" mostly refers to newspapers or magazines, but there are other ink-on-paper options such as flyers, circulars, inserts and other assorted vehicles. The options, in fact, can be endless depending on your product and its industry.

Advantages: Print has one significant advantage that both television and radio don't. As broadcast vehicles, your advertising message is a series of auditory and visual waves that disappear once they've reached your television or radio. A print ad can be referred to again and again. It's hard copy that takes a long time to change. Ads that appear in magazines have about as much staying power as the issue itself, which could last a week, a month or a lifetime on the coffee table or in the library. As a daily medium, newspapers replace magazine staying power with frequency, and we all know the value of repetition in advertising.

Print also can take the time and space to be more informative, providing product details about which a broadcast ad can only hint. That factor helps give the ad much greater staying power than any electronic impression. And, as we mentioned earlier, the proliferation of print products makes target marketing not only possible, but easily achievable.

Disadvantages: Print advertising, by nature of the media, is less dynamic, vivid and interactive. The best often operates in concert with broadcast media, offering a one-two punch, but some effective ads have been developed and launched without the aid of electronic support. Depending on the publication, it can be expensive and easily lost in the clutter of other imagery. It appeals to one sense—sight—that is as overloaded these days as any sense can be. And it requires active involvement, also known as reading, to communicate its message, whereas radio and especially television require passive participation from recipients.

MIXED MEDIA

The best strategy for any ad campaign is a mix of media that appeals to as many senses as possible and is appropriate to the product and industry. Print and radio can be cheap and still appeal to the senses of sight and sound. Television appeals to both, but you may still want to draw print into your campaign to bring a lasting impression to augment the ephemeral nature of broadcast transmissions. And all campaigns will want to include some form of bargain basement marketing alternatives to augment the more expensive, media driven campaign aspects.

There are some guidelines for any integrated campaign that should be followed for maximum impact:

- Make sure there is conceptual and graphic equity from piece to piece and media to media. Your goal is to make a memorable campaign that makes a variety of types of impressions. If there is nothing linking the pieces that the public can easily recognize, then it's not a campaign.

- Make sure the campaign elements are balanced and targeted appropriately to the audience. One space ad, tagged to 36 television spots, is not a very good use of resources or impact points, no matter how conceptually linked the pieces may be. Use all media effectively and in an overall strategic structure that makes sense to the audience.

- Remember why you advertise. Industry awards are nice, but if your ads aren't effective, then they're better off not existing. In the '80s, a luxury car company created a series of ads that featured woodland scenes, soft music, intriguing commentary, and not one shot of the car itself. Industry experts thought they were remarkable and revolutionary, but to this day people have a hard time remembering the name of the car those ads were promoting.

BEFORE YOU BEGIN

In a minute, we're going to talk about how to go about executing an effective media buy. But there are steps to take before that happens:

- Your media purchase strategy should match your overall strategic marketing plan and goals. If you haven't already done so, define that goal as precisely as possible and make sure your media buys will support it. Without it, no media purchase will be the right one.

- Define your target market and pick your media appropriate to that target market. Knowing the target market will help you decide which media will work best in helping you achieve your goals. Again, if you haven't defined your market, then you don't know what buys to make.

- Develop your media objectives and focus them on accomplishing your goals. These objectives will help define frequency and reach and will dictate the number of buys you make, how many times they are run and the size of your target market. Media objectives support, but are not the same as, your strategic goals. Think of media objectives as the roadmap to your media buys.

    The right frequency is a tricky thing to define. It has to be frequent enough to make an impression, but it can't be too frequent because of the risk of turning audiences off. Generally, one to two hits is too few to make a difference, while seven to eight may be too many.

MARKET RESEARCH

Before you can walk the media buyers' walk, you have to talk their talk . . . literally.

Media placement and market measurement have their own set of jargon and definitions that you'll need to know before the next time you talk to your ad rep. Here's a sample:

- *A.D.I.* means "area of dominant influence." It's a geographic area as defined by Arbitron that indicates that a certain county(ies) are tuned to a certain station most of the time.

- *Avails,* slang for availability, are the time slots available in which your commercial will run.

MARKET RESEARCH
(Continued)

• *C.P.M.* means "Cost per thousand" and it's the average cost for reaching 1,000 readers, listeners or viewers.

• *Dayparts* is the segments into which various periods of the day are divided and into which advertising is slotted. In television, there's daytime (sign on to 5 P.M.); early fringe (7 to 9 A.M.); access (7:30 to 8 P.M.); prime time (8 to 11 P.M.) and late fringe (11 P.M. to signoff). For radio you can purchase morning drive (sign on to 10 A.M.); daytime (10 A.M. to 4 P.M.); afternoon drive (4 to 7 P.M.) and night (7 P.M. to sign off).

Generally, three to four buys per campaign seem to be about right.

MAKING THE MEDIA BUY

When it comes to media buys, all rates are negotiable. In the same way you'd never pay sticker price for a car, you should never buy off the rate card for your media space. Consider those a mere starting point from which your negotiations can begin. Then take the following steps:

• Be direct in telling the rep what you're willing to pay for the campaign, but never negotiate on a "cost-per-spot" basis. You'll end up paying more and receiving less. Negotiate your fee based on a cost-per-thousand viewers (CPM) or, in the case of television, on the basis of gross rating points. You will get a better return for your investment.

And don't buy right away! Ask for a proposal and examine it against other proposals.

• Negotiate as far in advance of your need as possible. Like airline tickets, the price is lower the earlier you buy them. First-quarter buys can be especially economical because retailers who saturated the airwaves during the previous year's fourth-quarter holiday season likely aren't buying any more. Watch for value, but be wary of first-quarter format changes that could alter the station's demographics.

• Remember that you negotiate from a position of strength most of the time. Unless yours is an unusual market, there are very few "must buy" stations, channels or media. The proliferation of avenues can make media a buyers' market. Know that when you go into negotiations.

• Play by the (ratings) numbers, but know that those aren't your only consideration. Each media has its own unit of measure. Television has its Nielsen ratings, radio its Arbitron. Quarterly reports issued by each of those firms can tell you a lot about the market placement of a particular station or channel and can offer very valuable information when making a media buy. There is also qualitative information to consider, however, that includes the following:

• What type of editorial ambience does the station have and is it appropriate to your company and message?

• Are the station's other advertisers reputable and are their messages compatible with yours?

• Do your target audience members care about the medium you are choosing and will they be aboard to hear your message?

• Is the station operationally sound and able to maintain the audio integrity of your spot?

Buying the right media is critical to your campaign's success, but it's more than a statistical exercise. To choose the right vehicles for your market takes as much creativity and insight as any other aspect of advertising and marketing.

But unlike art and design, it also takes a calculator and a little negotiation savvy to get the best possible advantages for your advertising.

MARKET RESEARCH
(Continued)

• *D.M.A.* means "designated market area" and is the Neilsen company's version of A.D.I.

• *G.R.P.* means "gross rating point," a unit of measure that refers to one percent of a potential audience segment.

• *H.U.T.* means "homes using televisions" and defines an area during a specific rating period.

• *Rating* is the number of homes capable of receiving that same program.

• *Share* is the percentage of households being measured that are listening to a specific program.

*The fact that you have to classify me
means you don't understand
a damn thing about me.*

—Typical Response From Generation X

17

The New Demographics

In the art and science of marketing, even creativity leaves little to chance. No move is made without good reason and no product unveiled unless there is a likely market segment either clamoring for it or ready to be educated about it. In marketing, more than any other business discipline, the environment in which the company and its products live and work makes a big, big difference.

Seat of the pants strategies have given way to exhaustively researched data from which trends, patterns, behaviors and responses to social issues are monitored, analyzed, interpreted and turned into marketing intelligence. Welcome to the world of demographic study, the science of how we all think, act, walk, talk, sleep, play, work and do hundreds of other activities, from the exciting to the mundane, that make up our lives. From bungee jumping to brushing your teeth, someone somewhere is charting the activity, if not of you, then of others in your age group. Chances are they know as much or more about you than you do yourself.

But take heart. If Big Brother is indeed watching us, then it's only because he wants to sell us something.

ANALYZING THE MARKET

Social scientists have always studied population trends as a way to anticipate social behavior and its relationship to the needs and desires of individuals and population groups. When the early settlers bought Manhattan island from the Native American residents for $24 worth of what, in those days would have constituted expendible consumer goods, they indulged in a value exchange based on perceptions drawn about the supply-and-demand nature of that economic system. By providing a modest amount of what, for them, were plentiful goods, those settlers utilized early needs analysis based on what limited knowledge they may have had about the current residents.

In addition to meeting the needs of those "consumers"—the Native American residents—they undoubtedly thought they cut a good deal in the process. Had they thought about things like garbage strikes, theater ticket prices and apartment rents, perhaps they would have reconsidered their offer.

The science of demographics really didn't take hold in a big way until the group we call "Baby Boomers" reached the "discretionary income" stage of their young lives and advertisers suddenly realized that the largest generation ever to populate the world might be a pretty good market for soft drinks, fast food and a host of other consumables that their parents' generation had spent so much time and energy creating and building into lifestyle choices. With the advent of the science of segmentation in the late 1970s, marketers suddenly got serious about generational analysis as a way to target their marketing message and get the most out of their promotional dollars.

That science has continued to evolve outside the marketing realm to become a serious form of both business and social analysis. And marketers have found the information drawn about groups and individuals to be invaluable in its application to the marketing process.

When it comes to market analysis, numerous mechanisms and engines exist to cull the information needed to develop new products and propositions for companies. Labels for different population groups abound and profiles of what researchers say are "typical" consumers within these markets are plentiful. Looking for Early Adapter World War II Era Conservative Christian Coffee Drinkers? Undoubtedly some researcher has a neat profile in his or her market analysis file, complete with the information you'll need to sell your wares to this group.

For our introductory purposes, however, we'll focus on the three basic building blocks of social research that were touched on in an earlier chapter. Each is a sort mechanism in and of itself and each has an increasing level of application based on the depth of your market knowledge need and the nature of your applications.

The three types are as follows:

• *Geographics* is the study of populations based on where they live. It's based on the assumption that people tend to live in close proximity to other people like themselves in terms of social and economic identity. Of the three categories, it's the least precise because it uses one relatively gross measure to draw assumptions about an increasingly complex marketplace.

• Demographics itself refers to more complex social variables and patterns to draw its conclusions. It's also the word used to describe the overall science of population studies and refers to population analysis that goes beyond geographics to include other aspects of population distribution, including age, education levels, income strata, racial and ethnic influences and other more refined analytical points.

• Bore down to the next level and you have psychographics, the individual preferences that make up the mind, emotions and value system of the individual. In the same way geographics is the easiest data to gather—generally it's a zip code sort plus a little more—psychographics attempts to chart trends based on personality characteristics linked to social class and strata. A good psychographic study can show just how misleading geographic and even demographic data can be.

In a now classic example, two young women graduated from a prestigious Ivy League school at the same time with relatively the same level of academic achievement. Each was from a white, upper middle class family, each had the same quality of education and opportunity. Presumably, each was brought up with a similar values set, had many of the same life experiences and shared many of the same beliefs.

But that's where the similarities end. One of the young women was Grace Slick, who went on to become lead singer of a San Francisco-based acid rock band Jefferson Airplane and energetic spokesperson against the war in Vietnam and the establishment in

general. The other young woman was Tricia Nixon Cox, daughter
of Republican president Richard M. Nixon. Such is the nature of
psychographic research.

DEFINING THE AGE COHORT

What we'll focus on for the balance of this chapter does not delve
quite so deeply on an individual level. For the sake of expediency,
demographers have arrived at the age cohort as being the most critical in defining ideals, beliefs and values right along with social
trends, income levels, average educational achievement and other social characteristics. Both categories evolve out of the shared experiences members of specific generations have at key points in their collective personal development, as well as the values transmitted to
them by previous generations.

As you can imagine, offspring of large farm families growing
up during the Great Depression have a significantly different outlook on life than that of latchkey kids of the 1980s. By focusing on
age as a unit of measure, social scientists are able to blend similar
experiences and beliefs into a composite character that then extrapo-
lates into purchasing, saving and other social habits. Its convenience
is only exceeded by its accuracy in providing a base of information
for your marketing efforts.

According to *American Demographics,* a leading journal in the
study of this science, the five age cohorts currently alive and func-
tioning in a socially and economically meaningful way from oldest
to youngest are:

The World War II Generation.   This is the oldest body of living
Americans, all of whom were born before 1933. The values and beliefs were formed by the two most cataclysmic events of the 20th century—the Great Depression and World War II—and you can't over-
estimate the impact the two events have had on this group of people.

Thanks to rapid post-war economic expansion, generous government benefits programs, and conservative values driven by the
fear of loss fostered by Depression-era experiences, this generation is
highly affluent and may hold that title long after its members are

gone. The generation's inherent conservativism tends be based on religious values and its members less well-educated than the offspring they created precisely because a high school education was often enough for a person to make his or her way in the world successfully. This education gap has proven historically significant in society's changing points of view.

The Swing Generation. Born between 1933 and 1945, this generation was caught between the profound influences of the Great Depression and World War II and the rise of Baby Boomer dominance of the marketplace. This fact has driven a schism between members of the generation itself, which is among the smallest of the four age cohorts. Some members align with the conservative values of their generation of elders, others with the more liberal, indulgent tendencies of the generation to follow. Changes in economic status and balance may make this group, also known as the Silent Generation, the last affluent retirement-age group the world will know for a long time.

The Baby Boom Generation. We've heard so much about this group that one tends to forget there are other types of people in the world. Born between 1946 and 1964, Boomers constitute the largest social segment and likely will well into the 21st century. They are the living representation of the post-World War II expansion period, and many were raised by young, stay-at-home mothers who utilized the liberal leanings of Dr. Spock to offset the stricter disciplines felt by previous generations.

The Boomers were catered to by advertisers from the beginning and fortunes were made anticipating their every need as they moved through their various stages of life. They are better educated than the previous generations and much more the focal point of society than their elders had been during their formative years. Social trends like the anti-war movement of the 1960s and early '70s and the materialism of the '80s are a direct outgrowth of Boomer growth periods. Even when they're old they will demand society's attention, just because there are so damn many of the little buggers.

Generation X. Even the name is a departure from the others, usually based on the physical environment which shaped their values and behavior. This is a media-driven generation whose values tend to be the byproduct of much of the advertising messages they've received throughout their lives, coupled with the liberal, anti-establishment leanings of the Boomers, many of whom are their parents.

The cohort is further defined as anyone born between 1965 and 1976 and tends to be well-educated, but ambivalent about the future. This has a lot to do with economically uncertain times in which this generation was born and the relative pessimism regarding their own success and future. For the first time, advertising is viewed as a transparent, irrelevant attempt to get society to part with its money. They can be critical about the status quo, but not to the degree of the previous generation. They're also the generation that has helped drive the technology revolution, and that's an entire value structure unto itself.

The Millennial Generation (Also Known As Generation Y). If any group was ever heir to the Baby Boomer throne, it's this generation. Made up of members born between 1977 and 1994, the Millennials are the next largest generation to come down the road and seem to be among the first born in the 20th century in sync with their parents' value systems. They favor liberal causes raised in the '60s and have taken those causes—especially ones that directly affect their peers like racial and sexual equality—to the next level. Despite social and economic gains over the last two decades of the 20th century, they know they live in an uncertain world and respond accordingly.

Unlike previous generations, there are few gaps in education or values between Millennials and their parents. Technology has been a way of life from the beginning and this is truly the first completely wired generation, making them prime to move headlong into the 21st century.

SIZE MATTERS

So what's the makeup of these various groups? When it comes to influencing social, economic and marketing trends—and marketing, as sifted through an ever growing media presence, is a major social influence—the five generations make up the following pieces of the economic pie as we enter the new millennium:

World War II Generation	12.0 percent of the total population
Swing Generation	11.2 percent
Baby Boomers	28.8 percent
Generation X	16.4 percent
Millennial Generation	26.0 percent

In order of social influence based on size, that deck reshuffles and shows the following:

Baby Boomers	28.8 percent of the total population
Millennial Generation	26.0 percent
Generation X	16.4 percent
World War II Generation	12.0 percent
Swing Generation	11.2 percent

There is little doubt who the market leaders will be in the coming decades. In the same way the Swing Generation lost its social identity to the stronger influence on either side, Generation X could lose its economic identity to marketers ploughing new ground for 21st century products. Fortunately, the social difference likely will blur more over time, since the generational differences in key areas like economic strata and education tend to be less dramatic than those of the previous generations.

In the end we may all end up wanting the same color automobile as the Millennials because that's the only thing the car companies will be making. Better get used to it.

COMING TRENDS

There is little that happens to any of us anymore that isn't in some way measured. The science of demographics has proved an invaluable tool to marketers who need to know the size and scope of potential audiences and their relative receptivity to marketing messages based on upbringing and values. Understanding how to reach certain audience segments, and through which medium, always has been critical to successful marketing. Demographics allows, to as great a degree as possible, pinpoint accuracy in accomplishing this goal.

Consequently, there is far more data available about the five cohort groups than we ever could hope to reproduce here. Entire books have been written just about marketing to Generation X. In addition, using our own experiences as a guideline, certain things suggest themselves through common sense or common experience for which corresponding data may not be necessary.

The older population members, those of the World War II and Swing generations, watch more television, especially TV news, than do Boomers, Xers or Millennials. Consequently, marketing messages targeted to that group would do well slotted in between the weather and sports. The overall education levels of that generation, if you recall, are less than those of the younger generations. That means any message too obtuse, obscure or less than obvious may be dulled in its impact. A straightforward, plain-folks approach, as long as it's not condescending, will speak with greater clarity to these generations' value structures.

Despite the lesser percentage they hold of the overall marketplace, however, World War II and Swing Generation members control larger portions of the country's overall wealth, making them very good prospects for the appropriate marketing messages. Couple that with longer lives and abundant good health enjoyed by those groups and suddenly what you may have perceived as quiet generations slowing down to enjoy the winter of their years become robust, active groups prime for products and services that suit their lifestyles.

Market accordingly and let your stereotype of the "old fogey" slip away. And remember that between the two groups, we're still talking about nearly 40 million Americans. Despite the encroaching years, that's a force that has significant clout.

Marketers have followed the ubiquitous Baby Boomers since the first one entered the world nine months after the close of World War II. Now 78 million strong, Boomers are, indeed, everywhere. And so is their need for consumer goods. They have been courted by marketers all along and are used to having the choice when it comes to anything they want. They've been followed through childhood and on into young adulthood. The generation is now beginning to mature and the oldest ones are talking about retirement. This opens up whole new markets for mature products and services.

The Boomers are affluent, but unlikely to be as affluent as their elders when they do enter retirement en masse. That's because they're used to having their cake and eating it to, often on time payments. However, they have enjoyed significant earnings over their careers, and that means the market for luxury and leisure goods will be even stronger than it is right now for their more conservative, cautious predecessors. And they'll live even longer than those who have come before them, so their purchasing years will extend even further.

But that's not to say they should be neglected now. Most are in their peak earning years and their better education makes that earning power significantly higher than that of previous generations. For marketers, the Baby Boomers always have been a strong market. And they're just getting better with age.

Generation X, on the other hand, tends to be a little problematic. At only 44 million strong, they are the least dominant of the younger generations, and they come from a mixed bag of Boomers and a few of the younger Swing Generation parents. That can provide them with a very interesting, and mixed value system background.

But Xers are well educated and practical in their thinking. That attitude isn't quite that far afield from that of their parents, so the generation gap tends to be narrower and more easily bridged. Like the World War II Generation, many Xers entered the world during a time of financial insecurity, which make them more cautious and more cynical than their predecessors. That, in turn, makes them tough and unyielding in their demands from the marketplace.

Xers also tend to be somewhat entrepreneurial and they're just now coming into their own as a potent market and social force. It's a market well worth pursuing, assuming that your firm can embrace the right attitudes, the right values and the right purpose. Xers care and they expect you to care, too.

When it comes to the next big wave of purchasing power, however, it's not going to be Generation X. The Millennial Generation, those born between 1977 and 1994, are roaring into the market. At 70 million strong, they fall behind only the Boomers, which means marketers are primed for the next great age.

The Millennials will be an interesting mix. The market has become much more culturally diverse, a facet the Millennials have embraced thanks to the social values of their more liberal parents. But those same parents are putting pressure on them to grab hold and take advantage of all the opportunities they themselves may have missed. Millennials likely will not be rebellious and tend to be straighter arrows than previous generations. If this holds true, with their great number they will be the next generation to build new and exciting inroads into American society and the world.

In part due to the booming economy, the Millennials already are a potent buying force for the products they consume. As with the Baby Boomers, marketing will be able to follow this next great wave into a prosperous and lucrative future.

WHAT TO EXPECT FROM THE GENERATIONS

As we said, there is a wealth of data on the five cohort groups that make up America's current demographic profile. Each brings with it unique characteristics and market demands that need to be satisfied. You'll have to match your product to the generation(s) it's aimed at and strike out on your own. But the least we can do is discuss relative levels of affluence over time and examine projected spending habits.

It's a bullish economy, but spending will continue to be cautious by all age cohorts and each group will target its own needs based on where it sits in its life cycle. Take a close look at the following, then decide which generation trips your trigger. But remember that peak earnings equal peak spending, so adjust your marketing expenses accordingly.

• In terms of spending habits, housing is and will remain the highest expenditure for all groups. Right now, most if not all Boomers should be well settled and Millennials are, for the most part, still too young to comprise much of a mass buying force for real estate. That means Generation X is in the marketplace, finding the appropriate love nest and getting ready to build a family. Xers are a smaller segment, which means that, while interest is high, demand overall isn't as high as it had been for Boomers and will be for Millennials. Those in their prime years spend in the neighborhood of 31 percent of their outflow for housing, while those at farther ends of the age spectrum spend as much as 40 percent. Adjust marketing for other goods accordingly depending on the age group in question.

• Needless to say, the dynamics change and pressures increase when children enter the picture. Young children at home can change behavior patterns significantly, with less money spent on entertainment and leisure activities and more spent on necessities like child care, kids' clothes and education. The fact that Xers, like Boomers, have delayed childbearing until a little later in life stretches that period over more years, altering those dynamics.

• As far as household expenditures, families with parents aged 35 to 44 account for the greatest percentage in this critical area. Depending on when the families got started, that household may contain older children or younger children, but all have more mouths to feed. These are primarily the later Boomers, but we do see Xers creeping into this equation. Target marketing and spending based on these social coordinates and you'll have better luck maximizing your marketing dollars.

• Householders in the 45 to 54 year old range spend the most in household expenditures. Changes in household makeup, coupled with entry into peak earning years, give this age coordinate more financial clout than any other segment. The majority of Boomers have entered this group, further enhancing the outflow of funds exponential to the sheer number of bodies in question. Some, however, are pulling in and beginning to accumulate wealth

MARKET RESEARCH

Marketing often follows common sense principles as much as it does demographic data, but the puzzle that still seems to be missing pieces is Generation X. With their unusual position in the demographic constellation, what is the best strategy to market to this sometimes challenging market segment?

• Present yourself as a source of information. As children of the Internet, Xers have access to a wealth of information. It's from this information that they make their ultimate decisions. Position yourself as a reliable source of desirable data and you'll have a foot in the door. This is especially critical for sales people, who need to educate first and sell second.

MARKET RESEARCH

(Continued)

• Emphasize convenience. Brand recognition is important to Xers, but loyalty to a specific brand isn't. When it comes to desirable product characteristics, convenience tops the list. This includes financing as well as purchase convenience.

• Offer lots and lots of options. Xers grew up with a wide variety of choice. If you don't have it, then you will lose their interest.

• Technology is a plus. Older consumers prefer the human touch, but Xers have grown up with cell

out of fear that the Social Security System will have collapsed by the time they're ready to collect.

• Householders 55 and older tend to spend less on consumer goods for several reasons. Some have cut down on work time or perhaps have retired completely, which usually means a reduction in spending. For those who haven't retired, there are the later years to think about and the need to stash money away for the time when there will be no work at all. Consumer goods expenditures drop by as much as a third, although outflow for things like mortgage and pension contributions may go away entirely once homes are owned and pensions drawn upon rather than contributed to. For those with money, however, personal expenditure increases. Couples with big RVs bearing bumper stickers, "We're spending our children's inheritance!" fall into this category.

The very old—aged 75 and over—spend most of their money on health care and other necessities. There is little left for discretionary spending after that.

SHOW ME THE MONEY

Who has the most wealth available for marketers to tap? Pre-retirees who own real estate seem to have the highest level of net worth overall. That's not counting investments into Social Security, which most generations Boomer and younger believe to be an unlikely source of retirement income for them or their children. That means greater interest

in investment instruments, including participation in the stock market.

Stock ownership, in fact, is the growing
source of wealth development. Older householders generally show less activity in this
area, since they have fewer investible assets
and less time left on the planet to ride the Wall
Street roller coaster as stocks rise and fall. The
very young have yet to spend enough time in
the marketplace or accumulate enough investible income to become serious players.
That leaves the slightly older generation,
specifically the Boomers, as major players.
Since that group also is in its prime earning
years, such involvement only makes sense.

AND WHAT DOES
ALL THIS MEAN TO ME?

Like the stock market, marketing is a very
uncertain game, an investment that can yield
great returns or bottom out with no apprecia-
ble response after all your money is gone. A
business can't afford not to market, but it
also needs to market wisely and make the
most of its investments.

Solid demographic data can go a long
way in reducing the uncertainties in your
marketing efforts. Consider this chapter the
start. Seek out other quantitative and qualitative data about current and prospective audiences for your wares. The better you are able
to leverage this information in your favor, the
more effective your marketing efforts will become and, ultimately, the greater sales your
products will have.

MARKET
RESEARCH
(Continued)

phones, PCs, auto-
mated teller ma-
chines and other
forms of high-tech
service delivery.
They're not only
comfortable with
these options, they
often prefer them.

• Don't mix up Xers
with Boomers. The
two generations
don't automati-
cally like each
other just because
they're adjacent. If
Xers perceive your
message is aimed
at their parent's
generation, they
will turn off, tune
out and walk
away.

Apparently,
some things never
change, no matter
how sophisticated
we may get.

Watson, come here. I need you.

—Alexander Graham Bell to his assistant over the first working telephone line.

You ain't heard nothin' yet.

—Al Jolson in The Jazz Singer. *He may well have been talking about the Internet.*

18

Online Marketing
Part 1~Background

In a television commercial for the Dodge Intrepid, actor Edward Herrman, in voiceover mode, describes the car's features and benefits as you might expect any automobile ad to do. At the commercial's end, he invokes the product's tag line: "This changes everything."

Edward might also have been talking about the Internet. Since the introduction of online communications as far back as 1969 with ARPANET (a vehicle that linked government agencies to researchers), what has become known as the Internet has spread its tentacles around the globe and sunk its hooks into the public and private sectors, as well as the operations of businesses and the lives of consumers worldwide.

In the seventies and eighties, exercise physiologists warned us against becoming "couch potatoes." These days, the greater fear is the proliferation of "computer potatoes," a phenomenon largely due to the growth and application of the Internet, whose graphic counterpart, the World Wide Web, brings entertainment, information and communication to anyone with a PC, a modem, enough money to afford the monthly server fee, and hours, days or even weeks to spend online. An increasing number of marketers are discovering that their messages can flow over the same medium, augmenting their other marketing strategies and finding yet another way into the consciousness of the consumer.

Sounds simple enough, but realize the profound impact that the Internet has had on users and the entire marketing equation. Unlike most other remote media—television, radio, print and display advertising—the Internet offers the first truly interactive medium by which marketing messages can be sent and receive an almost immediate response. The couch potatoes may sit back, sip soft drinks and soak up the TV spots about the new, improved Whoozit Warfler. The computer potatoes, on the other hand, are accessing the Whoozit website, reading design specs, participating in online discussion groups, asking questions of the CEO, and basically querying the universe as to whether the advertising claims can hold water under close scrutiny.

It's that type of interaction, candid discussion and immediate contact found on the Internet that changes everything about marketing. In the book *The Cluetrain Manifesto*, a variety of authors make the case that the Internet has revived the idea of communities, this time in an electronic discussion format, and enhanced their abilities a hundredfold to literally make or break an idea, an ideology or a marketing or advertising campaign through acceptance or rejection. In 1969, the social cry was, "Power to the People!" Online communications may have finally taken us there.

WHY MARKET ONLINE?

In 1969, only a small cadre of propellerheads were involved in building the first online communications network. Today everyone from school kids to education administrators, New York stock brokers to little old ladies from Pasadena (and elsewhere) are online, hitting Web pages and talking up a storm in chat rooms, as part of newsgroups and through e-mail. It took radio 38 years to reach 50 million listeners and TV 13 years. The Internet was there in four years, and its rapid rise has even prompted educational systems and government bodies to call for a PC and modem in every household. By 2005, experts predict Internet access for more than 300 million households, with South American and Asian growth helping fuel that phenomenal rise. The vast majority of those may well be your current and potential customers.

Part of this growth has to do with the captivating effects of the World Wide Web. Ever since ham radio operators dialed in international overseas broadcasts, we've been fascinated with inside looks at other places and faces. The Web provides that in real time and at the cost of a local telephone call. It's open for business 24 hours a day, seven days a week and its shelf space for information is limitless. Entire libraries of information are available on the web, with browsers able to access data from sources users never knew existed. That information is delivered with words, pictures, sounds, even music. There is no better information source; never has been and probably never will be.

For marketers, a virtual identity has become critical to continued growth and development. Consumers have now become attuned to dialing up

www.yourcompany.com

and having the most recent information at their fingertips. Other companies already are there and many have been for quite some time. They have found a way to utilize the Internet's interactivity to their advantage, building a greater affinity among their customers. Online coupons, special recipes, additional "inside" information and a direct electronic pipeline to administrators are just some of the ways even old-line companies have made their presence more compelling on the Web.

Remember the old Red Ryder Fan Club that encouraged you to send in cereal boxtops and receive a membership card, badge and secret decoder ring? That strategy is back, refreshed for the new millennium. And the secret decoder ring is the Web itself.

WHO'S OUT THERE?

The Web is worldwide, but the U.S. leads in Internet usage by an electronic mile. An estimated 30 percent of all households have Internet access, which means roughly 50 million users nationwide. Canada is next. While they have a higher percentage of penetration —39 percent—they have a much lower actual number of users, about 9.7 million. Australia, Spain and Ireland all follow.

What's good about those numbers is that most users no longer see the Internet as an option. America Online and Roper Starch

Worldwide surveyed users only to find out that at least half of them consider the Internet a necessity in their daily lives. In fact, the same survey revealed that two-thirds of them would sacrifice their televisions and telephones rather than give up their Internet access. And the demographics of that group have moved away from its original profile of males aged 24–35 to a cross-cultural spread that represents an active online segment for virtually the entire population. This makes the Internet fertile territory for all sorts of marketing activity.

The breakdown in the gender of users is almost dead even between men and women. Children have been known to be more adept at going online, but seniors are joining the ranks in increasing numbers. What it all means is that the demographics and usage on the Internet are diverse and growing. High-tech delivery doesn't mean exclusively high-tech recipients—not anymore. That makes the Internet a viable marketing option and one that fits well within just about any company's marketing strategy because, large or small, we're all the same size online. When it comes to competition, the Internet has become the great equalizer.

DEVELOPING THE RIGHT
ONLINE MARKETING STRATEGY

Like any aspect of marketing, the Internet also requires a specific marketing strategy. But that strategy must, first and foremost, represent the overall marketing strategy of the company itself. If there is no integration between online and offline strategies, then there is no effective marketing effort, period.

The Internet is the consummate form of direct marketing. It exceeds telemarketing in its immediacy and direct mail marketing in its content and impact. However, it needs to exist as a part of the overall direct marketing strategy. When all is said and done, however, the Internet is merely one more medium—albeit the most profound and powerful medium—through which to interact with customers and the general public.

Part of what you'll need to communicate is clear identification and application of your product's or your company's brand. That's easily done over the Internet, which offers unlimited potential for content. Because of that vast scope, however, the main emphasis of the medium is informational rather than promotional. People visit Web sites to gain knowledge, not to be sweet-talked into making a purchase. That means your marketing efforts will have to be subtle to the point of being almost benign. Sell too hard and you will drive visitors away from your Web site. Provide the type of information they seek and they will return again and again.

As part of that effort, you'll have to decide whether your Web site should be used as a customer recruitment or retention tool. Are you providing information that keeps current customers interested or are you taking a proactive stance to convert new visitors to regular customers? That will guide the approach of your content and how that site is marketed and used.

Internet marketing is really the best example of one-to-one marketing, the new effort by marketers to communicate value propositions that are specific, not to groups or population segments, but to actual individuals reading the online message. There is no more intimate marketing medium than the Internet and nothing as well equipped to offer personalized contact between supplier and user. If you can tailor your efforts to appeal to individuals first, then those efforts will be more effective. We'll talk about one-to-one marketing in Chapter 21.

First you need to know what the competitive context for your product or industry looks like. One of the best lessons you can give yourself is a visit to your competitors' Web sites. By identifying their positioning strategy based on the way they present themselves online, you may be able to uncover a little more than they may have wanted you to know about their perception of their market positioning. Does it replicate yours, or is it something completely different? You'll need to decide before going in just what you may be up against. But that identification may be able to give a little more edge to your effort.

FIRST STEPS

Once you grasp the nature and purpose of the Internet, developing a marketing strategy and applications isn't that difficult. The concept for online marketing is best spelled out as follows:

MARKET RESEARCH

In addition to the Internet, companies also have developed their own intranets and extranets, each of which offers opportunities for marketing.

An *intranet* is the online equivalent of a closed-circuit internal TV channel that companies large and small use to keep employees informed and enable them to access internal departments, policies, issues and information. Many companies market such things as charity drives and personal interests through their intranet, some of which even boast online classifieds. A

Information + Interactivity =
Consumer Interest/Involvement

Creating and updating a compelling Web site while keeping it easily navigable should be the goal of any online marketer. The other challenge is finding a domain name that is easily identifiable and enables current and potential customers to find you amid the clutter and noise of the Web.

Your domain name—the identifier by which users "log on" to your Web site—should be reflective of your brand identity. This not only supports the brand but allows consumers easier access because of their familiarity with your product. I might not remember the identity of the Mars Candy Company, but I will know enough to type in www.snickers.com if I want information on one of my favorite confections. If your brand development work has concentrated on identifying the company—like United Airlines—then the Web site should highlight the company name, initials or acronym—www.UAL.com. If the product is the focus, as it is with Snickers, then it works better the other way.

This is a good way to test the recognition of your brand, but be careful that it doesn't scuttle your online development efforts. If your brand isn't as well known as you think it is, then using it as the domain name for your Web site might undermine development efforts on both sides. And don't get overly cute or too obscure with your site name if it supports an existing product or firm. If you do, you may end up having to build brand identity for the site name. Many people are intrigued enough by unusually named sites to dial them up. Many more, however, simply want to find your site and get the information they need. Helping them cut down on their search time will help you reach more current and potential customers.

DESIGNING YOUR SITE

Personal computers are powerful engines that are your window to understanding and accessing the cyberworld—that realm of Web pages, e-mails and other electronic communications options that literally do function within their own realm. Understanding how that world functions and using its attributes to your advantage will mean the difference between success or failure within your online marketing efforts.

Your face to that world is the home page of your World Wide Web site. It's what consumers see when they access your site and, like the real world, it's the attractiveness of that face and the accessibility of its components that help them decide whether they want to know you better or move on to another page. And this becomes a delicate balancing act between what you can do and what you should do in designing your Web page.

Computer technology is a multimedia technology involving text, graphics, sound and even motion, all of which become more complex within themselves as technological development streaks forward. With the right equipment, there's no end to what a clever page designer can do to make his or her page sing, dance and just behave in a really cool

MARKET RESEARCH
(Continued)

growing number are allowing access for internal product marketing or even selling banner ads to outside firms with an interest in that particular audience segment.

An *extranet* is like a private label Internet channel open to a select group of outside companies and individuals that have an intrinsic interest in the sponsoring company or firm. Once again, the quality and demographics of the audience may stimulate interest on the part of marketers and product promoters, making ad sales on the extranet not only attractive, but lucrative.

manner in hopes of attracting hits from web surfers looking for the latest and greatest that the Web has to offer.

Unfortunately, many Web page designers have the equivalent of NASCAR racers sitting on their desks while most of the rest of us are still putt-putting around in Model Ts. That dichotomy means only that the designer's really cool stuff will take longer to download on my machine than I care to wait. And that means that I will putt-putt on to the next Web site.

Here are some tips for good Web design that can help make your site both compelling and accessible:

• The Web offers an infinite capacity to store and show information, but that doesn't mean you should use it all. Too many Web page owners take the concept of providing complete information too seriously and wind up with text-heavy pages that are unattractive and cumbersome. Surfers will pass these by at lightning speed, something you definitely don't want to happen. Provide the information necessary, primarily through sub pages, and keep your home page attractive and inviting.

• Balance graphics and text, but keep the home page clean and streamlined to draw people in. There is a school of Web page designers emerging who know that design balance for a Web page is as critical as it is for a print ad and any other graphic product. The design should enhance brand development, but it also must be pleasing on its own. Avoid designs that are too busy or lack a graphic focal point. Make sure the concepts and elements are easily accessible and that the components aren't obscured either by the technical requirements of the page or the desire to over-communicate.

• Unlike print, Web pages must be easily navigable. Otherwise the surfer is going to get frustrated and move on. Unlike print ads, which are ends in and of themselves, Web pages are doorways to subsequent pages, e-mail access for the sponsoring company and hot links to other, related sites. As such, users will have to be able to understand page structure at a glance and move effectively through the sub pages and other components through the use of pop-up menus, buttons and other devices to promote and invite access. Making these avenues self-evident while still graphically attractive is critical.

Once the user loses his or her grasp of how to navigate the site, they quickly sail away to other, more inviting portals.

• Minimize motion features. The coolest thing about Web technology is the ability to spin, twirl and otherwise move components around on screen. The designer is faced with the decision of what *can* versus what *should* be done. Graphic elements, particularly those that dance and sing, still make a strong impression on site visitors. But those that are too complex take too long to download. Those compelled by your product or firm may be content to sit and wait. Those passing by will simply move on. Some graphic spin, like tastefully chosen jewelry, can be very effective. Too much, however, and you lose the subtle effect you were trying to reach. And you will look cheap.

• Finally, make the site appropriate to your product, your company and your industry. Your Web site, remember, is part of your image or brand campaign. If you're selling upscale products to a conservative crowd, then the site should reflect that in style and taste. If you're a popcorn wholesaler or run children's parties or events, you can afford to have a little more fun with your site. And you should definitely do so because your home page sets the tone for your firm and product in the eyes of the public. That tone should reflect your company's goals and strategies.

Despite all that, however, realize that the Web is still an exciting new medium for many users and one whose development and use has been driven by the 20- and 30-somethings in the crowd. If there is a time or place to take a more contemporary, "fun" approach to your marketing efforts, it's through your online marketing efforts. The nature of the medium has changed the way consumers and suppliers think about the customer equation. Many of the tenets of good marketing still apply, but the Web revs them up to a higher level.

While you don't want to appear tasteless or frivolous, you also can't afford to appear stodgy or behind the times, especially with your online marketing efforts. Look for opportunities to enhance your marketing efforts in ways encouraged by the new media. You've already broken down some boundaries through increased interactivity. Because of that, you may discover the need for a new look and feel for your company and its products. And that, in turn, may open doors for new products and ideas.

It's a brave new online world and the Internet is making it smaller every day.

BEYOND THE WEB PAGE

Most Internet marketing takes place on the Web page, and we'll spend the lion's share of Chapter 20 talking about development, placement and marketing technique. It's true that the Web page itself serves as a powerful, interactive ad for your firm and deserves as much attention as you need to give it in order to make it effective. But there are opportunities for ads on other Web sites, as well as ample ancillary opportunities in and around the net to maximize. As we said, we'll get to those in the next chapter.

But there also are several other options and opportunities that deserve mention here, if only so you understand their purpose and use as marketing options. They, too, offer inherent advantages as part of the new media. And they, too, have their own rules of the cyber road to which we all must pay attention.

Enter E-mail

The now-familiar Web page wasn't the first instance of online communication. That occurred in October, 1969, when UCLA computer science professor Leonard Kleinrock attempted to send the first electronic message to a colleague at Stanford University and suffered from one of the earliest computer crashes. The future of both aspects of the technology was born that day.

Electronic mail, or e-mail, is now one of the most common uses of personal computers. More than five million e-mails are sent each minute and some 293 billion each day worldwide. Friends, family, consumers and first-generation online marketers can't get enough of it, stirring up a constant storm of communications. It's the ultimate in one-to-one communications, a cross between a phone call and a letter that allows an immediate response or lets you wait before getting back to the sender. In today's overwrought got-to-have-it-now-but-don't-have-the-time society, it allows for selective responses dependent on the immediate need of the information.

One of the best things about e-mail is the urge we all have to respond. Sending an answer is easier, faster and cheaper than licking a stamp or picking up a telephone. And, since response is the goal of all forms of direct marketing, e-mail marketing seems to be a perfect vehicle, especially in a world weary of incessant telemarketing and mindless, vapid advertising, right?

Be aware that e-mail has its own protocols and its own view of marketing. Some people get offended when marketers attempt to reach them through their telephone, which they consider their personal instrument. That resentment triples when it comes to e-mails. Junk e-mail is called *spam* and is often jettisoned without even being opened. And electronic communications disposal is even easier than hanging up on a telemarketer.

But there are types of marketing e-mails that are not resented by recipients. Companies that remember that the Internet is, first and foremost, a communications medium and treat it as such from the start may find their contact welcome and the information they share not only well-received, but also acted upon, usually within hours of receipt. There are really four areas in which e-mail can be used as an effective marketing tool:

• Companies and organizations of all types have used e-mail to deliver electronic "newsletters" and other information they deem useful about their firm and its products. Some of these communiques are more sales oriented, consisting of notices of sales and specials. The more effective ones tend to be more informational, however, with news and information about the industry or special interests of the recipients. A manufacturer of cookware may offer cooking techniques, recipes or articles about various types of cuisines. Toy manufacturers may focus on educational and learning issues, or, for that matter, toy safety.

The underlying theme is the same: Next time you're in the market for whatever it is that we sell, we hope you'll remember this service we brought you at no charge and think of us. That theme isn't lost on anyone but, at the same time, respect for the rules of e-mail and sensitivity to the customers' perceptions of what the media

MARKET RESEARCH

As a communications medium, e-mail is the hottest thing going right now, but there are specific strategies you can employ to make your efforts more effective:

• *Think before you write.* Too many of us simply fire out queries, comments or kneejerk responses without taking the time to evaluate their effectiveness or even see if all the words are spelled correctly. Remember this is not conversation lost to the ether upon completion. E-mails can and have been used as evidence in courts of law. Proceed cautiously, professionally and with full understanding of the impact of your message.

should and shouldn't be carrying go a long way toward continued acceptance.

• E-mail also has become especially popular with companies that have a strong or exclusive online presence—you know them as "dot.com companies"—as a service medium to provide additional information about purchases. Those who order from Amazon.com can expect to receive an e-mail that confirms their order, followed by another e-mail that informs them when the product is shipped, how it was shipped and about how long it will take to arrive. Chances are there will be a follow-up e-mail a few days later that makes sure the product has arrived as well as countless scads of notifications in the future of sales and special offers.

Are the service e-mails necessary? Probably not, but they do make it seem like the company cares enough to keep the customer informed. The real reason, of course, is to reinforce the purchasers' relationship with the company, driving the impression a little deeper with each contact. The depth of that impression will make a difference the next time it comes time to make a similar purchase, but the e-mails aren't perceived as intrusive because, once again, they are positioned as information (or service) as opposed to sales.

• Customer service is a little different in that it's most often responses to orders placed by consumers themselves. It's not quite the same as the other initiatives, but allows the company to respond via return e-mail and use the medium to once again deepen the impression created through contact. Assuming those contacts were effective, each positive exchange helps build loyalty with the customer involved. It also allows two other things to happen:

1. Through continued e-mail and Web page involvement, the customer moves closer to a self-service environment that reduces company staff and resource involvement, thus overhead and expenses. In the best cases, it gives the customer a feeling of greater involvement and/or ownership in the firm with which he or she is doing business.

2. It presents the customer in an interactive environment that not only allows but encourages the submission of personal information. Some firms maintain interactive sites just to build better databases about current and potential customers. The Internet, especially in its pursuit of one-to-one marketing, trades heavily on information, and the more the better. By taking the time to solicit additional information at every encounter, Internet and e-mail contact with customers can contain value beyond that of the purchase.

• Finally, there is direct e-mail marketing itself, a.k.a. *spam.* It's cheaper to produce and send and usually elicits better responses than its direct mail counterpart. A lot of Web users don't like it and it can work against the company that's sending it. Moreover, it's a lot easier to change your e-mail address than it is to move or even change your telephone number, so lists become quickly outdated. There is greater skepticism about the legitimacy and

MARKET RESEARCH
(Continued)

• *Start and end your message effectively.* That means writing a compelling subject line to draw attention to your e-mail, likely one of dozens the recipient will receive that day. Close with an effective signature that identifies you completely. Many systems have auto signs that can be set up like a business card. Although this may seem impersonal among friends, it's a good idea in a business situation.

• *Keep it short and to the point.* The advantage of e-mail is immediate attention and quick response time. If you're planning a long diatribe, it might be better to

MARKET RESEARCH
(Continued)

issue it as an at-
tached memo or re-
port. Your friends
will thank you for
your efforts.

• *Make it useful.* The
most annoying
e-mails are those
that attach as a
one-line response
to a long, previ-
ously sent message.
If you're sending
an e-mail, make
sure it offers value
to all recipients.
You're asking
them for the time it
will take for them
to read the mes-
sage. The less of it
you waste, the
more you will be
appreciated.

• *Create a library.*
E-mails that are ef-
fective, just like let-
ters, may be used
again for different
audiences. Archive
yours so that you
have them at your
disposal and ready

honesty of the company at the other end and
some companies have enabled mechanisms to
block their employees from receiving spam. It
would seem the hurdles and opposition are
too great to make this method effective.

Despite that, some companies choose to
pursue e-mail marketing just the same. If you
are one, make sure your message contains
complete return contact information and
a link to your Web site. A footnote at the
bottom allowing recipients to decline future
e-mails shows you're legitimate and sensitive
to the position your firm has established in
the recipient's mind. And remember that information, not sales, is the medium's proper
context and at least try to appear that you're
playing by the rules.

The end result might be better than you
think.

Using Newsgroups

Newsgroups offer another, different kind of
marketing opportunity. Newsgroups are discussion groups among e-mailers who come
together to discuss similar interests. There are
more than 24,000 newsgroups on the net that
trade up to a million messages each day. Participants haggle about politics, seek out information about the best fly rods on the market
and trade recipes. From the marketers' point
of view, they offer invaluable access to potential sources of information and research.

The right newsgroups can provide the
candid thoughts and ideas about you, your
products and your competition that you may
get nowhere else. You can't proactively market to these users, but you can ask them ques-

tions, either innocently or deliberately, that can uncover questions you never thought to ask, problems you never thought your product had and research you never thought you'd find.

Some newsgroups will appreciate knowing there is an actual company representative online and make no bones about spouting off. Others will clam up or disappear like wraiths into other newsgroups, leaving you with nothing. It will be up to your masterful marketing-intuitive powers to determine the best approach before becoming actively engaged.

Listen and learn and you may be ready to take your online marketing to the next level.

MARKET RESEARCH
(Continued)

to go after minor adaptation. A stitch in cybertime now, saves nine later.

• *Develop effective server lists.* As an augment to your library, make sure frequently e-mailed addresses and marketing lists are on an automated server. That will save you time and allow you to concentrate on content development.

• *Use but don't abuse the technology.* Like other forms of marketing, e-mails should be used strategically. If you overuse them, recipients will delete them without opening them. That, obviously, is what you do not want to happen.

The Internet is a lot like the weather. Everyone talks about it, but no one has figured out how to make money with it.

—Overheard at a recent dot.com conference

19

Online Marketing
Part 2~Application

In the previous chapter, we learned a little bit about the Internet, its characteristics and opportunities and a few reasons to market online. If there is any reason not to market online, we'd like to hear it. Cases could be made that the cost of the reach doesn't yet justify the end results. And we've heard about the shifting sands on which some of the dot.com companies have built their empires. When it comes to the online world, we're all walking down some mean cyberstreets.

But as far as most companies go, a presence online is simply another avenue to attract customers. The nature of the medium, and perhaps even the message, has changed to meet the needs of the sometimes hypercharged cybercrowd. It offers a different avenue into the company and its strategic plan and for many firms, right now, that's enough. You need a presence before you can become a player, and it pays to sign on once you have a little better idea of what all the rules of the game are.

We'll spend the balance of our discussion describing ways to market effectively on the World Wide Web. We touched on e-mail and newsgroups and won't be returning there unless it specifically supports Web development, marketing and advertising. This chapter will focus exclusively on the Web and its abilities to reach consumers for two primary reasons:

1. As a business, every contact you have with current and potential customers is a marketing opportunity and those who take advantage of it, no matter what the approach, will be better off than those who don't. Marketing is built on a base of forward motion and when you're not moving forward, you're moving backward. A missed marketing opportunity is backward motion, in the eyes of the company *and* the customer.

2. Marketing online offers the best possible opportunity to practice effective one-to-one marketing. It's the ultimate niche program because you're customizing, as much as possible, your marketing message to the single individual who will be receiving it. Only database marketing and the power of the Internet make this possible. We'll talk more about one-to-one marketing in the next chapter. First we'll talk about how to create effective online messages.

MARKETING ONLINE: BASIC CONSIDERATIONS

We'll make the assumption that this is not an *if* question, but merely a matter of *when* to start and *how* to proceed. If it isn't, you can skip the rest of this chapter and move on. When to start is as soon as possible and preferably yesterday. Chances are your competitors are lightyears ahead of you if you don't yet have a Web presence. Commit the necessary resources and, for heaven's sake, get online.

How to proceed will be the focus of the balance of our discussion. First and foremost, remember that good Web marketing is intimate, integrated and interactive.

• Remember the nature of the Web ultimately is intimate. It is as infinite as the universe and as intimate as the image you put on your customers' home PC screens. They may be able to ride their computers to Katmandu and back, but when they've dialed up your Web site, yours is the only image in front of their face. Make sure that image is compelling enough to get them to stay and friendly enough to help them drop their guard and open their minds to your message.

• Integration of effort is crucial. Online marketing may well be the next and, someday, the only wave of advertising consumers will receive. The future of marketing may well rest in the laptop that all your customers will someday be carting everywhere with them. For now, however, the Internet is just one of the media available and must be integrated within, not isolated from, your marketing plans and strategies. In any type of marketing, plan integration is critical to success and the more logical components you have that come into play, the better and more effective your efforts will be. Remember that even dot.com companies like America Online have included more mundane delivery mechanisms like direct mail in its marketing plan. You should, too.

• Finally, the key advantage of doing anything on the Web is interactivity. Good marketing efforts utilize interactivity to promote interest, involvement and ownership in the company and its products. The Web is not a passive medium and marketers who treat it as such are missing a huge opportunity. Find ways that customers can interact with your site and you:

- increase the time they stay on the site;

- improve retention of the images they gather and the information they acquire;

- enhance their receptivity to future contacts with your firm or its products.

MARKET RESEARCH

Where else do Internet companies advertise? According to statistics collected by The Intermarket Group, 55 percent advertise in newspapers and 54 percent in magazines. Forty-nine percent gain exposure from marketing on other Web sites and 47 percent do their own online advertising. Radio (35 percent) and printed catalogues (25 percent) follow.

Direct mailers discovered decades ago that pieces that involve tearing, cutting, sticking and stamping have a greater participation and response than those that are no more than a passive read. The Internet increases those opportunities tenfold.

Most businesses have advertising or marketing agencies on retainer to help them develop their overall plans. Similar needs exist with Internet marketing as well and, while not necessarily more complicated or complex, those needs come with their own set of considerations:

• The agency you choose should be able to help you with clean, effective Web page design and recommendations about other online avenues for your product message. Web marketing is more about strategy than it is about graphics, but graphics always get top billing because it's the most evident component. The agency of choice should be able to develop a plan based not only on individual design taste, but also on an integrated and effective strategy that covers the cyberfront.

• In the same way traditional agencies have media buyers that handle broadcast and air time purchases, your agency needs to be able to advise you on the best possible Web site for your message as well as equitable arrangements in the cost-versus-value department. Is cost-per-action, cost-per-click or cost-per-sale a better unit of measure for you? Your agency should help you make that buying decision. (And you can check the end of this chapter for definitions of each of those terms.)

• There is a great deal of Web advertising space that goes unsold, which means savvy buyers often can pick up space for a fraction of the normal asking price. Your agency should be attuned to these opportunities and keep an eye out for Web ad auctions that will enable you to find the space you need at the best possible price. You can also check out the Web site www.adauction.com for other opportunities.

In that same vein, check out www.b2bworks.com. That's the business-to-business ad network which offers vertical market ad placement for specific industries and disciplines. Need to be a part of all sites related to aeronautical engineering and no others? Chances are this site can offer you some options.

WHAT TYPE ARE YOU?

The Internet's reach is limitless, but its opportunities for types of ads is not as plentiful as you might think. Sure, you can buy a spot on hundreds of thousands of sites that reach millions of people worldwide. But the type of spots available are surprisingly mundane. And, since they fall under the behavioral protocols of the Web, they also can be extremely limited. Understand that here we're not talking about your company's or product's own Web page. Instead, we're referring to the opportunities that present themselves on the Web pages of others. These are the ones that can bring you increased reach, but that reach only grasps the site visitor within limited parameters.

• *Banner ads* are the most popular type. Those are the ones that stretch across the top of many home pages, often with moving images and always with directions for followup actions. Since the space in banners is extremely limited, more emphasis is placed on drawing Web site visitors' attention with a compelling question, a moving graphic or a combination of the two. The banner then usually offers links or sources for more information.

DEFINITION

In the world of Web advertising, you'll come across the phrase "rich media." That has nothing to do with wealthy advertisers or luxury products. The term simply describes an ad that's rich with features—music, motion, glitz and twirl. Rich media is a lot more fun than flat images, but the same cautions about download time still apply.

MARKET RESEARCH

Unlike other media, your customers may find they need some help finding you among the myriad sites available. That's where search engines come in. They are your unofficial marketing partners and sales "bots" when it comes to getting consumers through your electronic "door." Without the help of search engines, people will never find you, no matter how much flash and pop your site may have.

• *Spot ads* are the much smaller squares or rectangles also located on the front page. Spots offer room for little more than a product name, logo graphic and maybe a few words or tag line. Spot ads don't say much other than "We support this Web page so don't forget us the next time you need our type of product."

• *Interstitial ads* are one of the inventions of the Web, but they have their roots in short television spots and radio tags. Interstitials are the ads that come on your screen, seemingly unannounced, as you move from one page to another within the same Web site. They are triggered by the visitors' movement from one page to the next, taking the seven or eight seconds between page loads to display their message and invite the viewer in for more information.

For the uninitiated, interstitials can be intriguing or confusing at first, driving a compulsion to open them up and see what's going on inside. Some interstitials make it difficult to exit without taking the desired action. After awhile those very factors can cause visitors to click them off without even opening them up.

• *Pop-ups and daughters* are two terms that are worth knowing, even if you don't want to pursue the strategy. Pop-ups are another type of interstitial, ones that pop up in another window located within the main window, thanks to the power of embedded HTML files. Sometimes these embedded ads pop up after you click on a banner ad. The pair, working together, are known as banner and daughter. Content-wise they're no different from banners or other interstitials. The difference simply comes in how and where they are deployed during the visitor's experience with the Web page.

• *Sponsorships* are tried-and-true opportunities for a variety of media, and the Web also has embraced them. Entire Web sites are now sponsored by corporate America, as are subsets of home pages in a wide variety of industries. Consistent support links the sponsor with the product or service and is a very effective means to assuring financial stability on both sides of the equation. A year-long sponsorship contract can assure constant financial benefits to the host site as well as keep the costs in check for the sponsor if the site suddenly gets hot and the price goes up.

Whichever approach you choose, remember that the best ads are the ones that download quickly for the end user, make a positive and vivid impression and result in actions or activities that lead to a sale (or whatever the desired outcome might be). Remember our comments in the last chapter about keeping Web page images compelling without making them technically complex? The same holds true for Web page ads. If your image takes too long to download, then the Web surfer already has passed on to the next page and your opportunity is lost.

One last note: As you might imagine, banner ads and spots have a tendency to be

MARKET RESEARCH
(Continued)

Search engines operate with a set of complex algorithms, scanning pages for text and trying to locate key words. You will need to register with several search engines, indicating the key word(s) that people might use in searching for your site. Those key words also should appear in any Web directory listing that's published and throughout your home page.

MARKET RESEARCH

To navigate your way through the rigors of online marketing, you will first need to understand the vocabulary of the discipline. Here are a few choice words and terms for you:

• Clickthrough— what consumers do when they click on a banner ad that takes them through a Web site. It provides more precise statistics than the number of "hits" a Web site takes because it measures interest in the ad product rather than a mere touchdown on a Web site. It's the differ-

less irritating to Web page viewers than pop-ups and interstitials. Formal and informal surveys reveal, in fact, the pop-ups are twice as irritating as stationary ads that give the viewer a choice of response. Pop-ups call for interaction, of course, but may be switched off quicker than their message can be digested. Use them wisely. It's the risk you run for capitalizing on the technology of the media.

AD BASICS STILL APPLY

Whether you use rich media or poor media, banners or interstitials, the basics of good advertising still apply to the Web. Before getting caught up in technology and reach, give consideration to the following components in creating your online ad:

• Develop an ad that sells features, not benefits, and make sure it meets some human need, not just your company's need for more revenue. Consumers buy the sizzle, not the steak; and they buy the hole, not the drill that made it. Make sure you answer a desire before it's stated and offer a benefit without being asked. That's the way to capture and keep attention.

• Keep your ads brief, to the point and compelling. Remember that brevity is the soul of wit, as William Shakespeare liked to remind his audiences. This is also a good lesson for ad copywriters. Banners are little better than billboards, spots less so when it comes to the amount of content that can be included. Don't make the mistake of overloading yours.

• Any accompanying graphics should follow the same set of rules. More is less when it comes to either inspired or uninspired imagery. One core graphic or logo is about all you have time for, so make the most of it.

• Provide the necessary technical instructions if you want your audience to respond. Show a button and say, "Click here," if you want them to move to another screen. If you don't, chances are that they won't.

• Take advantage of the technology without overplaying your hand. Authors know it's easier to write long than short and ad creation is the same. Capture the essence, apply the appropriate graphic and get rich quick; that is, use rich media that will load quickly, pop interestingly then get out of the way of your marketing message. Like all advertising, this is a balancing act and not an easy one. But, like all advertising, it's worth the effort.

IDENTIFYING AN EFFECTIVE STRATEGY

Once your components are in place, you will need to know how you plan to deploy them and what you can expect in return. A lot of firms establish a Web site, sit back and count the number of hits and consider themselves successful if those hits exceed six figures. All in a day's work, they say.

The truth is that the number of hits, as we said earlier, are a deceptive and empty unit of measurement roughly akin to the

MARKET RESEARCH
(Continued)

ence between making a sales presentation and online window shopping.

• **Clickthrough rate (CTR)**—the numeric computation of the clickthrough patterns on your banner ad.

• **Cookie**—a small file used for tracking and verification purposes that often is used in place of your screen name and user ID once both have been established at the site.

• **Cost per action (CPA)**—the price paid by the banner advertiser to the

MARKET RESEARCH
(Continued)

site owner for each action delivered. Those actions may be a lead, a completed form or even a sale.

- **Cost per click (CPC)**—the rate the advertiser pays the site owner based on the anticipated number of clicks. Once that click number has been satisfied, the ad's duration has been completed. This differs from other forms of advertising, which tend to base contracts on time periods (days, weeks, months) rather than impressions.
- **Cost per sale (CPS)**—a buying model that charges the advertiser based on the number of actual sales

number of people who walk by your store and look in your window. Unless they come through the door and make a purchase, most merchants would not count them as a successful sales encounter. The Web is the same way. Data available about the type of traffic your site receives is endless. How the value of that data is interpreted is another story altogether.

The data forms the framework and the two key components are a) the number of hits the home page receives, and b) the number of clickthroughs on your Web advertising. From that foundation you can build an interpretation that will help you measure the success of your efforts against the goals you set forth. Despite the growing interest in the data, remember that direct mailers consider a piece successful if it generates a two percent response. Good results on the Web, despite its global reach, are bordered by similar parameters.

From that basis, you can analyze components like impressions per page on your site, which sections commanded the most attention (build on those) and which ones commanded the least (lose those). You can do a traffic analysis and discover which times of day are busiest for which parts of the site. You also can analyze the common entry and exit points—in other words, what draws visitors to the page and at what point do they leave (the latter could be indicative of a problem page). Finally, find out which is the most visited page and why. All of this contributes to your market understanding, hence your ability to build and adjust an appropriate strategy.

This is all part of what's known as data mining, the analysis of raw statistical information for meaning in relation to marketing goals and objectives. If your site has 100,000 visitors a month you're doing well if your goal is half that. If your goal is twice that, however, you'd better find a new way to spark interest. And, no matter what the number, if your site isn't growing in visits... well, it soon will be retrograding in just the way we described earlier.

Your Webmaster may be the one who tracks these stats. That's the person responsible for the development and maintenance of the page and its application. Generally, this person is a tekkie, rather than an artist or content specialist. That means you will need additional staff to fill the page and keep the content fresh. Customers don't visit your Web page because you understand and apply the technology. They visit the page because it contains news and information they can use. Keeping the news fresh and interesting is another way to keep them coming back.

DESIGN YOUR OWN SHOWCASE

When all is said and done, your Web site is your company's online showcase and sometimes the first and last impression that customers have of your firm and its products. Developing a good one is money well spent and critical to your successful marketing efforts.

MARKET RESEARCH
(Continued)

made, versus either the CPA or the CPC model. Tracking cookies is often the way these costs are computed.

- **Cost per thousand (CPM)**—a more traditional unit of measure universal to other media. The advertiser is charged for every 1,000 times his ad is displayed as measured by the number of hits a site takes.

- **Effective frequency** —how often the same ad should be shown to the same person without negatively affecting its impact.

- **Effective reach**— the number of people who see this ad.

MARKET RESEARCH
(Continued)

- **Hit**—the most familiar term on the Web, this is the number of times a home page is downloaded by a consumer. Despite its popularity, its frequency of use exists in inverse proportion to its accuracy as a measurement tool.

- **Impression**—a unit of measure that links one consumer to one view of the Web page or its material.

- **Return on investment (ROI)**—the principle of value judgement of the marketing cost undertaken. In other words, are the cost of your banner, interstitial and other ads on the Web worth the investment?

What's more, it's a necessary competitive tool in an increasingly competitive world.

You've heard that last part about competition ever since you entered the marketing field. But what you may not realize is that the Web has leveled the playing field for *all* businesses out there. Design considerations being equal, the site for Bob's Bait and Tackle Shop, which he runs out of the back of his lakeshore cottage, can be as compelling as the site for General Motors or Kraft Foods. On the Web everyone looks the same, which means you suddenly have competitors from around the globe you never knew existed and never had to worry about because your customers didn't know they existed, either. It's a whole new ballgame now.

This has been taken to its logical extreme by the financial services industry. When you consider what that industry offers—savings, loans, investments and insurance products pretty well sum it up—you quickly realize:

1. in an online environment, Citibank will look pretty much like the State Bank of Chicken Switch;

2. product desirability is determined by rates and delivery time, not the purveyor of those services; and

3. all of those products can be delivered electronically, which makes the physical presence of a brick-and-mortar structure obsolete.

What does that mean? It means that smart entrepreneurs already have created cyber banks that exist only as online entities. There is no building, no vault, no smiling tellers. All transactions are done online and all funds transfer are done electronically. That's an advantage that goes well beyond mere marketing in demonstrating the power of the Internet. It also makes the point that, no matter who you are or where you're located, you need to be on the Web in order to compete.

And that goes for Bob and his bait store as well as General Motors.

New business is nice,
but repeat customers pay the bills.

—Marketing Axiom

20

From Branding to Bonding

When I turn on my computer, dial up the World Wide Web and visit the Amazon.com site, the company's home page greets me by name. Knowing what I last purchased and when, it offers me some new items that roughly parallel my previous selections. If I haven't made any purchases in a number of months, the firm sends me e-mails with special offers and sale information. It attempts to anticipate my interests and suggests ways of getting back into the buying groove.

The local Honda dealership where I have my car serviced sends out quarterly postcards reminding me what the next level of service is that I need. The card patiently explains the importance of ongoing maintenance and includes dated coupons for service discounts to spark me to action. When I need minor work done—say a knob replaced on the dash—I no longer have to make an appointment. I simply can show up at my convenience and the service writer will do the installation for me at no cost other than that of the part.

When I hop on a United Airlines flight, my Premier Executive status has already alerted the gate agent to place me toward the front of the plane in the Economy Plus section that offers passengers more leg room. If the flight isn't full, the agent also will block the middle seat to give me and whoever else may occupy that row a little more space to spread out. And, if I have chosen to upgrade to First Class, I will be able to do so 72 hours prior to flight time through a quick call to their 800 number.

When I call my local Pizza Hut restaurant, the person who answers the telephone knows exactly what my previous pizza purchase was, when it was made and whether it was delivered or picked up. "Do you still like extra cheese on that pie, Mr. Muckian?" is what I hear.

All of the above are examples of the type of data mining that has become possible thanks to computer technology and its applications to marketing. It's also what marketing consultants Don Peppers and Martha Rogers call "the 1:1 future."

Capturing market share for your product or company is no longer enough, Peppers and Rogers say. Today, competition and opportunity have driven marketing well beyond that level. Instead of market share, what companies now must strive for is "share of customer," increasing loyalty by deepening penetration levels into how many products those customers buy, how often those purchases are made and how much that customer is willing to spend with the company.

United Airlines does it every time I fly. By offering me double the miles as befits my status in their Mileage Plus program, they have assured my loyalty even in the face of delayed or cancelled flights and sub-par performance because they are paying me for my inconvenience by giving me increased opportunities for free airline tickets. Surveys have shown that, in the last 10 years, airline passengers in general have increased the tolerance for delayed flights from 30 minutes to more than three hours thanks to such reward programs. When I travel, all other things being equal, it will be on United Airlines.

My Honda dealership is the same way. They have taken over the maintenance stewardship of my car. I no longer have to think about what needs to be done and when. I know they have a complete service file on my vehicle and will remind me when the car needs servicing. When it comes time for me to sell the car, I can request a printout of my service record to show how well the car has been maintained and use that to increase the price I am asking for the vehicle. When it comes to repairs, I don't even think of other options because they have made it easy for me to maintain my automotive "investment."

In point of fact, both of these companies have deepened their share of customer in me because they've taken extra steps to make sure I am getting the most I can from my relationship with their services. Through their automated systems, they have been able to keep tabs on my buying behavior and know when to take action to assure that my next purchase is made in a timely fashion. The fact that this service is automated makes little difference to me because, in the end, I ultimately benefit from this soft sell approach. And even though I may pay a little more by not shopping around, the convenience to me and recognition of my needs as a consumer makes this a very effective way to keep me as a customer.

And, as Peppers and Rogers point out, that is a relationship that results from financial investments on both sides and brings rewards to both customer and company.

BUILDING RELATIONSHIPS

There are different buzzwords and catch phrases to describe this phenomenon, but it all boils down to one thing—building mutually beneficial relationships with the customer. If you recall as far back as Chapter 3, that relationship is the heart and soul of the branding concept. In its purist form, branding is not a logo, an image or a measure of quality. Branding classically defined is the relationship between the customer and product or company. It is the expectation promised and the level of quality or service delivered that contribute to brand development. But it is the way the customer feels about that product or service that determines the effectiveness of the brand itself.

I feel good about my Honda because it's a well-engineered, high quality automobile that blends elements of both comfort and service that contribute to my satisfaction level. When I first purchased the car a number of years ago, it raised my personal standards in overall expectations of automobile style, performance and reliability and has served as a benchmark in that area of consumer development. Due to its high quality of engineering, routine maintenance will extend the life of my Accord, making the original purchase a sound financial investment. And I enjoy the look and feel of the vehicle when I drive it.

As far as this customer is concerned, the Honda brand has delivered and I won't give the concept of engineering quality a second thought when it comes time to purchase a new car. Even if I switch to a different brand, the level of performance, style, reliability and, subsequently, value that I enjoyed in my Honda will become the new basis level for all future automotive performance.

That's branding at its most evident and ubiquitous level. Despite my enjoyment and loyalty to the brand, however, I know that the people in Marysville, Ohio, where my vehicle was manufactured, haven't a clue as to who I am, what my likes and dislikes are, what level of service I expect and how much frustration I will tolerate from my service provider. But my local dealership, with whom I have my vehicle serviced, knows all that and probably a little bit more. They have taken my brand loyalty and cultivated it to a different level, one that ad man Michael Knapstein calls "bonding."

It might also be called a symptom of Peppers' and Rogers' 1:1 future. But whatever sobriquet we apply to it, it all boils down to getting to know the customer, not by geographic, demographic or even psychographic type, but as an individual purchaser. An audience of one, if you will. And then tailoring the product or service to meet that individual's needs.

That's not the way of the future. That's how business is being done today, thanks to an inordinate amount of data mining and manipulation. And, like marketing on the World Wide Web, if your firm isn't moving in that direction, then it soon may not be moving anywhere at all.

Think of it the way you might have thought of the village grocer a century ago. He knew what type of supplies—flour, sugar, yeast—that your grandmother or great grandmother needed to run her household and cook for her family, and he made it a point to stock those supplies for her. When a drummer came through town with something new, he had a pretty good idea whether Grandmother would buy it and if Grandfather would let her do so. He became not just the local merchant, but in many ways the personal buyer for the village folks who shopped in his store. They learned to trust his judgement and, in many cases, surrendered the dry goods decisions of their lives to this man.

That's not so different from my Honda dealership. They know what's good for my vehicle and when it needs servicing. I have come to trust their judgement and have been rewarded with sound performance and an extended life to my vehicle. As Knapstein says, I have bonded with them as a provider and moved beyond the Honda brand to an even greater level of involvement with the product and its manufacturing and distribution network. When it comes to me, they have an excellent share of customer that could well last a long, long time.

REDESIGNING YOUR APPROACH

Adapting to the bonding principle is not difficult from an external point of view. Like me, many of your customers already are there in their thinking because so many of your competitors have found ways to build such relationships cost effectively with an eye toward keeping and maintaining them in perpetuity. This somewhat elliptical progression that boomerangs back to an earlier concept of customer service really was made possible by the growth of mass marketing and subsequent brand development in the post World War II economic boom.

At the time, the village grocer concept could no longer stand up to mass distributors as the product demand swelled and providers grew to meet that demand. The return to the individual buyer concept has not been due to a reduction in that market, but rather to greater sophistication in the audience sorting mechanism and continued market growth, making the development of that sort of mechanism not only possible but critical to survival.

The economic size and strength of the various players have helped drive the technology—in this case databases and interactive online relationships with customers—that have taken us forward. But the development of the technology has enabled much smaller players to enter the market, creating a boutique world in which even corporate giants like General Motors brand their product lines individually, as opposed to an affiliation appendage of the GM empire.

For many consumers, General Motors is a corporate entity that weathers union problems, posts gains and losses, hires and fires high-powered and highly paid executives, and generally helps drive the U.S. economy. When they're buying their Chevy Blazers or their Cadillac El Dorados, however, these consumers pay little heed to the GM connection, instead concentrating on the features and benefits of the product itself. In reality, most wouldn't care if their cars were made in Detroit, Michigan, or on the red planet Mars as long as they delivered the same quality and cachet they have come to expect from the product.

That's branding as it leads to bonding. The point of that example is to show that most companies are closer to one-to-one marketing than they may think and many already have the mechanisms in place to begin treating their customers, not as slices of market share but as individuals. And that's critical because, frankly, that's what the world has become.

The two chapters we spent on online marketing barely scrape the surface of what has emerged as a profound change not only in the way people do business, but also in how they relate to each other as individuals and en masse. During the post World War II economic boom, society attempted to fulfill America's "melting pot" notions and homogenize its citizens into one vast social type separated by economic strata. Governmental and business bodies at large found hard standards much easier to legislate, mandate and market to, of course, and the race was on to make this a gray flannel suit world.

Society, which is based on the people within it who, in turn, all are biological entities, began to naturally deviate and subdivide from the norm like so many conceptual amoeba splitting and spreading. Despite the power structure's best efforts, delineations along racial, ethnic and philosophical lines simply couldn't be morphed out of existence. We were people, not product, and couldn't be managed simply as human inventory. Rigid standards notwithstanding, things began to change.

The invention of the Internet took that concept a quantum leap forward, allowing further delineations and, most compelling of all, the ability for people to communicate with each other freely, economically and completely. Suddenly it was no longer social norms, tribal laws or family rules that measured the breadth and depth of consumers; it was individual characteristics themselves. Mass marketing gave way to niche marketing, which in turn, has delivered us to where we are today.

The companies who have embraced this and adjusted their point of view to accommodate this concept will succeed. Those that haven't will languish until some stronger, swifter, more facile competitor comes along to eat their lunch. In today's world that happens to every industry every hour of every day.

The main challenge for a firm moving in the direction of bonding, then, is two-fold:

• The company itself has to change its mindset and focus on effective one-to-one marketing and service. That's what consumers now expect and progressive providers have raised the bar accordingly. The hardest thing for some firms to swallow is that the old, comfortable and currently profitable way of doing business no longer is sufficient. Reengineering corporate attitude is often more difficult and costly for a company than reengineering its physical plant. Those that fail to do so, however, may find that comfort zone pulled out from under them like a threadbare rug as profits erode and the old way of doing things suddenly becomes antiquated and inadequate for survival.

• Success in pursuing this new approach is based not only on developing the proper attitude, but also having access to the data necessary to make change successful. Computer power and PC access by company and customer alike go a long way to amassing that data and sorting customers into an infinite number of types. Through the Internet's interactive communications capabilities, those types then can be modified and communications tailored to individuals, who can be addressed by name and preferences, much the way Amazon.com approaches me.

Direct mail has, for a long time, been able to simulate this approach through mail merge technologies that have personalized mass mail by name, date of birth, address and other factors. These days, by providing key information, you can even order kids' books that have been personalized to the life milestones of the child. The Internet takes this further, enabling a two-way communications link that allows for continued updating and refinement of that information to a central database that then crafts and distributes communiques based on the data that simply grows more personal over time, much like any real relationship would.

The net result? A bonding between company and customer that allows for anticipation of needs prior to having them stated and fulfillment based on customer desire, not corporate policy. My Farmers Insurance agent sends me a birthday card each year. Does he really care about me? I'm sure he does as a policyholder, but even he can join the one-to-one revolution through simple manipulation of his own rudimentary database, along with the appropriate response. It's really that simple.

CORNERSTONES OF DEVELOPMENT

When it comes to developing any one-to-one marketing approach, the cornerstone behind the concept is knowing the customer and knowing what to do with that customer that helps you both cross the bridge from branding to bonding. The United States Constitution states that all people are created equal. Unfortunately, this edict doesn't extend to your company's customers. Some are better than others in certain intrinsic ways and it's those with whom you want to begin your efforts.

Any entity creates spheres of influence, structured roughly like ripples in a pond once the stone has been thrown. Those closest to the point of impact resonate and ripple most rapidly, providing the firm with the greatest response. As subsequent rings reach further away from center, the spread gets broader and the vibrations lighter. In short, the firm has less influence over these individuals and may have no sway at all.

Consider the airline frequent flyer clubs as an example. Anyone can join and anyone who has ever been on a commercial airline more than once probably has. This population represents the primary market for such programs, one that is maintained with no special effort other than minimal, periodic (usually quarterly) contact. In some cases, when the relationship is dormant for too long, the customer file is maintained but contact ceases.

As frequency of product use increases, those flyers move up the ladder of influence. In most clubs, those that travel 25,000 miles per year enter a higher level of status with more amenities. They have proven themselves customers of some constance and are rewarded with bonus miles, check-in privileges and other benefits designed to stimulate support of that usage level. Keep flying 25,000 miles a year with us and we will be happy to maintain that level of preference, the airlines say. Drop below that and you will lose those privileges and rejoin the unwashed masses in the rear of the aircraft.

The next level usually breaks at about 50,000 flight miles per year and accounts for the biggest benefits jump. There is another subsequent level for even more frequent flyers where the benefits package becomes complete. No matter which level a flyer falls into, however, the strategy is clear. The better customer gets more benefits and more attention because there is a greater likelihood of increased patronage and airline usage. And that translates into more revenue for the firm.

Customer value revolves around product or service usage, of course. But most marketers realize the value of word-of-mouth customer support. A frequent flyer plan, no matter what the benefit scale, is rendered less valuable if the airline itself suffers from late departures, lost luggage and cancelled flights. If the inevitable happens, as it did with United Airlines as discussed earlier in this book, the best strategy is to acknowledge the error, apologize and, most importantly, up the benefits to compensate for the inconvenience. Flyers will still grumble and complain, but they'll have even more incentive to fly and a vested interest in suggesting the airline to others, if only by virtue of telling them of all the additional mileage they received in compensation for the airline's screwups.

The lesson here is to target your good customers and spend your time and effort pleasing and retaining them. In many companies, the major marketing effort focuses on acquiring new customers, which can be anywhere from six to 10 times the cost of maintaining current relationships. You will need to concentrate on new customer development to stem the tide of natural attrition but your primary marketing effort should come from deepening product usage within your current customer base. Then work on gaining market share.

Recognition of the important role customers play naturally leads itself to the proposition that customer relationships need to be managed first and products need to be managed second. You already know quite a bit based on past buying patterns and other communications you've had with your customers. Your individualized marketing can be enhanced by strengthening the relationship and making customers collaborative rather than combative.

Once again, this involves knowing what your customer wants at the deepest level to which you can penetrate, and then seeking to fulfill that need. By appearing to care, you also can build greater trust, which strengthens the relationship but also may open the doors to information about your competition and how much apparent share of customer they have. This knowledge adds to your competitive database and allows you to segment a portion of your preferred customers that may be patronizing one specific competitive brand. By understanding the unique selling proposition of that competitor, you may be able to execute a flanking maneuver and offer this subgroup special considerations that will drive more of their business back in your direction, thus deepening share of customer to an even greater level.

Once again, it all depends on the level and quality of the information you have and the ways it feeds the value proposition you offer. Fail to use that information wisely and you will lose that share of audience and perhaps the audience itself.

FUTURE REFINEMENTS

The social factors driving us all to individualized marketing will only increase as time goes on. And so will your refinement in finding ways to bond with your best customers. In fact, is there any question in your mind that any of the following will not occur?

• Society will continue to segment as new social and ethnic groups grow and gain prominence within the confines of your general market. Marketing in Spanish has been a given for the past decade, but will there be a time for mass marketing efforts in Chinese, Korean, Hmong and other Asian languages? This continued diversification will not be accompanied by cultural homogenization, either. Emphasis will be on keeping cultural traits and tendencies intact, forcing marketers to accommodate a variety of components if they want to succeed.

• The speed of life will continue to increase, making personal time a premium commodity. Less time will be spent by consumers "shopping around" and more time building relationships with trusted merchants who can deliver merchandise at a time and in a way convenient to the buyer. In many cases, convenience will become as important as quality, if not more so, in determining merchants of choice.

• Alternatives to traditional product shapes and delivery methodologies will proliferate, changing the old ways in which we do business. Remember the example in an earlier chapter of the first "cyberbank" that exists only as an online entity, has no brick and mortar facility, no vault, and no drive-up windows? Whenever it's possible, it's highly probable that product providers will not only find new ways to market and deliver, but also to produce the very products and services that they're selling in an electronic format.

• Individuals—that's all of us—will begin to see life in new ways. Whether it's something as mundane as "casual Fridays" in our offices or the increased ability to telecommute from a mountain top, the nature of the way we work, play, socialize and raise our families is changing at a profoundly intrinsic level. Telecommuting from a mountain top may not initially determine whether we drink whole or skim milk, but it will determine who we buy it from. Eventually it will also alter how much we buy and, inevitably, if we continue to buy it at all. This shift in the awareness and identity of the various populations we market to is, indeed, the most profound adjustment of all.

At the end of the 19th century, the Industrial Revolution altered the way we lived and worked, changing society from an agrarian base to an industrial one and bringing people from the country to the city. Currently, we are in the throes of the Digital Revolution that is fractionalizing society while, at the same time, drawing elements together that otherwise wouldn't have known each other. It allows players to compete in a market they otherwise wouldn't have known existed. The change is at least as profound, and probably significantly more so, as all the movements that have come before. What's more, it's still in process and may be that way for a long time to come.

Had he been more commercially inclined, Aldous Huxley might have called this a brave new marketing world. And he wouldn't have been far from wrong.

The future can't wait; no place to hide.
So climb on aboard. We're goin' inside.

—Firesign Theater

21

Brave New Marketing World

In comparison to the rest of the world, the United States is said to excel in the production and distribution of just two products: marketing/advertising and Hollywood motion pictures. That makes you, as a marketer, an international ambassador of business, a shining example of the best the U.S. has to offer, a gold medal athlete in the Olympics of global commerce.

Pretty frightening, isn't it? This is especially true when you consider the fact that both of those industries specialize in the creation of image and illusion while helping guide the creation of public perception in pursuit of commerce. Once you think about it, however, you will realize that's the foundation behind not only economic growth, but also human evolution.

Few professions other than marketing—except, of course, politics—would wholeheartedly accept the phrase "perception is reality." But most of us would admit if pressed that we judge each other not based on who the other person really is, but on who we think that person is in relationship to ourselves. That's perception, not reality. But that perception becomes more real to us than reality ever could be. And that's the essence behind effective marketing.

Times have changed since the first broadsides were pinned to the sides of buildings announcing some new notion or dry good or that the circus is coming to town. We've traveled light years from the time when the first public relations officers suggested that big businesses might want to develop a social conscience to ease the sting of public criticism. We no longer create a product, hoping someone will buy it. We now measure market share, test customer receptivity and disect the competition before we even think of entering the product stream. Marketing has become not only an art, but a science and must be treated as such.

That requires a foundation of basic skills balanced by a scientific approach to strategic and corporate development. You must have a complete knowledge of the tools available, and have the market identified before product launch as well as during the post-launch assessment phase. There still is no guarantee you'll hit the target, much less surpass your goals. But at least you'll be in line with the competition and have a better chance of not only surviving, but thriving.

And today, there are more options available than any past marketer ever would have dreamed.

A CLASSIC CASE STUDY REVISITED

When one can't quite figure out the future, the old saying goes, one is tempted to tinker with the past. Hindsight is 20–20 and we're all certain that, with a little time and effort, if a past opportunity had been presented to us, we certainly could have made a success out of what had been a marketing flop. After all, if some enterprising entrepreneur can realize market success with products like the Pet Rock and the Wacky Wallwalker—the sticky, octopus-like toy that you threw against a wall and watched roll slowly down—then it should be relatively easy to re-engineer the marketing for a more legitimate and useful product and turn it into a success, right?

Let's test this thesis. For the sake of argument, let's assign you to the Ford Edsel account. Let's see what the value of hindsight, along with 21st century marketing tools, might have done in your hands to save one of marketing's greatest blunders. We'll even help you cheat a little by giving you access to 21st century technology and marketing thinking. Given your busy schedule and many challenges, it's the least we can do.

It's difficult to imagine a Dearborn, Michigan boardroom circa 1956 filled with anxious Ford Motor Company executives poring over the results of public surveys that identify a public preference for a new, strange-looking sedan. But the data was there and it looked too good to ignore. It was time for one of America's automotive titans to get off his bucket seat and forge ahead with this new product. Based on the numbers, the team was confident it would have a winner on its hands, thumbs tucked under his suspenders, company scion Henry Ford Jr. chose to name the car after his son, Edsel Ford. From a mass-market perspective, all systems were go.

We all know what happened next. The car was manufactured and introduced and the buying public stayed away in droves. The odd car with the odder front end proved to be just that and, despite the survey results, no one wanted it. In mass market America, there was no room for such failure. After a short stay, the Edsel went away.

Of course, as the newest marketing junior executive at Ford, that doesn't let you off the hook. In fact, the elder Mr. Ford decides that if anyone can save the Edsel, it must be you. (That also means that if it turns out no one can save the Edsel, then Ford will have a scapegoat. Isn't that how life works?)

Given this new opportunity—as well as access to 21st century tools—what can you do to save the Edsel and turn it into one of America's hottest new motor products? Based on what we've learned throughout this volume, here are some steps that you undoubtedly will follow:

• The first thing to do is to review the marketing plan and decide if either the plan itself and/or the product fits into the overall strategic goals of Ford Motor Company. Is the company's goal to create another widely accepted mass-market vehicle, or does it need niche products to round out its line and gain extra market share in areas where it otherwise lacks penetration? An honest assessment of how the product fits into the scheme of things is critical to progress in the right direction. That, in fact, may have helped Ford from the beginning.

• In the same way, you'll need to scour the research results with a fine-tooth comb and understand exactly what respondents were saying. People often think they want things because they're new and/or different and their involvement in the conceptualization and

development of these products—passively, through survey participation, of course—makes them feel like they are on the cutting edge
of economic development.

For many, however, it's no more than a much-needed intellectual exercise. When it comes right down to it, many people are
happy in their comfort zones—some would call them ruts—and
want products with familiar elements and uses so they don't have to
further complicate their lives. An odd-looking car might be fun to
think about and take for a test drive, but I sure as heck wouldn't
want to own one. Understanding how what they say relates to what,
ultimately, they will accept, and applying the appropriate salt grains
of extenuating circumstances to the process is a critical next step.

• You'll need also to re-examine the competition's marketplace positioning and find out whether they have closely competing products
in this area. If you're the first to market this novel vehicle, it means
a) you're ahead of your time or b) there's no market for it. In both
cases, your product may suffer from the same lack of public acceptance and sales malaise, meaning you'll have to create the market for
it as well as fill the need you've created. That requires a lot more effort than the standard, "Here it is, folks! Come and get it" approach
many established companies are used to expecting.

• Your discoveries in these areas will contribute to your overall understanding of the product and its overall place within it. Clearly, it
will be an uphill battle, especially in the period's *Life* magazine mass
marketing culture. Undoubtedly, however, there will be people eager
to escape the great American homogenization effort who will be
likely candidates for purchasing this product. Inventing the concept
of niche—relatively new at the time—and finding the people to fill
that niche could make you the hero of Ford Motor Company. But
you'll have to clearly delineate that niche and all it entails, then hope
like hell there are enough people to make the product at least pay its
production costs, if not turn a profit.

• From this information, you will need to begin developing the Edsel
"brand" by identifying the key attributes of both product and audience and positioning the car in response to those attributes. Subsequent efforts will help you build a relationship with those owners and
potential owners that is the key concept behind brand development.

A strong brand, of course, is the relationship between customer and product and will help override public resistance to the new and unusual.

• Mr. Ford will need to allow you an adequate budget because you're not only introducing a product, you're creating a market for it. That will take longer and cost more, but it could put Ford Motor Company into an enviable competitive position by taking an exercise simply meant to move merchandise and making it a new strategic initiative. The meter is running and the financial statement is filling with red ink, so this may be tougher than you might think. Without adequate support, however, you'll simply be throwing good money after bad. Marketing successfully without adequate funds is akin to turning water to wine, and that isn't likely to happen.

The need for financial support speaks to a louder, more pressing need of corporate support for the entire effort. In order to be successful, the Edsel needs to be more than the ugly stepchild of a major manufacturer. It needs to be supported and heralded in the same way the company's mainstream top sellers are. This may be hard for some executives to swallow, but the gain in market share alone should give them ample reason to promote and support the success of your efforts.

• Standard media will be a key consideration, especially in light of the dual needs stated above. You know from niche development that expensive television spots aimed at the mainstream will have marginal impact. Instead, you'll need to practice your very best niche marketing and look for unique avenues to reach the people you're convinced will be the real buyers of this vehicle. If you've decided that the unique design will attract the intellectual crowd, ads in the appropriate scientific publications may be what you want, along with college campus immersions and direct mail to leaders in a variety of industries. Since we're talking about new market development, heavy emphasis on automotive media will be critical. They will want to know what the industry is up to and why. Qualitative analysis of the product, its features and its audience will provide valuable information.

• Since you're developing a new identity for this product, it will be essential that the communications channels you choose will go far beyond mere advertising. Public relations will play a key role here. You will want support from the media in terms of discussion of why niche marketing is the way of the future for the automotive industry, both from a customer service perspective and as a corporate development strategy. You will want to earmark the growing social and cultural diversity you know to be coming down the road as the key to increasing automotive market share. By becoming a social seer of sorts, you will be better able to position your product in development of the market you need to create for it.

• Online marketing, too, is critical. But remember to keep the efforts sublime and aimed more at gathering and disseminating information than selling product. An Edsel Web page, of course, is a must. Content should be aimed at serious discussion of the car's attributes, as well as input from owners and those interested in becoming owners. Online chats and "cyber conferences" devoted to the Edsel will be critical in building interest in the product and momentum for future sales.

In addition, you can begin to refine your database of potential clients by finding out more about what they have in common, what the competition is doing to position itself against you, and what product characteristics are the most attractive about the car. You also can use the medium to market branded merchandise and communicate information about activities and ralleys held by the Edsel Owners Club, which you have created and which is flourishing through the U.S. even as we speak.

• What it all boils down to, of course, is how closely your customers bond with the product and the company. That means using technology to treat them as individuals, not merely a slice of the market pie, and make them feel that their ownership of an Edsel and their personal involvement in the Edsel mystique is the key factor contributing to the success or failure of the brand. Marketing individually will be critical to creating this customized niche.

In the end, your strategy will have worked. The Edsel will have been repositioned and reintroduced as the quirky new vehicle that has both nostalgia and sex appeal. Its drivers will be creative, unique individuals who are able to make a statement about themselves with their cars much as others do with creative and colorful wardrobes.

As a boutique product, supplies will be limited, so you'll be able to charge a premium price and won't need to carry inventory. The Edsel is suddenly hot, the subject of talk shows and trade industry analysis. In the end its relaunch is not only a sound financial investment for Ford, bringing more than adequate financial returns, it's also a good image investment, positioning Ford as being in touch with the new generation and the company the public automatically will turn to for the next "statement" vehicle that promotes the pleasures of motoring.

Congratulations, you've become the hero of Dearborn! Mr. Ford gives you a fat bonus, a generous raise and promotes you to Senior Vice President. You're written up in all the trades and receive numerous requests for speaking engagements and articles. The greatest honor comes when rival General Motors steals you away by doubling your salary and offering all kinds of executive perks.

Your future has been set, all because you followed the principles of marketing science and committed yourself to proper product development, positioning, pricing, packaging, promotion and placement. Your new boss at GM already has your first big assignment ready for you: reposition and relaunch their new economy model, the Corvair. He hands you a stack of phone notes "from that pesky Mr. Nader" and you're off and running.

WHAT ABOUT YOU?

If you can market the Edsel, you can market anything. Are you ready to drive your career ahead by utilizing basic and advanced marketing principles to accomplish the strategic and operational goals that have been set before you?

The time to start is yesterday.

Index